T0285640

ISBN: 9781627311472

FERAL HOUSE
1240 W Sims Way #124
Port Townsend WA 98368

www.feralhouse.com

Designed by Ron Kretsch

LEMURIA

A True Story
of a Fake Place

Justin McHenry

For Sarah, Lilah, and Clara

INTRODUCTION:

The Lost Continents of Perception

CONTINENTS ARE NOT SOMETHING YOU LOSE. IT TAKES EFFORT TO MAKE a whole continent vanish. If nature has a hand in the disappearance, then the land breaks apart and is consumed by the sea or by other landmasses—a gradual death. Millions upon millions of years of slow, tortuous dissolution. However, if we humans (or in some cases, proto-humans) do have a hand in the losing of a continent, then that takes generations of wickedness. Those deeds building upon one another. Choices, all the wrong ones, being made time and time again, until that weight proves too much for a land to bear and it succumbs to its inherent vices.

When that scale finally tilts and the day comes, at least the destruction comes quick. Violent too. Volcanoes. Floods. Comets. Death, then submersion, with the ruination of the land. Only the faintest wisps of its existence haunting the remaining world. No, continents are not ever lost. They have earned their right to disappear.

What follows is the story of a place earning that right to exist and disappear. Lemuria was a proposed land bridge put forth in the nineteenth century to try to explain how lemurs ended up on Madagascar. Once proposed, this idea, which was given the name Lemuria, quickly found itself in the middle of everything. People threw this theorized continent into the fury surrounding evolution. It got thrust into the discussion on the permanence of the continents and the seas. And into the forging of alternative spiritual thought in the West. Lemuria became the pivotal cradle for the cradle of mankind. The cradle of spirituality. The cradle of all civilization. Lemuria got sent into outer space and populated by denizens from other worlds, as well as astral figures, conspiratorial ones, persecuted enlightened beings, cyclops, dinosaurs, and everything in between.

This created world of Lemuria gets inhabited by its own race of super humans. These Lemurians would then play outsized roles in the creation of myths surrounding Mt. Shasta in California, the conduits for New Age channelers, and the basis for modern contactees. The evolution of the idea of Lemurians and

Lemuria offers a glimpse of how alternative narratives get formed, turned, shifted, and manipulated. This story will show how one such narrative gets chiseled out of the bedrock by decades of use by various forces and factions, demonstrating how scientists debated and used Lemuria for their purposes. And when they wiped their hands of its existence, the story of how esotericists and occult practitioners tried to use the Lemuria that was created by science for their own means. What started out in earnest entered into more mystical realms, which Lemuria has not shaken, and it has been contorted into what it is today: a land of seed crystals and a cautionary tale that QAnon followers hold up to demonstrate what happens when the Demonic Cabal takes over and destroys an entire continent.

Lemuria, taken as a reality, has a curious chronology. Madame Blavatsky has it existing 80 million years ago, while her disciples Besant and Leadbeater put it around five million years ago. James Churchward has his great continent of Mu at its peak around 50,000 years ago. But what all of those agree upon is that Lemuria had broken up and was destroyed no sooner than 12,000 years ago. There is no continuity surrounding when it did exist. But what remains relatively consistent is how it disappeared: a violent catastrophe sank the land to the bottom of the ocean. During this process, Lemuria became all but unrecognizable from its inception.

Lemuria gets aided in this journey by its proponents tacking racial identities on to the land and its people, in what will quickly turn into racist rhetoric propping up a white superiority dogma. Science kickstarted this fascination with tying Lemuria to race, and those that followed kept on the racist plight of Lemurians. Prominent nineteenth-century scientists such as Ernst Haeckel would do this by first equating those from Lemuria with the "lower," "darker" races that were not seen to be as evolved as the white Aryan races, with the native races across the globe being the direct descendants of Lemurians and evolving along a different path from the white race. The racial descriptions of Lemurians morphed as Lemuria became a more idealized society, an advanced civilization, leaving it primed to be inhabited by classic white Aryan gods. Tall, blond, intelligent, spiritually attuned. These deific-Lemurians are whom white Aryans are really descended from. At every step throughout the Lemurian story, the question of race is not far behind.

Along with the question of race comes the obvious appropriation of various Eastern cultures and religions by the likes of Helena Petrovna Blavatsky, better known as Madame Blavatsky, and more explicitly by her adherents Annie Besant, C.W. Leadbeater, and Alice Bailey, who came after. The appropriation of these ideas and cultures by white Westerners is still going on today. Unabashed and unashamed theft of ideas and cultural beliefs added to a patronizing diffusionist belief that culture and civilization poured forth from not these cultures or native ones but by a higher, more advanced white one.

At the beginning, the sciences created and defined Lemuria. Some of the leading scientists of the nineteenth century took the concept under their wings to breathe vague reality into its existence, which aided in the coming of Lemurians to America, settling within the majestic peak of Mt. Shasta in California. Not content burrowing into one mountain, this led to a whole underground civilization, and their conspiratorial plans formulated in the pages of a pulp magazine—until new religious movements got their hands on it, imbuing the idea of Lemuria with the alien and prosecuted overtones it lives with today.

Lemuria is the protagonist here. It is the one that undergoes multiple changes and grows in complexity, from its birth in 1864 to today. In a way, it goes through its own hero's journey. Escaping the ordinary, heeding the call, offering some resistance, but Lemuria loses itself on that journey, never to find its way again. And when Lemuria looks in the mirror, what do you think it sees? Is it proud of what it has become? Or does it say: *Who am I? How did I get here?* Somewhere it got led astray, and now it is time to try to untangle the knot of this odyssey and find its true reality.

Whatever Lemuria has become, this ultimately is a story about people. People invented the idea. People carried Lemuria out into space and around the oceans on this planet. People filled this land with beings, both human and extraterrestrial, godlike and evil. Individuals guide Lemuria every step of the story. These are flawed people too. Humans, just like you and me. Many are honest and genuine in their beliefs, while others took advantage of the vagueness Lemuria provided to gain attention, further their agendas, or warn mankind. Good and bad hustlers, hucksters and schemers fill this book and write Lemuria's story. This is as much their story as it is the Lemurians'.

Which gets to the heart of the book. I call Lemuria a "fake place" because it was an invention by people. Theories and the channeled memories of ascended masters do not a continent make. That did not stop a select few from trying to prove that an actual Lemuria, or Mu, existed; however, if there did exist a long-lost advanced civilization out in the Pacific or the Indian Ocean or the many other places people located Lemuria, it is not something that will be explored here. People and their stories—their Lemuria is the focus, for if anything, it will show how we are susceptible to creating alternative narratives and believing in them. If for no other reason than being connected, and feeling connected to one another. Building a bridge.

CHAPTER 1:

A Bridge Not Far Enough

LEMURIA WAS BORN FROM SCIENCE. WHATEVER IT CAME TO BE, OR BE known for, cannot or should not be divorced from its origin story deep within the heart of a number of different fields of science, whether that be evolutionary theory or paleontology, zoology or geology.

It is science that has theorized, proven, disproven, and argued over the existence of Lemuria for over 150 years now. And it is science that will keep doing so for many more decades, if not centuries, to come.

It appeared. There. The last word. A last word of a paper buried in the middle of the Linnean Society's publication of papers of 1864. Lemuria's father, Philip Lutley Sclater, followed his creation with a well-earned or retrospectively pertinent exclamation mark.

The anomalies of the Mammal fauna of Madagascar can best be explained by supposing that anterior to the existence of Africa in its present shape, a large continent occupied parts of the Atlantic and Indian Oceans stretching out towards (what is now) America to the west, and to India and its islands on the east; that this continent was broken up into islands, of which some have become amalgamated with the present continent of Africa, and some, possibly, with what is now Asia; and that in Madagascar and the Mascarene Islands we have existing relics of this great continent, for which as the original focus of the "Stirps Lemurum," I should propose the name Lemuria!

Sclater proposed Lemuria as a means of explaining lemurs' presence on Madagascar, going into detail to describe their characteristics and how similar they are to other such animals on other continents. To Sclater and a whole host of others, the only possible explanation could be a long-lost sunken continent that encompassed South America, Africa, Madagascar, and India. This was Lemuria.

Quarterly Journal of Science N° 2

Illustration of the different types of lemurs and mammals found on Madagascar that accompanied P.L. Sclater's article where Lemuria makes its first appearance.

At the time, Sclater was a noted zoologist who was making several contributions to the world of nineteenth-century ornithology as well as serving as the secretary of the Zoological Society of London. However, his continental naming prowess and his idea of Lemuria as a land bridge managed to burrow itself into a sort of collective imagination that sparked generations of scientific debate.

You cannot have Lemuria without lemurs. Wherever this road leads us, however far astray we veer, the lemur will always be there in the name. Anchoring us to a thing. An animal.

It is, upon reflection, only fitting that these diminutive ancient primates are the source of so much mystery and so much fantasy. They live up to the hype. Found only on Madagascar, where you will find over 110 species of lemurs, as well as fourteen genera and five families. Such impressive diversification for a species inhabiting but a small area of Madagascar. While lemurs are only found there, sister species are found all over the world, from bush babies in Africa to lorises in India. They range in size from the diminutive pygmy mouse lemur, the smallest primate in the world with its head and body measuring less than two and a half inches and weighing about one ounce, to the largest, the indiri, which stands at three feet and weighs up to twenty pounds.

As a whole, they are incredibly vocal animals: the brown lemurs grunt, while sifakas get their name from the swears they belt out ("Shi-fack! Shi-FAKH!"), and the indiri's eerie wailing call is part police siren and part humpback whale song, echoing around the forests of the island.

Lemurs typically have small monkey-like bodies and limbs, with most having bushy tails often as long as their bodies. A distinguishing characteristic is their large, lemon-like eyes set in heart-shaped faces that captivate the first time you look into them or they into you. Within the realm of primates, lemurs are considered inferior, most likely because if our ancestors from millions of years ago were here today, they would probably resemble the lemur. Small-brained and reliant upon their sense of smell rather than sight, unlike what more evolved primates—and those huge peering eyes—lead you to believe.

Whenever lemurs did arrive on Madagascar, their traits evolved quickly, and they diversified as quickly as they spread out throughout the island. Madagascar became a distinct biosphere in which 90 percent of the species located there are endemic, and where lemurs filled all the niches that monkeys did elsewhere and in astonishing shapes and sizes. Madagascar is among the richest countries on Earth in primate diversity, with lemurs accounting for 20 percent of the world's total primate species and nearly a third of the global families.

When most think of lemurs, the image of a ring-tailed lemur comes to mind. Ring-tails are queer creatures. Traveling less than a kilometer a day and staying mostly to their small home territory, they are not opposed to raiding tourists' bungalows for sodas and bananas. And they love nothing more than to splay out, happily snuggled against a sister lemur, purring and napping the hot afternoon away.

They are formal to the point of ritual, such as the hierarchy of their grooming practices and importance placed on grooming infants. Unique among all primates is the male ring-tailed lemur's submissiveness to the females—an inherited deference not experienced elsewhere in the world or in civilization. Males never claim rights to food or space, only accepting it upon entering a female group. When challenged by females, they retreat and will approach a female group timidly, performing submissive vocalizations in an attempt to be accepted into the female family.

As males throughout the natural world are wont to do, male lemurs battle one another in stink fights and jump fights. Stink fights are where they draw their tails across their wrist glands and shake them over their heads to allow that scent to waft up into the nostrils of their foes, while jump fights feature serious battles, pitting whole groups of males leaping in the air at one another, swiping and attacking with their wrist spurs, and winners of these fights earn the chance to mate with the females. But then again, females do get bored with such mating shenanigans, and on such occasions, they will simply go up and bop the hapless males on the nose to express their displeasure.

Precisely how lemur female dominance developed, when all other primates and non-primate mammal males are the dominant sex, is one more mystery of these creatures and of this place.

The females are definitely the more interesting of the ring-tailed lemurs. Their femininity is treated like virility among humans: an enforced trait where their dominance is flaunted. Together, they gather into family groups or troops that develop and shift in dramatic circumstances. Typically, one female emerges as the leader of the troop. Abrupt changes in troop leadership happen with some frequency as new generations of females test older power structures. Now, this doesn't mean that harmony reigns supreme among the females. Internal strife and conflict are abundant with these female troops. Even if a female leader gets usurped, she will stay with the group, never choosing to leave it, taking whatever treatment the new leader will dole out rather than venturing out on her own.

Along with the internal conflict exists a tremendous amount of external conflict. Troops create defined territories fixed by a tradition of generational lemur memory, scent posts (gouging the barks of trees with their wrist spurs and then performing a handstand to press their privates against the tree to rub their scent into it), and by fending off challenges from rival female troops—territories that they defend with their lives.

Those challenges from rivals turn into gangland turf battles. Brutal fights over territory and resources, an all-female primate battle royale. These can be intense battles with vicious wounds accumulating on both sides; however, sturdy creatures that they are, lemurs and their wounds have a way of zippering up on their own.

A couple of females from either troop usually do the fighting, sometimes with their babies clinging upside down on their mother's bellies, where they too become casualties though they exhibit the same high amount of toughness as their mothers. Parry and feint, parry and grapple. Breaking holds, only to reestablish them. They struggle with one another in a generational discord for the long-term ownership of resources. A soap opera with its tragedies but also with its care and support of one female for another. What becomes clear is that the males fight for sex, while the females fight to survive.

WHILE YOU CANNOT HAVE LEMURIA WITHOUT LEMURS, YOU CANNOT HAVE lemurs without Madagascar. The island nation is very much a world unto itself. Mysteries have a way of finding themselves there, and surrounding Madagascar to make it feel like a place out of time. Noted lemur researcher Allison Jolly remarked how it is as if "time has broken its banks and flowed to the present down a different channel." Medieval Arab geographers and traders traveling to the island came away referring to it as the "Island of the Moon."

Madagascar is a massive place, an island larger than California. Madagascar's girth and ecological makeup lead many to claim it is its own continent. The size distorts the fact that at the closest point, it is 250 miles off the coast of Africa.

So many animals, insects, and plants exist on the island that cannot be found anywhere else on Earth—including not only lemurs but other mammals and plants. Because of this, the island provides a glimpse of the world as it looked during the age of the dinosaurs. A lost world. Particularly lost because so little of the fossil record has been found on the island, partly due to the soil composition not being conducive to the fossilization process.

Given its size and closeness to Africa, it's astonishing that no evidence of human habitation from before the time of Christ exists on the island. And those first peoples of Madagascar originated not from Africa but from Indonesia, some 3,500 miles across the Indian Ocean. The descendants of these first people are the Malagasy, whose customs and language all originate in Indonesia, with examples of this Pacific culture being found in terraced rice paddies, outrigger canoes, and ancestor worship all over the island. How they managed to reach the island before peoples from Africa or even the Middle East or India is remarkable unto itself.

Adding to this strangeness is that not a single artifact from any early archaeological site on Madagascar points toward Indonesia, and nothing in

Indonesia suggests a connection with Madagascar. Linguistically, the Malagasy language is closest to a Malayo-Polynesian tongue spoken in the Barito Valley in southwestern Borneo. While no one knows when, how, or why these people came to Madagascar, once settled on the island, it took them roughly 1,300 years to venture into the center of it.

Over the past few centuries, a mixture of African, Arab, South Indian, and European people in addition to the Malagasy settled on Madagascar. Arabic traders were probably the next group of people in the Middle Ages to venture to the island. Europeans first noted Madagascar on their cruises in the sixteenth century, and over the following centuries they began the baby steps toward European colonization. The British tried first, but attempts by the French took hold in the nineteenth century. This led to a century or more of French rule. With the collapse of African colonialism, Madagascar has been an independent nation since 1960.

Much like all other things that humans touch, the environment of Madagascar has suffered terribly. Farming and the introduction of herd animals wreaked havoc on the soil. Rampant deforestation and large-scale grazing sterilized much of the grassland that covers the majority of the island. These environmental woes meant hardships for the people of Madagascar, who have to somehow balance the beautiful but delicate ecology of their homeland with survival and prosperity.

The deterioration of the environment of Madagascar has already led to extinctions (such as the elephant bird) and endangered the habitats of large swaths of the island's fauna population. Particularly those of the lemurs.

Before we kill off the lemurs, let us get to the crux of the matter, and that is lemurs getting onto Madagascar in the first place—the problem that led Sclater to suggest Lemuria as a land bridge. This might not seem all that much of a mystery, with Africa being right there. Madagascar and Africa both have similar primates that lemurs could have evolved from. If only it were that simple. Paleohistory seldom is.

To get lemurs on Madagascar, we have to begin with a time when there was little to nothing on the island. Back to a day when the world changed: the Cretaceous-Tertiary Extinction event. Not only was this event responsible for the extinction of dinosaurs, but it also extinguished most life on Madagascar. Few of Madagascar's fauna at the time survived, and what did survive does not offer much in the way of conclusions. Or so we think. The fossil record prior to the extinction event is sketchy at best.

That was 66 million years ago. Other milestones to keep in mind are that the common primate ancestors appeared around 79.6 million years ago, lemurs' ancestors branched off between 62 to 65 million years ago, and the diversification of lemurs into differing species, genera, and families started around 50 million years ago, with diversification happening all on Madagascar.

Lemurs—or more accurately, their ancestors—could not have arrived on the island before the extinction event and not after diversification started. Scientists estimate that lemurs came over between 70 to 41 million years ago. It should be noted that it is not only lemurs we are talking about but all the mammals of Madagascar as well as birds, insects, lizards, and so on. All of them needed to colonize Madagascar at some point, somehow.

There is a belief of a single source ancestor for lemurs, creating the possibility for a single colonizing event of Madagascar. For many years, debates among scientists called for a need for multiple colonizations to account for the differing families of lemurs. If there are five families of lemurs, then each one needed to make its own way to Madagascar.

However, recent DNA sequencing linked all current lemurs to a single common ancestor, meaning all that was needed was one lone pregnant lemur ancestor or a lemur couple to survive the trek from Africa to Madagascar in order to create the modern line of lemurs.

Now, once on Madagascar, those lemurs diversified quickly. They got bigger. They got smaller. And they grew into their own families and species and developed their own traits and came to be what we see today. Lemurs had no real predators until man stepped foot on the island a couple of thousand years ago, and they spent that time adapting freely. As we have seen, Madagascar is a big, ecologically diverse place, and it should have more diversity of species than it does for an island its size.

This is the heart of the matter: How exactly did these lemurs get to Madagascar? It is probably a mystery that will never be solved, at least definitively. But that does not stop scientists from trying to figure it out.

Since the twentieth century, there have been two primary schools of thought concerning how lemurs managed to travel from Africa to Madagascar, though both camps seem to agree that they started off in Africa. (Except for a few who think it possible they arrived via India, but more on that later.) One camp sits firmly on the rafting side. Yes, rafting, on literal rafts from Africa to Madagascar. The lemurs sailed out across the Mozambique Channel on rafts of knotted-up vegetation and other debris kicked up by storms that pushed it toward the promised land of Madagascar. The anti-rafters fall into the camp of believing in a type of temporary land bridge that connected or quasi-connected Madagascar to the mainland—all brought about by the exposure of the Davie Ridge. Over the years, the two sides have been arguing among themselves.

The idea behind lemur rafting became popularized by George Gaylord Simpson, a paleontologist and evolutionary thinker who worked at the American Museum of Natural History in New York City. In 1940, working on the backs of previous scientists, Simpson took on the subject of mammal migration and land bridges. He makes a few compelling arguments against land bridges being at the center of mammals living on islands, which had been the theory *du jour* for a century or more at that point.

Simpson rationalized that land bridges do not permit only one kind of animal to pass over it, nor permit travel in only one direction. They are two-lane roads. Animals from Madagascar had as much opportunity to migrate to Africa as African mammals like lemurs had to travel to Madagascar. Land bridges are a simple solution to a complicated problem.

In practice, migration over land bridges becomes more predictive and not all that mysterious. The Isthmus of Panama provides a good example of a "filter bridge" (another way of saying land bridge) at work. Once that connection formed, uniting North, Central, and South America, this bridge increased the number of similar fauna in both the north and south. A balancing effect followed to what we see today between the continents. A land bridge in action. A back and forth of species, and for Madagascar, it would mean not just lemurs crossing over, as there was no land bridge tollbooth operator in this theory to keep out the lions and elephants.

Because of this, Simpson proposed a sweepstakes, specifically the African-Malagasy sweepstakes. Lemurs for whatever reason scored a winning lotto ticket that carried them across the Mozambique Channel and onto Madagascar by rafts. Not of their construction, but created and shipped out because they were holed up in a tree or other vegetation by a massive storm and flung across to the island.

While this means of transportation seems improbable, that does not mean impossible. Any improbable event becomes slightly more probable once you allow for tens of millions of years for it to happen. An epoch's worth of dice rolls. Who crosses? When do they cross? All chance. And that chance crossing better explains the distribution of Madagascar's mammals than if a land bridge existed that was open to each and all of Africa's mammals. The randomness of this distribution suggests over-water dispersal and not any land bridge connection.

To further his point, Simpson argues that the expanse of geologic time helps to negate any barriers that exist. So, of course, given enough time, lemurs will eventually make it to Madagascar despite less-than-ideal conditions in the Mozambique Channel, or any biological inhibitors of lemur hibernation or lack thereof. What does it matter when you have millions upon millions of years to get there? That there were only a few colonizing events (lemurs, rodents, et cetera) leads to rafting sweepstakes as they are low-probability events, as opposed to land bridges, which lead to greater dispersal.

In the wake of Simpson and rafting sweepstakes, many scientists have spent a considerable amount of time and effort exploring the idea of rafting, whether working out the logistics of floating islands or wind vs. current in the propulsion of rafts or looking at ancient single origins for lemurs. Also, current studies of lemur behavior have led some to use that as evidence for rafting, stemming from observations of small lemurs gathering in groups in tree holes and undergoing prolonged hibernation, with their metabolic rates and body temperatures helping to explain how they could have survived such a journey.

For much of the last half of the twentieth century, rafting was all but accepted as the most probable way for lemurs to migrate to Madagascar. And that is when the dredging started. French underwater geological surveys along the Davie Ridge (a submerged mountain range that cuts under the surface of the Mozambique Channel halfway between Madagascar and Africa) in the late 1990s and early 2000s began showing signs that the crests of the ridge remained above sea level until the Eocene period, or around the time lemurs are thought to have made it to Madagascar. From this dredging sedimentation data, scientists began putting forth theories that a land bridge ran along the Davie Ridge several kilometers wide. These unsubmerged crests created islands or a pathway in the middle of the channel that aided lemur migration. These discoveries have led to increased interest in researching possible land bridge connections—a process that includes poking as many holes as possible in Simpson's raft sweepstakes.

Focus shifted to probability math and demonstrating the unfavorable current patterns in the Mozambique Channel. These scientists worked toward showing how historic data of cyclone paths and current and wind directions would make it easier to come from Madagascar to Africa, which led to questions about why there isn't more talk of lemurs migrating from Madagascar to Africa.

Anti-rafters attack the rafts themselves and how they need to provide the resources necessary for those being rafted over to survive. These vegetation rafts often break up easily, particularly in rough seas and surf, which would be needed to propel them from Africa to Madagascar, while their shape needed to be hydrodynamic enough to reduce drag through the water. Critics have run simulations of particles and how long it takes a particle to reach Madagascar from Africa, and they came to the conclusion that at a minimum, it would take seventy days.

They generally believe that primitive mammals were not more suited to rafting than modern ones. The seasonal hibernation observed in modern lemurs could have been something that evolved post-colonization. Plus, how deeply did they hibernate? These scientists make the point that hibernating lemurs would be awoken by their hibernating tree falling and being pushed out to sea.

To explain why more animals did not cross over the land bridges created by the exposure of the Davie Ridge, their answer to that is draughts. A global cooldown led to draughts in Madagascar and Sub-Saharan Africa, which then led to extinctions and eradication of species. Coupled with the issue of Madagascar's soil not preserving bones very well, there is no real proof that some species were even there.

Another avenue to combat the theory of rafting is to focus on other non-lemur species and how they managed to make it across the Mozambique Channel and onto Madagascar. This includes studying pygmy hippos and their lack of swimming prowess. Pygmy hippos once did inhabit Madagascar but have since been killed off on the island. How they managed to make it over on rafts is unknown; though pygmy by name, they are still husky creatures not quite suited for a seventy-day rafting adventure. They are poor swimmers who paddle, shuffle, and bounce along the bottom of the body of water to get where they need to, so 250 miles is awfully long for them, and the Channel is over 1,000 kilometers deep in places, making their method of swimming rather difficult. Finally, Asian lorises probably originated from Africa too. Now, did they raft all the way from Africa to India and all points east?

This modern discussion of land bridges stretches across the centuries, and it ties not only to Madagascar but to the whole concept of the existence (and disappearance) of continents and the seas and the historical relationship between the two. Scientific discourse during the nineteenth century was primarily focused on the global distribution of plants and animals. What is most relevant to Lemuria is how the wide variety of plants and animals were related to each other and why they existed where they did.

Many scientists fell under the spell of land bridge theory, and the problem seemed to be twofold. On the one hand, many legitimate scientists were adherents of James Hutton and Charles Lyell's ideas on the gradual, consistent change of the Earth over long periods of geologic time—a theory known as uniformitarianism, which provided an intellectual basis for those scientists to pass off any kind of change such as land bridges or continents rising or lowering. With this incredibly powerful tool uniformitarianism afforded scientists, it became so much easier for them to answer complex problems like getting lemurs to Madagascar—along with the belief in the nineteenth century that continents and seas were permanent. They did not move. The seas may rise and cover some continents, or recede to reveal others. However, the continents remained where they have always been and always will be.

With the continents being firmly in place and change being gradual, this granted any scientist with a ruler and a pen the opportunity to create a land bridge or even a sunken continent and become a paleozoologist themselves.

What is striking is that these were the leading scientists in their fields for their day, earnest folks trying to piece together these mysteries, and the best they could do is build elaborate networks of land bridges here, there, and everywhere. This involved creating multiple Atlantic continents to explain faunal similarities between North America and Europe, or multiple lost Pacific continents connecting New Zealand and South America, or enormous tracts of land connecting New Zealand to Antarctica and other Southern Hemisphere locales.

Even with this emphasis being placed on connecting land bridges all across the globe, Madagascar still received significant attention. Many others after Sclater explored the idea of Lemuria but gave it more scientific names, like "Africano-Indian Continent," "Indo-Oceania," "Indo-Madagascar peninsula," and "Indo-African Continent." Lemuria was useful to attract attention to the very real problem of fauna distribution, proving to be a catalyst, not a solution.

Many in the latter half of the nineteenth century expressed doubts over sunken continents, but many of those doubts took the form of dismissive lines here and there throughout scientific journals and letters among themselves. It was not until the prolific scientist and all-around renaissance man Alfred Russel Wallace, who at one time was a naturalist, explorer, geographer, engineer, surveyor, anthropologist, biologist, socialist activist, paranormal investigator, and xenologist, took a red pen to the idea of Lemuria and provided scientific reasoning to refute its existence in his 1880 tract *Island Life*.

Wallace was a man with remarkable curiosity. The breadth of his writings and topics to which he dedicated his life and talents bear witness to that. Upon entering adulthood, Wallace took up surveying, which led the way to a teaching gig at the University of Leicester in England, where he befriended entomologist Henry Bates and became intrigued by insects. As he continued surveying, this allowed him to explore his newfound passion and collect as many insects as possible. Tired of the workaday world and filled with insectile wanderlust, Wallace boated off to Brazil with his friend Bates and spent a handful of years there, collecting specimens and exploring the people and places in the wilds of the rainforest.

A longer journey next took him to the East Indies and the Malay Archipelago, which also served as the name of his highly successful book about his years there. While there, he collected over 175,000 specimens, many of which he sold to finance his research travels.

It is on these travels that he began developing his ideas around evolution and natural selection, becoming second to Darwin in terms of nineteenth-century evolutionary thinkers. While they disagreed over many details and theories revolving around evolution, Wallace and Darwin shared a hard, fast dedication to the importance of natural selection. Wallace would even write a book titled

British naturalist Alfred Russel Wallace, who developed the theory of natural selection concurrently to Charles Darwin.

Darwinism to promote natural selection and silence any detractors. In later life, he became interested in many different concepts, such as whether life could have existed on Mars, disproving flat-earth claims, and getting active with land reform movements in Great Britain.

Wallace himself at one point dabbled as a land bridge proponent, going in depth in a lecture given to the Linnean Society in 1859, agreeing that the Indian Ocean once housed a continent, and calling for a "great Pacific Continent" based on his extensive travels in the South Pacific:

> *They point to the time when a great continent occupied a portion at least of what is now the Indian Ocean, of which the islands of Mauritius, Bourbon, &c. may be fragments, while the Chagos Bank and the Keeling Atolls indicate its former extension eastward to the vicinity of what is now the Malayan Archipelago. The Celebes group remains the last eastern fragment of this now submerged land, or of some of its adjacent islands, indicating its peculiar origin by its zoological isolation, and by still retaining a marked affinity with the African fauna. The great Pacific continent, of which Australia and New Guinea are no doubt fragments, probably existed at a much earlier period, and extended as far westward as the Moluccas. The extension of Asia as far to the south and east as the Straits of Madagascar and Lombock must have occurred subsequent to the submergence of both these great southern continents; and the breaking up and separation of the islands of Sumatra, Java, and Borneo has been the last great geological change these regions have undergone.*

He believed that gradual geologic changes would have raised and lowered landmasses, which could have expanded the footprints of the islands and provided stepping stones for fauna to travel from the African continent to Madagascar. However, a whole sunken continent stretching out across multiple oceans was too easy a solution. Plus, there is no direct evidence that the land and sea underwent any radical change at least during the periods when lemur migration would have taken place.

Wallace applied multiple disciplines (climatology, geography, paleogeography, oceanography, biology, botany, et cetera) to explain how different fauna and flora were distributed to islands across the globe, and he found that every continent and every island offered similar problems of greater or lesser complexity.

For Madagascar, Wallace makes the same arguments that are passed around today, such as the islands surrounding Madagascar could have easily been larger and aided in the distribution. What is remarkable to Wallace (and to us still) is that the biological elements of Madagascar have more in common with the Americas than with Africa. And the current crop of African mammals would be more prevalent if there were some sort of land connection. He speculates about when Madagascar separated from Africa, saying that it had to happen before Africa separated from Europe and Asia. A sunken continent would be "so easy and pleasant," but his experiences had led him to know faunal distribution is seldom so easy.

While he makes a rather strong argument against a sunken continent around Madagascar, he fails to provide a compelling one for how lemurs got onto the island, going all over the place from era to era and building some sort of connection with Africa in the process (while also acknowledging the depth of the Mozambique Channel making it improbable). This is what would lead to later problems, as the scientists of the day were offered less than definitive arguments for a problem they had no clue how to solve.

Throughout the latter half of the nineteenth century and into the early twentieth, scientists discussing faunal distribution danced around the idea of whether or not the continents moved. The thinking of the day did not allow for that concept to be understood in any scientific way. Continents were where they were, and oceans were too. This permanence was backed by the likes of the Wallaces and other prominent men of science. They would say things like "If oceans and continents were permanent," already hedging their bets as to not truly declare that were the case but also avoid disputing it.

Even critics of Lemuria still relied upon other sunken landforms, such as sunken islands, to explain bird migration from India to Madagascar. One person's sunken islands are another's submerged continent. This does not help to dispute sunken continents, when scientists would turn around and then say there were sunken connections, just from another direction. This vague scientific theorizing allowed the "quasi-scientific writers" to swoop in and make the claims that they did.

THE FINAL AND MOST LASTING LEMURIA-ADJACENT RELATED CONTINENT

was proposed by Austrian geologist Eduard Suess in his work *Das Antlitz der Erde* (The Face of the Earth published in multiple volumes between 1885 and 1909 with the first English translation appearing in 1904, which has been called the greatest book that geology has ever seen. Suess named this amalgamation Gondwanaland (now referred to as Gondwana), a name that stuck. Gondwanaland would overshadow Lemuria in the scientific world and provide a theoretical bridge between land-bridge adherents of old and modern science.

Suess set about the lofty challenge of describing not only the current face of Earth but the ancient face as well, which is how he ended up theorizing the existence of Gondwanaland, a continent that included all of South America,

Africa, Madagascar, and India, and came to encompass much of the area that Sclater proposed, the only difference being that Suess approached it geologically first and zoologically tangentially. And even he seemed mystified at the presence of some flora and fauna on Gondwanaland.

Suess' shifting continents helped pave the way for the work of German astronomer-meteorologist-polar explorer Alfred Wegener, who right after the Great War would revolutionize the way we think about continents.

Wegener spent a considerable amount of time on expeditions in Greenland, mostly studying Arctic climate. Between two such expeditions, he became fascinated with the concept of isostasy, the idea that Earth's crust sits on a viscous layer, which in theory would allow movement of the continental shelf.

Using that interest, and looking at a globe and seeing how all the continents look like they could fit together as a massive puzzle, he got to work laying out his theory, which would come to be known as continental drift theory. It is in *The Origins of Continents and Oceans* that Wegener provides the basis for the drifting of continents. An interesting work, because he spends much of it quoting others saying how right he is. The impetus for Wegener was distribution of fauna and land bridges. It was a 1911 report of paleontological evidence of a land bridge between Brazil and Africa that set him down the path making arguments against land bridges, saying what others will echo—that land bridges are not for one species but for all. Also, the appearance and disappearance of these bridges would cause a displacement effect that has not been seen.

What connections there were between continents were formed with the existing continent shifting and moving, and not by the sinking of land or intermediate continents like Lemuria. Permanence exists, but as the area of the ocean and continental blocks as a whole and not of individual oceans and continents. What could be considered sunken continents only exist in coastal waters and continental shelf regions.

Lemuria plays a significant role in Wegener's theory. He is literally moving whole continents around to disprove its existence, and then labels the movement of the breakup of Gondwanaland as the Lemurian Compression. This compression shows how India broke away from Africa, peeling Madagascar off with it. India traveled and pushed into Asia. The ensuing collision (a very slow, drawn-out collision) created the Himalayas in the process and was felt all over, from Abyssinia, Somalia, and Burma to Mongolia and Russia. This action managed to set Madagascar off on its own journey, allowing it to travel down toward Africa and settle in its current location. Once again, Lemuria found itself at the nexus of some serious scientific thinking.

After nearly forty years of ridicule in the scientific community, continental drift theory began to be taken seriously in the mid-1960s, providing the inspiration for

Fig. 28.

Der lemurische Zusammenschub.

Figure showing Wegener's theory around the "Lemurian Compression" from his work Origin of the Continents and Oceans.

some true Kuhnian paradigm shifts. The breakthroughs came with the ideas of seafloor spreading and plate tectonics. These two geological advances created the equations whose outcome was continental drift theory.

However, this has not meant the end of sunken continents. On the contrary, it has led to a boom in recent years, brought about by the ever-progressing advances in technology. These modern devices have the ability to detect key paleomagnetic readings that signal seafloor spreading and plate shifts—and have picked up fractured chunks of sunken continents. Since plate tectonics became the new norm, more and more lost continents or chunks of lost continents are being discovered. Nary a year goes by without some new lost continent being called out either in Iceland or Australia, New Zealand or underneath Europe, or off the western coast of Africa or underneath the Mauritius Islands, just a hop, skip, and a raft away from the shores of Madagascar.

All of this certainly leaves the possibility open for there being more continental activity in and around Madagascar. Particularly since many have commented on Madagascar being a continental island—that is, made up of a broken hunk of another continent and not the creation of volcanic activity. The latest discoveries of other sunken continental fragments in the Indian Ocean relatively close to Madagascar do not rule out the possibility that there may have been more to Madagascar in the ancient past. Enough that it turns the theories of lemur colonization on their head.

Even all the newfound continents buried deep under risen continents or islands would have little impact on Madagascar, as it was already in its current location or at least as far from Africa as it currently sits. The presence of a Mauritian continent creates possibilities for further colonization of lemur ancestors from Madagascar to India, either through the same debates which got lemurs to Madagascar from Africa. But it is all relatively tight time frames and small geological windows of five or ten or fifteen million years to get lemurs to Madagascar and then out into India to help explain lorises there. Maybe that is the point that proves the rule. All it took was a couple of days in those millions of years to get the job done. By raft, by bridge, by whatever means necessary.

And where does that leave Lemuria? Who knows—maybe something similar did exist in some sort of bastardized piecemeal version. Small lanes of exposed land here, strips of land poking up there, and an ancient lemur could walk from Africa to Madagascar to India, though they more easily could not have made such a trek. And they peered longingly out to sea wondering what lies beyond or how they were brought here.

Almost from its inception, science hit back hard against the existence of Lemuria. If the physical continent does not exist, then Lemuria ceases to exist, but that is not what has occurred. Lemuria never existed. Even if such a land was there, no one knew it as Lemuria. It was a name given to a supposition. No more real than Gotham or Wakanda. Science went to great lengths to prove that it did not exist, never was real, just a bridge to nowhere. But sometimes trying hard to disprove a thing has the opposite result.

If all of this seems muddled, confusing, and less than definitive, that's because it is. And has always been a morass to wade through. Maybe that is the moral to this particular part of the story. When you deal with theories, however factual or scientific, they are just that: theories no more concrete than any other. This allowed Lemuria to live on a lot longer than some theorized faunal highway and ceased being about lemurs at all, and started being about people. Those gaps or openings pave the way for other more out-there, hurtful theories. The gyre widens. The center will not hold. It all falls apart.

CHAPTER 2:

The First Mammals to Wear Pants

ONCE YOU PLACE PEOPLE SOMEWHERE, IT BECOMES INCREDIBLY DIFFICULT to pry them off of that place, whether by nature or by other humans. We are natural colonizers, glomming onto a piece of territory with every fiber of our lazy industrious being and never letting go.

So when Germany's most famous Darwinist, Ernst Haeckel, put people, however primitive he might have made them, onto this place called Lemuria, he opened up a Pandora's box that still refuses to be shut. Using Sclater's idea of Lemuria he made that continent the cradle of mankind, while turning it into some sort of "evolutionary paradise" that led the way for others after him to have people—actual humans—and some not-so-humans inhabiting this now lost continent.

Haeckel's suggestion, aided by a map he drew of Lemuria that served as a distribution center for the hereditary ancestor to mankind, became a vital turning point in the Lemurian saga. He created the idea that Lemuria was a paradise—a special place where the missing link of human evolution was allowed to develop, and it finds itself at the heart of the debate on Darwin's theories. For after this, or really because of it, is when pseudo-scientists step in and hijack the narrative, sending Lemuria hurtling off into other directions and realms.

This is a long, meandering process deeply rooted in the history of the fight to promote and prove human evolution, which simultaneously devolves into scientific racism. And where there are Germans and racism, inevitably Nazis get dragged into the conversation.

FOR HOW MUCH TROUBLE IT WOULD CAUSE, HAECKEL SPENT VERY LITTLE time discussing Lemuria. He gave it a cursory mention in his seminal work of popular science, *Natürliche Schöpfungsgeschichte* (The History of Creation), providing glowing descriptions of Lemuria. Though he did refer to it as a paradise, in the same breath he also implied the land was a stand-in for any kind of paradise. This turned out to be an important idea, though, because it stuck, much as people did

German biologist and early champion of Darwin's theories, Ernst Haeckel.

on Lemuria. In every iteration of Lemuria that appears afterward, the land would remain a paradise. It all started with Haeckel's suggestion. But for the German Darwinist, there needed to be a Goldilocks land somewhere allowing the ideal conditions for humans to evolve. Lemuria was just as good as any in that regard.

A piece of deflection he throws out there that has been ignored by more esoteric thinkers is that right before mentioning Lemuria, he makes it abundantly clear that he is only offering his own theory: "any answer to this question must be regarded only as a provisional hypothesis."

Just as there was a need to create bridges to explain animal migration, there needed to be a way to move early man around. Lemuria served this purpose for Haeckel. At the time of his writing in the late 1860s and subsequent English translation in the early 1870s, *Lemuria* was newly coined. A scientific buzzword that had not yet received much scrutiny (that came later), it served as a perfect tool for Haeckel, ready to be used and to provide the means to transport all of man's early ancestors.

Haeckel was a monogenist, meaning he believed in a single origin for mankind. Because there was a single origin if you go back far enough, and he would go back all the way to tracing mankind to bacteria, the *urschleim*, to prove that there was one primeval home. And Haeckel made that home Lemuria:

But there are a number of circumstances (especially chronological facts) which suggest that the primeval home of man was a continent now sunk below the surface of the Indian Ocean, which extended along the south of Asia, as it is at present (and probably in direct connection with it), towards the east, as far as further India and the Sunda Islands; towards the west, as far as Madagascar and the south-eastern shores of Africa…. Sclater has given this continent the name of Lemuria.

By assuming this Lemuria to have been man's primeval home, we greatly facilitate the explanation of the geographical distribution of the human species by migration.

With that, people first appeared on Lemuria. Haeckel's Lemurians were the missing link in the developmental stage of mankind. Not quite apes, but not yet man.

It is a short passage and rather inconsequential in the grand scheme of the whole book. And that is it for Haeckel and Lemuria. Haeckel's Lemuria had little to no impact on the scientific community. While his use of Lemuria made no impact on science at the time, Haeckel himself made a huge impact, and his idea

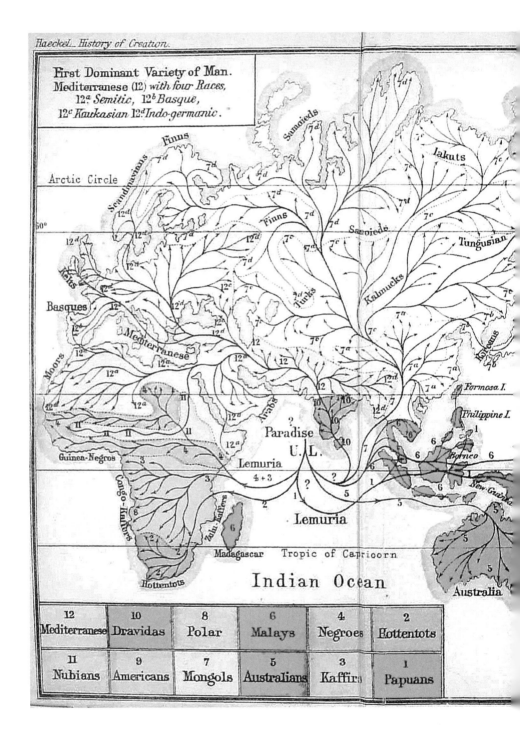

First Dominant Variety of Man.
Mediterranese (12) *with four Races,*
12ᵃ *Semitic,* 12ᵇ *Basque,*
12ᶜ *Kaukasian* 12ᵈ *Indo-germanic.*

Arctic Circle

Finns

Scandinavians

Samoieds

Iakuts

60°

Finns

Samoieds

Tungusian

Turks

Kalmucks

Basques

Moors

Mediterranese

Guinea-Negros

Congo-Kaffirs

Zulu-Kaffirs

Arabs

Paradise
U.L.

Lemuria
4 + 3

Lemuria

Formosa I.

Philippine I.

Borneo

New Guinea

Madagascar   Tropic of Capricorn

Hottentots

Indian Ocean

Australia

12	10	8	6	4	2
Mediterranese	Dravidas	Polar	Malays	Negroes	Hottentots
11	9	7	5	3	1
Nubians	Americans	Mongols	Australians	Kaffirs	Papuans

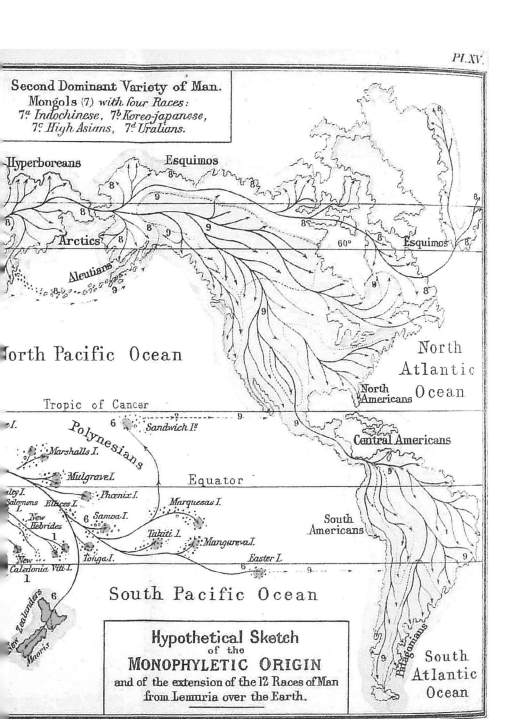

Haeckel's Map from The History of Creation *that shows the distribution of humans from Lemuria to around the world.*

of the Lemurian as a missing evolutionary step in humanity's origins would be key and is at the heart of the nineteenth-century debate on Darwin.

This idea most likely would not have been remembered if he had not put his artistic talents to use and drawn a stunning map, showing Lemuria and the migration out of it. He did what others had not yet done, and that is to visualize Lemuria, making it look good in the process. This map helped sell the idea far more than his words did. It made it all too easy to see how early protohumans shipped out of Lemuria and moved into Africa, Asia, India, and Europe.

The map also played a significant role in dislodging Lemuria from the original Sclater placement as having stretched out from South America to India. Haeckel's Lemuria sits squarely in the Indian Ocean, a position that allowed for these man-apes to migrate out of Lemuria to the other continents. He gives no real reason for doing so, and it appears to have something to do with finding a good central distribution point and area with a climate that would support a tropical paradise. The Indian Ocean provided both. And just like an inhabited Lemuria would have long-lasting effects, the movement of Lemuria would do the same, as later theorists would move the continent across the Pacific until it finally made its way to America.

The map stayed right up to the last official edition in 1920, and he never stopped saying that it was not hypothetical throughout, until fossil records started appearing in the 1890s, which led to some vindication on his part. While the map stayed, Lemuria did not. In a telling bit of erasure, in the eighth edition that came out in 1889, the name *Lemuria* disappeared. In between the publishing of the seventh and eighth editions, Helena Petrovna Blavatsky published *The Secret Doctrine*, throughout which she not only continually attacked Haeckel but also offered up her distinctly nonscientific take on Lemuria. As a move to cut off a new source of criticism, Haeckel simply excised Lemuria from the map. But he still mentioned the possibility of Lemuria, though his tone and ideas shifted to there possibly being two homes, one in Africa and the other in Southeast Asia.

Unlike his evolutionary compatriots, Haeckel was heavily ensconced in the German romantic scientist realm, seeing and styling himself much in the same vein as notable eighteenth- and nineteenth-century writers and scientists Alexander von Humboldt and Johann Wolfgang von Goethe. Goethe in particular heavily influenced him. His stature as a "nature philosopher" was one Haeckel hoped to ascend to.

Interplays of nature and philosophy filled Haeckel's writing and thinking, leading him to popularize monism as a belief structure in the late nineteenth century. His monistic beliefs, something he held tight to throughout his entire life until he passed away in 1919, were so influential that a Monistic Society was founded and prospered in Germany in the late nineteenth and on into the early twentieth century. His monism rejected the notion of "supernatural" events and transcendental intelligence having provided the universe with any sort of order or purpose—an outright rejection of religion. To Haeckel, humans have no immaterial soul or unique qualities setting them apart from the rest of nature. It is this belief in natural laws and materialism that would raise the ire of both the opponents of evolution and occultists alike.

Born in Potsdam in 1834, Haeckel began his educated life as a physician, studying medicine in Berlin and earning his M.D. in 1857. His sojourn into medicine lasted but a brief period, for he found his true calling in zoology. There he dedicated his life, working under the noted anatomist Carl Gegenbaur at the University of Jena, a university with which he would become synonymous, and his house there would be turned into a museum.

It was radiolarians, a form of protozoa characterized by the tiny, intricate skeletons they leave behind, where he made his early, important contributions to zoology and evolution. His monograph on them, *Radiolaria* (1862), laid the factual background for Darwin's theory, so much so that when the young Haeckel sent the English evolutionist the monograph, it brought forth a genuine enthusiasm for the work. He would keep sending Darwin positive press clippings that he received and other works of his that were published. Haeckel was not only known for his work with radiolarians but also for research on calcareous sponges, corals, and medusae, and for discovering and describing hundreds of species—an impressive showing that has led some to call him possibly the greatest invertebrate zoologist of all time.

Haeckel first read *On the Origin of Species* in 1864, during a radiolarian research trip to the Mediterranean. And something inside of him clicked with a passion and a fury. It cannot be overstated how much unbridled enthusiasm he showed for Darwinism, a passion that burned for the rest of his life. Evolution provided him the means to ascend to be the nature philosopher of his heroes. This exuberance survived and outlived him. Infecting others. Sparking curiosity.

What helped to elevate him over his peers were his keen artistic abilities. Each work exhibited intricately illustrated representations of the miniature marine forms, brightly colored and quite spectacular—enough so that collections of these illustrations have been published separately as *Art Forms in Nature* and *The Art and Science of Ernst Haeckel*. On top of all that, Haeckel knew how to turn a phrase and coined many key scientific terms, such as ecology, ontogeny, and phylogeny, as well as being the first person to use the phrase "World War I." In a great bit of Lemurian synergy, he was awarded the prestigious Darwin-Wallace Medal from the Linnean Society, the same place where Sclater coined the term *Lemuria*.

While all of these are key contributions to science, none of the accomplishments mentioned can compete with his other life: being Darwin's biggest hype man of the nineteenth century. Nobody else—not in Germany, Europe, or the world—could match his enthusiasm for Darwin's ideas or his reach. In his day as an explainer of evolution, more people learned about it from his works than anywhere else. Darwin's works were not as widely read as his. Haeckel became the primary source of the entire world's knowledge on Darwin and his theories.

His *The History of Creation* underwent many editions in German and English and twenty-three other languages, selling hundreds of thousands of copies, and he updated the content with every edition, keeping the public informed of new discoveries in the world of evolution. This made him as much of an international science celebrity as there could be in the nineteenth century. Where Darwin was restrained and cautious, Haeckel was combative and controversial, not afraid to lash out at opponents. He was very much the attack dog that evolution needed in order to be explained to a wider public. His caustic approach and vehement attacks on organized religion brought much scorn but also much attention, which helped steer more eyes toward his work and subsequently that of Darwin.

Darwin's contributions to science are massive. His theories of natural selection and descent reverberated through the scientific community and most everywhere else. While on one hand you had Darwinists like Haeckel and Wallace, there were equally vehement opponents to him. Some came from religious sectors, but many also came from within the science community—scientists whose life's work, their careers, their livelihoods were upended by Darwin's ideas and their quickening influence in their realms. So they fought back hard, creating an opening for Haeckel to be as combative as he wanted in order to needle these adversaries.

> *Seek to make the important general results of it [scientific discoveries] fruitful to the mass and to assist in spreading the knowledge of physical science among the people. The highest triumph of the human mind, the true knowledge of the most general laws of nature, ought not to remain the private possession of a privileged class of savants, but ought to become the common property of all mankind.*
>
> — Haeckel, *The History of Creation*

Haeckel identified a large receptive audience: the ever-growing middle class in industrialized nations. These educated readers related to Haeckel's arguments of utilizing personal initiative and individual achievement in their quest to improve their social status. And this same Western, educated middle class was being told that they, white Europeans, were atop the racial hierarchy, receiving from science and scientists a verification of their racial superiority, which helped to raise the profile of Haeckel's work.

One thing that Darwin did not do in *On the Origin of Species* was touch on human evolution or what his theories meant to human evolution. He said afterward that he did not want the uproar over the idea of humans evolving from some ape to overshadow the theory and process behind it. Like evolution, it would take a while, but a dozen or so years after *On the Origin of Species*, Darwin tackled human origins in *The Descent of Man,* published in 1871.

In that interim is when Haeckel published *The History of Creation*, first in German in 1868, with the first English translation appearing in 1874. When Darwin read the English version, he made a point to add to later editions of *The Descent of Man* how highly he regarded Haeckel's work, noting that if he had seen *The History of Creation* beforehand, he would not have even bothered to write his book. Haeckel nailed it. He realized that what general audiences wanted to read about was where humans had come from.

THE BIBLICAL ORIGINS OF HUMANKIND ESTABLISHED IN GENESIS HELD

up for a remarkable amount of time. For thousands of years, from the time of Adam up until the nineteenth century, nobody disputed the creation story.

During this period, many prominent scientists were going out of their way to link their proto-evolutionary ideas to creationism somehow. Carl Linnaeus, Georges Cuvier, and Louis Agassiz all worked under the eye of a supreme creator. Not really until Jean-Baptiste Lamarck's *Philosophie Zoologique* (1809) do you have ideas that humankind developed—and was not created by a supreme being— starting to spring forth: "Life is purely a physical phenomenon. All the phenomena of life depend on mechanical, physical, and chemical causes, which are inherent in the nature of matter itself."

Few supported this theory directly, but indirectly, the likes of Erasmus Darwin, grandfather to Charles, as well as Herbert Spencer, Lorenz Oken, and Thomas Henry Huxley all contributed to the idea of evolution. These ideas were all swirling around in the opening decades of the nineteenth century, waiting for someone to make a connection, which is when Charles Darwin makes his appearance. His doctrine of descent was much more comprehensive, strict, and interconnected than his predecessors' ideas. And he also established a new theory on the natural causes of organic development, the active ingredient in producing organic matter, and a means for this organic material to transform over time, which he called natural selection.

When first presented, no one was fully accepting all of Darwin's theories. Scientists picked and chose the bits of his theories that would further their ideas, while rejecting aspects that did not fit their theses.

If descent is the "how," then natural selection is as close to a "why" as we get. Species were not formed according to fixed ideas; instead, organic change was driven by ordinary laws and the forces of nature. At its core, Darwin's *On the Origin of Species* created three fundamental questions concerning human evolution: when did humans first appear, who were their nearest ancestors, and where did they first appear?

In practice, human evolution is a huge thorny bramble, not so much a tidy diagram that shows apes evolving into humans. It is not that linear. There are dead ends, starts and stops, intermingling, and a plethora of antecedents that somehow fit together where the end results are us humans. Each new discovery further complicates matters—which makes the works by popular scientists like Haeckel then, or other works about it today, so important in smoothing out these complications, so we can begin to understand how humanity evolved.

It is generally agreed upon by most scientists that *Homo sapiens* evolved in southern Africa roughly 300,000 years ago. If *Homo sapiens* evolved around 300,000 years ago, they got there by evolving over several millions of years as far back as seven million years ago. Our early hominid ancestors included a whole host of primates (*Dryopithecus, Graecopithecus, Griphopithecus, Kenyapithecus, Orrorin, Sahelanthropus, Samburupithecus*, et cetera); from this entangled jumble, no true missing link exists, only a journey that involves dozens of species and many more questions.

These early hominins were very apelike in appearance, but they had one of the key attributes that separates apes from hominins: they walked on two legs. This bipedalism distinguished them from other apes at the time and developed as a key trait on the journey to humanity.

Along with walking on two legs, our brain size is much more expansive than our ancestral apes—three times the size. Interestingly, that growth happened over the past two million years, which coincides with the findings that there existed no older traces of hominins outside of Africa before 2.1 million years ago. Maybe the two go hand in hand. As the brain size increased, so did the ability to think long-term. Some have speculated there was a feedback loop created where advances in technology, such as inventing tools for everyday life, allowed them to hunt more efficiently and secure nutritious meat to fuel brain growth, which allowed them to think up bigger and better tools to get even more meat.

Further complicating matters was that there were many different hominid species walking the planet from about 15,000 years to seven million years ago. Many "evolutionary experiment" species came and went, evolving at different rates. These include body parts randomly evolving, like a very modern human-like hand being attached to the arm of an ape—discoveries that blow the doors off the notion of the steady progress of evolution. There were a lot more bumps in that road.

DNA analysis shows how similar we are at the deepest level with chimps and bonobos, sharing 99 percent of the same genetic makeup. By taking DNA samples from some of the more recent hominids like Neanderthals and Denisovans, we learn the story of how *H. sapiens* interbred with them—the offspring of which provided *H. sapiens* with certain traits like being able to handle higher altitudes, and the development of antibodies to viruses found in certain parts of the world. This crushes any notions of purity within a species, let alone a particular race, and while these species were interbreeding with one another, they were also sharing other things like culture, the ability to craft tools, art, et cetera.

Within the DNA of us, there also lie mysteries. While we have fossil records for Neanderthals and very scant records of Denisovans, we nonetheless have those records and have extracted DNA from those that give us insight into their genetic makeup. However, both of them disappeared between fifteen to thirty thousand years ago, and no one knows why. Some theorize that *H. sapiens* waged war on Neanderthals and Denisovans, wiping them off the face of the planet. But there also exist other traces of unknown hominids with our DNA, ready to be discovered one day. A whole slew of missing links—but maybe there will always be missing links, because we are dealing with millions of years of evolution.

All of this modern research makes Haeckel's suppositions of a Lemurian cradle for humanity and his development model of Lemuria as extinct as the continent itself. With multiple paths to the promised land, Lemuria is not needed to get you there.

A major discussion point within the human origin story is: Where did humans originate? In the nineteenth century, physical proof (fossils) was an important step needed in order to prove to creationists the validity of Darwinism.

Darwin, for what it's worth, was an outlier in his day, as he suggested Africa as the probable origin place for mankind due to the fact that humankind's nearest primate cousins, chimps and gorillas, could be found there. However, there was an overwhelming consensus among philosophers and scientists, and almost everyone else, that humanity came from Asia. For around 150 years between 1800 and 1950, most of the science community, from evolutionists to philologists and everything in between, believed that Asia was where the human race first existed.

In the eighteenth century, a British colonial administrator and amateur philologist, William Jones, set sail for India, where after some time spent researching there, he delivered a series of lectures that created the idea of an Indo-European field of study that encompassed a wide swath of sciences. It is during these lectures that he proposed a "central country" from which all cultures sprang. While he located this place in Persia—modern-day Iran—it was more the dual concept that stuck: both the idea of Indo-European culture tying everything to Europe, and an idea of a wellspring or cradle.

German philosopher Georg Wilhelm Friedrich Hegel likened the Indo-European concept to discovering a lost continent, and it enabled the building of bridges between people and places far apart and seemingly independent of each other. His *Philosophie der Geschichte* (1837) popularized the phrase *ex Oriente lux*, "a light from the East," which greatly helped spread the idea of Asian origins.

What helped in popularizing this idea was the discovery of ancient Buddhist and Vedic texts that far predated Western and Egyptian societies, which made many creationists start to question how it was possible for these societies to exist seemingly before the residents of Eden. So by the time it got around to Haeckel and *The History of Creation*, he was not making any outlandish statements when he suggested that there was a cradle of humanity and it existed somewhere east of Africa. The newly coined Lemuria perfectly fit both of these categories and answered many questions. How did early humans migrate? Especially if the oceans and continents remained stationary? A huge intercontinental central landmass connecting Africa, India, and Asia offered a means to ferry our ancestors between continents.

But back in the nineteenth century, the idea of a linear progress of evolution was still prominent, leading to the quest to find that "missing link" between man and ape. As Haeckel pushed a Lemurian-based Asian cradle of humanity, it inspired Dutch physician Eugène Dubois to go off in search of the elusive lost piece to human evolution.

Dubois became enamored with the wanderlust of science and chased that passion. For him, it was to prove evolution in humans. And he kind of managed to do that in the late 1880s, after becoming disillusioned with his academic career, where he had made a name for himself tracing the evolution of the larynx. Ernst Haeckel and others placed much importance on the development of speech as one of the key factors in the advancement of the human species. Since the larynx plays a significant role in the formation of the sounds to create speech, it was a backdoor means to solve that mystery of human progression. Wanting more, and motivated by recent Neanderthal skeleton discoveries in Spy, Belgium, Dubois became excited about the possibility of finding the fossil record needed to prove human evolution.

Using his trusty "Bible of evolution," Haeckel's *The History of Creation*, Dubois looked to Asia. Research and some rational thinking landed him in the Dutch East Indies. Soon, he enlisted as a medical officer and made his way to Sumatra. Once there, during his free time he would venture out to the caves of Sumatra in search of fossils, which he found in droves—but none proved useful in the hunt to prove human evolution.

His tactics shifted when he secured a transfer from Sumatra to Java and focused his efforts on recessed river beds. This yielded immediate results, as an ancient jawbone was discovered. Over the course of the next couple of digging seasons, Dubois' crew (for he did little digging or even overseeing himself, relying instead on forced labor among the native inhabitants) unearthed two monumental finds. First came the skull cap, which was too big to be ape and yet too small to be human. The following year saw the discovery of a femur not far away and in the same geologic layer. The femur showed this species to be an upright walker. Add the two together, bipedalism and increased brain capacity, and you get a new species of ancient ape, which he called "the first known transitional form." It took three days, two weeks, and five years, but in 1891, Dubois had his missing link.

He gave it the name *Pithecanthropus erectus* after the species theorized by Haeckel in *The History of Creation*. Over time, it came to be known as *Homo erectus*.

Criticism of Dubois and his findings came almost immediately: wave after wave of negativity left him to answer his critics constantly, year after year hardening him. As he became withdrawn, he took his bones and went home. There was a lot of praise, with the most stirring defense coming from Haeckel at the 4th International Congress of Zoology (1898) where he took on Dubois' critics:

> *These deplorable deficiencies of empirical palæontology are balanced on the other side by a growing number of positive facts, which possess an inestimable value in human phylogeny. The most interesting and most important of these is the celebrated fossil* Pithecanthropus erectus, *discovered in Java in 1894 by Dr. Eugène Dubois. Three years ago this now famous ape-like man provoked an animated discussion at the third International Zoological Congress at Leyden . . . The final result of the long discussion at Leyden was that, of twelve experts present, three held that the fossil remains belonged to a low race of man; three declared them to be those of a man-like ape of great size; the rest maintained that they belonged to an intermediate form, which directly connected primitive man with the anthropoid apes. This last view is the right one, and accords with the laws of logical inference.* Pithecanthropus erectus *of Dubois is truly a Pliocene remainder of that famous group of highest Catarrhines which were the immediate pithecoid ancestors of man. He is, indeed, the long-searched-for 'missing link,' for which, in 1866, I myself had proposed the hypothetical genus* Pithecanthropus, *species* Alalus.

At the time, Dubois' discoveries became the proof needed for human evolution and showed the development from ape to man. However, in more modern times, the

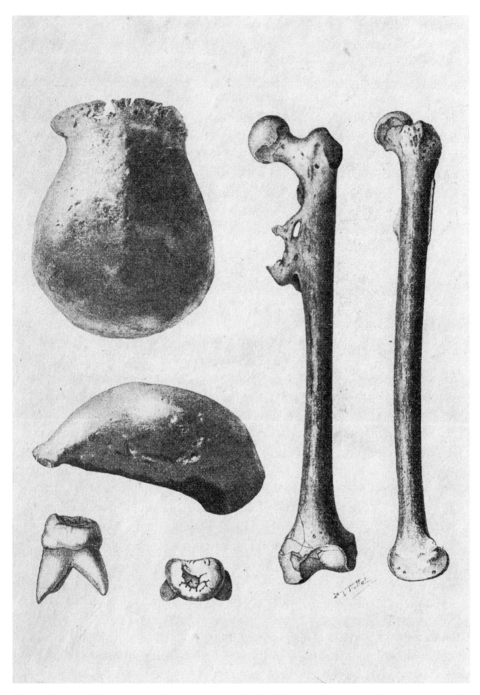

Illustrations of the bones discovered by Dubois' work teams, which he used to theorize a new evolutionary layer to humanity, which he called Pithecanthropus erectus *after Haeckel. During his life, Dubois kept tight control over access to these bones, and only allowed a select few to make detailed drawings of them.*

findings have come into serious question, with the femur uncovered by Dubois' team not bearing the same characteristics as more modern *Homo erectus* discoveries. There is some doubt existing around the skull cap; putting aside the legitimate questions whether or not the skull and femur came from the same creature, the skull cap has been described as possibly being that of a larger-than-normal gibbon. Despite these challenges, Dubois did create the analytical framework by which hominid remains are still studied and analyzed, 125 years later.

He also helped to vindicate Haeckel's ideas, as well as giving a veneer of science to those who had used Haeckel as the basis for their own theories.

IN THE NINETEENTH CENTURY, MANY SCIENTISTS HELD TERRIBLE VIEWS and espoused even more bizarre ones, while today scientists lean toward extreme specialization, staying in one lane to pursue those interests almost solely and the minutiae that stem from that. Yesteryear's science depended upon proving prejudices and preconceived notions. This is how race came to be at the heart of so many matters, with scientists determined to document the differences between races, no matter how ridiculous and far afield they happened to be.

Not only content on putting people on Lemuria, Haeckel brought races there as well. In his lead-up to mentioning Lemuria, Haeckel first lays out in depth his hierarchy of races, forever connecting the two: race and Lemuria. He created that through line, which would stick to the lost continent. Race and Lemuria are inseparable, with Lemurians later becoming their own race altogether.

Haeckel posits a twenty-two-stage development process that mankind went through, beginning with a common bacterium from which all life sprang and continuing through to the stage where we are now. Lemuria fits in at that twenty-first stage, the man-ape stage, and it is from there, after the diaspora from Lemuria, when man-ape turns into humans and then into different races.

Haeckel saw the many races as being different species, saying that if whites and blacks were snails there was no way that scientists would think that they came from the same species. He goes further and breaks down humans into twelve different species, with races falling under those species levels. The differences important to him were skin-deep and included skin color, hair texture, and skull shape, and that is what has led to the different species of humans.

Nineteenth-century scientists were race-obsessed and concentrated their attention on proving the superiority of white Europeans. While Darwin remained somewhat ambivalent toward race, at least in his public writings, that did not stop every other evolutionist out there from bringing race into the equation. When evolution came around, it proved to be a powerful tool in this quest to scientifically cement white Europeans at the top of the evolutionary ladder. And Haeckel was no exception.

In the same breath as discussing Lemuria, he places it within a racial hierarchy, drawing a fanciful tree of races. This tie-in would lead others to turn Lemurians into their own race, eventually into a variety of other beings, and back to being the ideal Aryans in the Nazi sense of the word. All of it starts with Haeckel and is deeply ingrained in the world of scientific racism.

Haeckel's hierarchy of races was nothing new—a regurgitation of all that came before him, starting more than one hundred years before, with Linnaeus devising the four "varieties" of humans (American, Asiatic, African, and European). This was followed by Johann Friedrich Blumenbach creating five races: Caucasian, Mongolian, Ethiopian, American, and Malayan. From here on out, scientists referred to these biological and physical differences among groups as races.

Nearly at the same time as race came into being, white European males started having opinions on which ones were the best races. Like Georges Cuvier saying whites were the most beautiful, or Francis Galton, Darwin's cousin, using observation to document the passing of traits from generation to generation, claiming that if we can see heredity in humans, then we could control its social impacts. Galton helped to form the building blocks of eugenics. He went a step further in his *Heredity Genius* and provided a statistical analysis of men of genius, in which he talked about inferior races losing the evolutionary battle against European countries. He claimed immigrants wreaked havoc with the gene pool of ancient Greece, which led to its downfall, and called on the government to take action and have the best people procreate "to keep the superior stocks from mixing with inferiors."

Haeckel lived, thrived, and influenced in this environment. Many times throughout *The History of Creation* when talking about Darwin, his theory of natural selection, or others' views on the science of evolution, he will manage to turn it back around to race—which immediately devolves into "lower races" and how they are incapable of a true inner culture or higher mental development. He is unable to discuss race without placing some sort of value on it.

When not being detrimental toward one race, he was elevating others—mostly his own, which he would call the "Indo-Germanic" race, "which has far surpassed all other races of men in mental development." These "Indo-Germans" showed off their superiority by spreading out over the entire globe, conquering it, and doing such a great job that they pushed other races to the brink of extinction, such as the decimation of the indigenous peoples of North and South America that followed after European conquest.

Since it was the English and Germans who figured out evolution and who follow monistic philosophy, that proved to Haeckel their superior developments. It just so happens that all of Haeckel's interests also fall in line with the superior mental developments of Indo-Germans.

All of this is coming seemingly unprovoked and does not fit into any of his arguments for promoting human evolution, other than that this is what people thought about when they thought about how humans evolved. They, being white middle-class Europeans or those Americans of European descent, wanted scientific validation that they were better than others, and—maybe more importantly—different from all the other peoples of color. Ultimate proof of white superiority. And Haeckel was all too willing to provide that.

Because of his dogged focus on race, modern critics of Haeckel leveled claims that he was an inspiration for Nazi racial policies. His biographer has struck back against such claims, but in doing so, he lets Haeckel off the hook for his racist views. There were other scientists during this era that escaped discussing races in the derogatory manner with which Haeckel approached it. Also, he managed to think freely and progressively on many other topics, but not about race. His influence upon the thought leaders of National Socialism is a mixed bag. The Nazis did not really need a singular racist inspiration to fuel their hateful, murderous ways. Assigning sole blame to a single scientist downplays the hundreds of years of prejudice that came before and ignores developments in and around that period of time. It is complicated and does not lie solely on the writings of Haeckel.

But it cannot be ignored that while much is made out of how popular Haeckel was in spreading the views of Darwin and evolution, that same text was also advancing a white supremacist viewpoint. While he may not have directly influenced Nazi policy, he did popularize, normalize, and scientificize white Aryan supremacy, and that, however inadvertently or purposely, could be introduced into the hearts and minds of the German middle class—who would then lend their support to the National Socialists, look the other way, and become complacent and complicit as they committed their atrocities.

This is the company that Lemuria kept, at the vanguard of evolution yet the nexus of racism. While others who came later, primarily Blavatsky and Rudolf Steiner, were ingesting Haeckel and his views on Lemuria—that it was a paradise, that it was a cradle—they also ingested these ideas about race, and they would go on to permeate their works and the works of their followers. Lemuria lay within the hearts of those seeking to understand humanity's origins and a means to prove the ascendency of a white Europa. Haeckel put people on Lemuria and also turned it into a paradise—two ideas that have stuck to Lemuria a century and a half later—while dislodging it from its mooring, which allowed the continent to travel the seas and roam where it's needed. While Haeckel's racial views and those of many other leading nineteenth-century Darwinists would twist and turn into twentieth-century nightmares, Lemuria kept on growing and receiving attention from very different sources.

CHAPTER 3:

The Congressman and the Continent

ALREADY EXISTING. ALREADY LOST. ALREADY CONSUMED BY THE OCEAN. There. Out past the pillars of Heracles. Once great, laid Atlantis, whose shadow looms large when there is any discussion about sunken island continents. It is the alpha of such long-lost places, and in order to tell the history of Lemuria, one must first pay respects to Atlantis. Because nearly every single time Lemuria gets brought up, Atlantis is right there with it, an oceanic marriage of convenience. Like marriage, it can be volatile, though this one will come to include nuclear bombs and imprisonment in deep underground cities. Atlantis was birthed from the mind of Plato, or relayed through him, and has been mystifying people ever since. However, the question is not whether or not Atlantis really existed, but whether people believed Plato when he said that it did. And it is at the same time that Lemuria was receiving consideration in the scientific world that Atlantis was being revived—being pulled out of the abyss and brought into the modern consciousness. The lost continent sisters had forever linked themselves.

The man at the heart of the nineteenth-century revival of Atlantis was a former United States congressman, a failed Populist, a doomed city builder, a purveyor of apocalyptic proclamations. He was Ignatius Donnelly, a distinctly American figure who proves that no matter how many times a person loses, they are never really a failure. And his road to salvation led through Atlantis, and more specifically laid out a popular argument for its actual existence. Popular it was, and proved to be incredibly influential, for in many ways, you do not get what comes next with Lemuria without Donnelly's study of Atlantis. He set the tone for this kind of DIY research that would thrive for those wishing to do the same for Lemuria. He also had small but dramatic and direct implications for Lemuria, continuing it on its seemingly endless mission to wander the oceans looking for a place to settle. And it does not happen without Atlantis.

ATLANTIS COMES FROM A SINGLE PLACE: FROM THE MIND OF ONE PERSON, Plato, the famed ancient Greek philosopher. No other writer before him ever mentioned a land called Atlantis, though the surviving written record is scant. The continent nation only briefly appears in Plato's dialogue *Timaeus* but gets explored more in depth in his next dialogue, *Critias*. Often, these two dialogues get lumped together due to their being written near the same time (around 360 BC) and covering the same contemporary period of time and event.

Timaeus was the first of these dialogues to be written, and proved to be a greatly influential work that was preserved through the Dark Ages. Up until the thirteenth century, the ideas found within *Timaeus* provided the general understanding of the natural world. The setup for the majority of the dialogue is taken up by Timaeus describing how the universe was created, the purpose of that creation, expanding on the elements and properties of the universe, providing details into the makeup of those elemental forces, and saying that the universe was shaped like a dodecahedron. However, before we get to this natural philosophy section, Critias chimes in to relate a story he heard from Solon, and it is here the world first comes across the story of Atlantis.

OFFERING BUT A GLIMPSE, CRITIAS GIVES A BRIEF SYNOPSIS OF HOW

Atlantis rose up, figuratively, as a nation based on a substantial island, "larger than Libya and Asia put together," out in the Atlantic Ocean (we assume it is the Atlantic), locating it out past the Pillars of Heracles. It was home to a powerful empire that ruled over other islands and parts of Africa and Europe. Not content with what they had, the Atlanteans came after Athens and the rest of the Hellenistic world. Athens led the way in a coalition against the Atlanteans. As the war dragged on, Athens' allies dropped off, and alone they defeated the island empire. Soon after, earthquakes and floods sank Atlantis in a day—forever lost down below the ocean.

In Plato's next dialogue, *Critias,* he goes further in depth into the Atlantis story, picking right up where *Timaeus* left off, relating that the events happened 9,000 years ago and that it was told to Solon while traveling through Egypt. Solon lived some two hundred years prior to Plato and was an important Athenian statesman who ushered in a series of reforms in ancient Athens as the Chief Magistrate, such as canceling debts and mortgages, standardizing weights and measures, opening up citizenship, and repealing the death penalty. When urged to become a tyrant, he instead retired and left Athens for ten years, traveled around, presumably to Egypt where he learned the tale of Atlantis. And he would not be the last person who traveled to Egypt and came back with occult knowledge, as it is a running theme.

Atlantis dates back to the age of the old gods, when the world was allotted to them. Being in the ocean, it fell under the purview of Poseidon, who mated with an island maiden, with the children from this coupling going on to rule over Atlantis and the other domains of its empire—ten kings in all. The oldest son and first king was Atlas, from whom Atlantis derives its name, "daughter of Atlas."

After providing the genealogy of the offspring from Poseidon, Critias gets into describing the natural resources of Atlantis, the mountains, lakes, and woods—all of which provided ample resources for the island nation, enough to support elephants, and included vast copper mines. The people prospered, building bridges and canals, temples and palaces, a harbor, and citadels.

He takes you on a tour around the city and its environs. Along the way, he provides a glimpse into Atlantean society, how leaders were found, how military service was handled, and the prayers to Poseidon. Most importantly, the kings were not to take up arms against one another and were bound to come to each other's aid.

As the generations passed, the godly blood thinned out, making the kings more human, which brought with it the human vices of avarice, power lust, and all sorts of unseemly behavior. So much so that Zeus intervened to punish the out-of-control Atlanteans, which is where Critias ends mid-sentence: "And when he called them together, he spake as follows."

That is it. A little over 7,000 words on the place, all of which launched centuries of writers and others down paths trying to prove, disprove, understand, and locate Atlantis. One thing that is for certain is how opaque it all is. While modern Platonic scholars can agree that Atlantis is a myth, that's about all they can agree on. What the myth refers to or is trying to say remains very much up for debate.

Atlantis shares details with many other nations, states, and cultures either at the time of Plato's writing or within the relatively near past of Plato. Corollaries have been made between Atlantis and Persia or Carthage or Syracuse or Attica or Athens itself, and the various configurations between them. It could also partly be true that Plato was harkening back to early Minoan Crete or Thera civilizations. Whatever the meaning is behind Atlantis is hard to parse out.

Plato lived eighty or eighty-one years on this planet, but his ideas have stretched way beyond and have lived on nearly 2,500 years after he died. Born in Athens in 428(7) BC, he was raised in a family of "public men," statesmen, and legislators, one of them being Critias (the younger), whose grandfather is the Critias in whose mouth Plato places the Atlantis story. But not much is definitively known about Plato up to his sixtieth birthday. His life is a bit of a blank slate, with the only discernible thing being the influence Socrates played in shaping his mind. Socrates was acquainted with Plato's uncle, so he might have been around for most of Plato's life, and the two eventually became friends. It was Plato who tried to help his friend out of Athens as he got into political trouble, which led to Socrates' execution. But the historical Plato does not make an appearance until he founded the Academy in his forties, and he dedicated his time and energy to organizing and directing the activities of the Academy. When he turned sixty, he became embroiled in intrigues involving the Syracuse and Carthaginian courts, which sparked his only known trip from Athens. It proved perilous and he got out just as there were plans on his life. He spent the remaining years at the Academy and pulled together his late dialogues, which *Timaeus* and *Critias* fall under.

All of his dialogues have apparently made it down over the millennia. There are no references to any that are missing or incomplete, which makes the abrupt end of *Critias* very conspicuous, and it seems unlikely that the ending was lost at all—more likely, it was purposely never finished.

There has been some interesting commentary on why Plato invokes history as he does, dedicating the entire dialogue to it, since he is constructing his own alternative history to comment on how and why we construct our own histories, and the transformations that happen to the facts when we do so. A fundamental lack of both understanding and agreement on the nature and existence of Atlantis has allowed for it to become debatably "real" and waiting to be discovered.

Atlantis, or the idea of it, interested some in Athens. Not terribly long after Plato wrote about Atlantis, Theopompus came around to offer his spin on the same motif, parodying the Atlantis story in his *Philippica*. His island of "Meropia" shares a lot of basic similarities such as the two opposing cities, and he took a step toward further heightening the irreality by having it relayed by a satyr-like creature, which might provide some insight into what he thinks of Plato. While his main goal might have been to poke fun at the idea of Atlantis, what he managed to accomplish is being the first to create an outright fictional Atlantis—a tradition that still thrives to this day.

Aristotle would also dip a toe in Atlantean waters by saying the lands outside the "Pillars of Heracles" joined up with parts of India, which could have much later provided inspiration for Columbus' journey to the New World. What is of particular interest is that he invokes the idea of a land bridge to account for elephants in Africa, Asia, India, and Atlantis—another first, this theorized land connection to explain similar animal species in multiple places.

For the remainder of antiquity, Atlantis would be brought up sparingly. It was used mostly as an example to discuss catastrophic events like earthquakes and islands being submerged. As BC turned to AD and Christianity spread, early church writers would use Atlantis as an example of possible proof of the biblical flood. But the writings offered nothing in the way of investigations or commentary, with Atlantis being but one example, a footnote, that may or may not have happened. Cosmas Indicopleustes' *Christian Topography* is the last such ancient text written in the late sixth century. This came some nine hundred years after *Timaeus* and *Critias*.

Nine hundred more years would go by before Atlantis made its way out of the depths and back into the imagination of writers, scientists, explorers, and

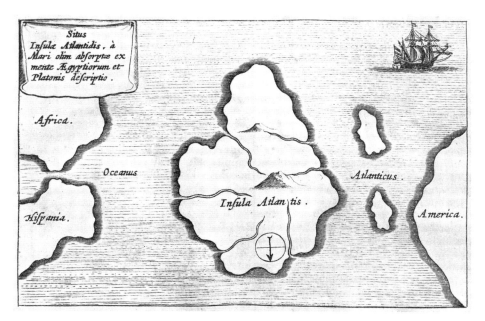

Image of Athanasius Kircher's map from his work Mundus Subterraneus, *which is the first known depiction of Atlantis.*

the church. A couple of things happened in the late fifteenth century to achieve Atlantis' resurrection. First, Marsilio Ficino would translate Plato's works, bringing new attention to them, and Ficino would come out and say Atlantis was real. Next, Columbus set sail into the Atlantic and came across the Americas, the New World. This began a long tradition of claiming Atlantis was the New World.

With the coming European exploration and colonization of the Americas, it brought new people to these continents and in contact—violent contact—with the native inhabitants. They began to study the indigenous peoples. From these works, we get allusions that the Americas were Atlantis, like the works from sixteenth-century Spanish writers like Francisco López de Gómara and Pedro Sarmiento de Gamboa.

The seventeenth century produced the first map drawn with Atlantis on it, by Athanasius Kircher. Sir Francis Bacon offered up an updated version of the Atlantis story in his posthumously released essay "The New Atlantis." Instead of the Atlantic, he locates his utopian island nation of Bensalem in the South Pacific. But it is very much a utopian world. The most intriguing development of this time was the work of the Swedish physician Olof Rudbeck and his *Atlantica*. Rudbeck was the leading physician in Sweden and made major medical breakthroughs, achievements, and great scholarly contributions, yet he became convinced to the point of obsession that Atlantis could be found in Sweden.

Rudbeck was the first to succumb to the infatuation with the Atlantis story. This began with compulsively investigating the continent and going searching for it like no one else would do until Donnelly two hundred years later. He compared Scandinavian runes to other artifacts, claimed Noah's son Japhet ended up in Atlantis, a.k.a. Sweden, and theorized that Atlantis became the cradle of civilizations—the exact idea that Donnelly would hit upon and make popular. The nationalistic approach made it somewhat popular in Sweden, and even Isaac Newton wrote Rudbeck to ask for a copy of his work. However, what publicity he garnered quickly dissipated, and his work has been all but forgotten. Donnelly makes no mention of Rudbeck in his work, and *Atlantica* never was translated into English, but Donnelly does reference Sweden a handful of times, and it would be interesting to find if he ran across Rudbeck's work in Scandinavian-rich Minnesota. The Enlightenment and the Age of Revolution did not leave much time to explore the topic of Atlantis, but in general it brought about more skepticism around the idea of a real Atlantis. One exception would be Jean-Sylvain Bailly, mayor of Paris during the Revolutionary era and eventual guillotine victim. Bailly also dabbled in ancient history and thought there had to be a "destroyed and forgotten" place where civilization sprang from, which he had tabbed to be Atlantis. What Plato was doing was describing a memory of a golden age that had made its way down to him, with Atlantis serving much the same use as Haeckel's Lemuria: a launchpad where civilizations spread out from all over.

The decades prior to Donnelly's work saw not much by way of direct research. Irishman Henry O'Brien's *The Round Towers of Ireland* helped set a diffusionist precedent by attempting to link those Irish round towers to the Egyptian pyramids, though he made no direct correlation to Atlantis. Just prior to the publication of Donnelly's book, amateur archaeology couple the Le Plongeons began spinning their tale of Queen Móo and Atlantis, taken from their discoveries at Chichén Itzá on the Yucatán Peninsula. The biggest development was the beginning of utilizing Atlantis in fiction, such as the fantastical flights of French occultist Antoine Fabre d'Olivet or in the poetry of Jacint Verdaguer. The most notable was the runaway success of Jules Verne's *20,000 Leagues Under the Sea*, where Captain Nemo takes his *Nautilus* on a ride around the ruins of Atlantis. Some have said this directly inspired Donnelly to go on his own hunt for Atlantis.

What is clear is that there existed no real intellectual environment for Donnelly to operate in. There was no consistent discourse on Atlantis over the previous three centuries, only isolated bursts from all over the Western world. Donnelly managed to popularize the idea of Atlantis by knowingly or unknowingly synthesizing some arguments that had come before, while creating a whole lot more arguments in the process.

Ignatius Donnelly, American politican, populist, orator, novelist, Shakespearean author doubter, and proponent of Atlantis. (Minnesota Historical Society)

THERE IS A CERTAIN KIND OF HUSTLER THAT IS NATIVE TO AMERICA.

Bustling with energy and near-boundless ideas (some would call them schemes), changing not so much with the times or with failures but upon the breezes of their whims, forever in search of that thing. That thing that has burrowed within them so long, long ago that they have been chasing after it ever since, as it floats forever out of grasp.

Ignatius Donnelly was a hustler. Not in the swindler sense, but in a romantic one—a gothic romantic one. Full of apocalyptic declarations that teeter upon the precipice of reason, dire political prophecies of class warfare, and the immediate collapse of civilization. To be a hustler, you must have supreme confidence in yourself, your ability to be right, to win. Donnelly held such views of himself, which is not to say self-doubt did not creep in, defeat after defeat, because it did, but the hope for something new, something better, always rested there ready to be grasped. His critics called him the greatest failure who ever lived. But defeats to a hustler are fuel: an unsatisfied, unrecognized fuel spurring him on to the next thing.

Born and raised in Philadelphia to an Irish immigrant father and second-generation Irish-American mother in 1831, Donnelly was mostly raised by his pawn-shop-owning mother after his father died of typhus. Out of school and needing a career, he steered toward law, apprenticing under Benjamin Harris Brewster, who would later serve as the U.S. Attorney General. He branched out on his own, a full-fledged twenty-one-year-old lawyer, and quickly became involved in Democratic politics, using his first public political speech to provide a phrenological reading of Horace Greeley's head. Becoming a champion of immigrants and the role government should play in accepting them into their society, at a time when nativist, Know-Nothing sentiment spread over the country, became his first cause, which put him at odds with Democratic views. And by 1858, he had switched his allegiance to the newly formed Republican Party.

Not showing much adeptness in actual law, Donnelly headed up co-ops to help German and Irish migrants finance and build homes. As altruistic as that all sounds, it included speculating in land, which netted him some profits and his opponents some ammunition. Combine the ill feelings of his opponents and no law practice, among other failures, and Philadelphia had lost its appeal, so he headed west to Minnesota in 1857.

The decision to move to Minnesota was one of money, or the potential for money. The Territory of Minnesota was expanding rapidly during the 1850s: the population went from 6,000 at the start of the decade to 170,000 by the end of it, becoming a state in 1858. Donnelly saw this boom and wanted a piece of it, partnering with fellow Philadelphia expat John Nininger to buy up land south of St. Paul with the intention of building a town there, Nininger City, where Donnelly threw himself into promoting the venture. It failed almost on arrival, with the one lasting thing being his house, in which he would remain.

More immediate success came through politics, where he ingratiated himself quickly into local Republican affairs, elbowing his way into state and then national politics. Donnelly was elected Lieutenant Governor of Minnesota in 1858 at the age of twenty-eight, followed shortly thereafter by a successful campaign to win a seat in the U.S. House of Representatives, where he served from 1863 to 1869. After losing the seat, he started to become more and more radical, eventually getting involved with many different reform movements of the day: the Grangers, anti-monopoly, anti-corruption, et cetera, forming much of the platform for what would come to be known as Populism. He would serve in the Minnesota state legislature and run as the People's Party (Populist Party) vice presidential candidate on a ticket with Wharton Baker in 1900.

His popular writing helped to keep him in the spotlight and elevate his political standing. *Atlantis: The Antediluvian World* came out when his political career was at an all-time low. In the previous decade, multiple political battles had turned against him; absorbing those slings and arrows for years and years can have an impact on a person. Some solace could be had by leaving politics behind and in tackling the Atlantis question.

After *Atlantis: The Antediluvian World* came out in 1882, Donnelly kept up with similar subject matters. Next came explaining how the Earth got so much gravel in *Ragnarok: The Age of Fire and Gravel*. It proved not to be successful, and he had difficulties finding a publisher for it. This was followed by his next most influential works, those on the Shakespeare authorship debate. He was firmly in the camp who believed that William Shakespeare had not written all of the works that had been ascribed to him. In the process of researching the authorship question, he "unlocked" an intricate, complex cipher developed by the true author, Francis Bacon, who had hidden clues throughout Shakespeare's work, which amounted to a series of breadcrumbs that led back to Bacon. He then moved on to writing straight-up sci-fi with the futuristic dystopian novel *Caesar's Column*.

Back to the winter of 1881, when Donnelly had reached the bottom, with his political influence veering toward nonexistent. His economic prospects were just as dire. He spent his days farming in the lonely husk of a town that was supposed to have been Nininger City. Now he and his family were the lone residents. This could explain why he threw himself forcefully into writing. The rapidity with which Donnelly produced *Atlantis: The Antediluvian World* is staggering, first making note of working on it in January of 1881; only two months later, he had a completed manuscript.

Donnelly was a novice historian and writer. That did not stop him from using an impressive breadth of scientific magazines and journals, world mythology, literature, and geography to craft his work. He had been interested in reading and following the latest scientific news all his adult life, and most likely influenced by Verne's *20,000 Leagues*—not the last time fiction will be used to fuel speculation in this story. He combined this sourcing with his paranoid political background to allow him to make connections between causes and events. His political experience as a Populist allowed him to see the influence that wealth and power had on the world, witnessing it firsthand while lobbying for the railroad elites who controlled much of the country, and his years as a lawyer all played into how he went about researching and arguing the reality of Atlantis.

With the completed manuscript in hand, Donnelly headed off to New York at the end of March 1881 to secure a publisher, which he did fairly easily. Harper and Brothers, his first stop, offered a deal almost instantly. Proofs, edits, and production took the rest of the year to complete.

Atlantis: The Antediluvian World was published in February 1882 and was an instant success. Positive reviews poured in. Coverage of the book and its topic appeared all over the country and the world. Days after the release, Harper was already planning a second edition. In all, there would be seven printings in 1882 alone, nearly unheard of for a piece of nonfiction. By the end of the decade, the book went through twenty-three editions in the U.S. and an additional twenty-six in England. The likes of British Prime Minister William Ewart Gladstone read the work and sent a congratulatory letter to Donnelly. It was popular and stayed popular. And it brought Atlantis to the forefront, so much so that it was the theme of the 1883 Mardi Gras. Well into the twentieth century, the book's popularity continued to spread, and as late as 1949 Harper would re-release another edition.

Why it touched such a nerve is probably as mysterious as Atlantis itself. It could have been the bold assuredness with which Donnelly proclaimed that Atlantis was real. Not stopping there, though, he made Atlantis the cradle whose colonies spread out far and wide to bring civilization to South, Central, and North America, Europe, the Mediterranean, and Africa. Donnelly's Atlantis was also the original paradise, the Garden of Eden, all in one place, whose kings and queens served as the ancient gods of all those civilizations it colonized—and whose destruction provided the source for all the stories of devastating floods like the one Noah survived in his ark. All popular topics that the general public could connect with.

How he managed to prove all of this was by tying together a wide spectrum of strings using an equally impressive number of sources that seemed awfully convincing, told with confident bravado that allowed no room for doubt: "There is nothing improbable in this narrative, so far as it describes a great rich, cultured, and educated people. Almost every part of Plato's story can be paralleled by descriptions of the people of Egypt or Peru." This mixture of cocksureness and scientific veneer helped to enhance the believability.

It did not matter that Donnelly would miss the mark often and by a wide margin: "There are in Plato's narrative no marvels; no myths; no takes of gods, gorgons, hobgoblins, or giants. It is a plain and reasonable history…" which skips over the whole part of the kings of Atlantis being sired by Poseidon; the ancient Greek gods getting together to complain about Atlantis; and Zeus, the god of gods, having to step in to smite Atlantis. All of that gets overlooked. And it pays no attention to how Plato clearly illustrates that there was a Greek civilization running parallel and in direct opposition to Atlantis, which suggests there was another human civilization on par with Atlantis and that even conquered Atlantis—one with just as much a claim to being the cradle of civilization as Atlantis.

Still, the sourcing is remarkable for how much he depends upon science to go about proving his conclusions, utilizing many different branches: volcanology, geography, human physiology, archaeology, meteorology, oceanography, and biology. This multifield approach would be used by many afterward, most notably James Churchward, and Lewis Spence doing the same for Lemuria decades later.

This is no more evident than in Donnelly's discussion on "The Testimony of the Sea," where he uses the latest findings of deep-sea soundings performed by scientific missions of the United States, Great Britain, and Germany. He focuses his attention on Dolphin's Ridge, now the Mid-Atlantic Ridge, a rise caused by the joining of two tectonic plates of which the Azores are a part and which conveniently marks the general location of where Atlantis should be, and where he argues Atlantis resided, with the Azores being the remnant of the larger island. It shows him using scientific discoveries to fuel his arguments, quoting *Nature*, *Popular Science*, and *Scientific American* to hit home how true this all is. He was not wrong about most of the things he cites throughout this chapter and many others, at least when it comes to what was known at the time.

Mr. J. Starke Gardner, the eminent English geologist, is of the opinion that in the Eocene Period a great extension of land existed to the west of Cornwall. Referring to the location of the "Dolphin" and "Challenger" ridges, he asserts that "a great tract of land formerly existed where the sea now is, and that Cornwall, the Scilly and Channel Islands, Ireland and Brittany, are the remains of its highest summits." (Popular Science Review, July 1878)

Here, then, we have the backbone of the ancient continent which once occupied the whole of the Atlantic Ocean, and from whose washings

Europe and America were constructed; the deepest parts of the ocean, 3500 fathoms deep, represent those portions which sunk first, to wit, the plains to the east and west of the central mountain range; some of the loftiest peaks of this range—the Azores, St. Paul's, Ascension, Tristan d'Acunha—are still above the ocean level; while the great body of Atlantis lies a few hundred fathoms beneath the sea. In these "connecting ridges" we see the pathway which once extended between the New World and the Old, and by means of which the plants and animals of one continent travelled to the other; and by the same avenues black men found their way, as we will show hereafter, from Africa to America, and red men from America to Africa.

And, as I have shown, the same great law which gradually depressed the Atlantic continent, and raised the lands east and west of it.

He shows an adeptness in using this information. If anything, Donnelly was great at creating the dots and making the connections between them. He is using the same land-bridge logic that permeated scientific thought at the time. But if science did not know whether these land bridges existed or not, how can we expect Donnelly to know? He was taking a very narrow look at a very specific region, around the Azores, and looking for connections to Atlantis. He showed no critical analysis and only latched on to specific passages in his cited works, while seeking out information that supports only his hypothesis and not any that could imperil his arguments.

What is important is Donnelly piecing together these tidbits to create the illusion of plausibility that there could have existed a larger landmass around the Azores. He uses an article from the *American Scientific Review* called "Glimpses of Atlantis" as the backbone of his theory and quotes from it extensively. He backs up these claims by revisiting the unproven land bridge or stepping-stone-esque island argument.

Donnelly is guilty of being selective of the information he is looking at and not as thorough as he could have been. But then again, he is not a scientist, and he is not doing independent research, only reporting what others have done and drawing conclusions to match his hypothesis. If you read this information while already believing Atlantis existed, then you are going to see Atlantis in the waters around the Azores. If you do not believe in Atlantis, then this information means something else, and you may lean toward tectonic plates and the shifting and pushing of them creating these ridges. Those ideas were generations away, though, and Donnelly was applying the essence of the science of the day. He was very much a prosecutor building and arguing his case. He believed in Atlantis, so he

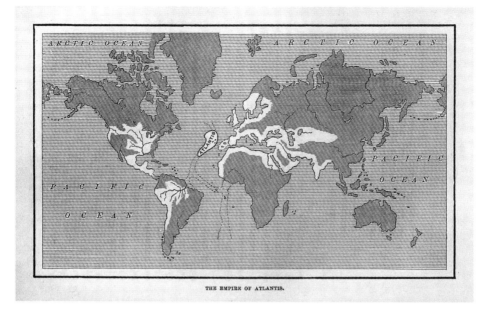

THE EMPIRE OF ATLANTIS.

Map of the Empire of Atlantis from Atlantis: The Antediluvian World, *which shows the spread and impact of Atlantean civilization across the world.*

was putting forth the ideas that adhered to that belief, and jettisoning those that might not line up or would hurt his case.

Another tactic Donnelly employs is history in the form of comparative cultural artifacts. He takes a tour of many ancient cultures, comparing architecture in one location to another—pyramids, for example, and also the Irish round towers—noting place-name similarities between Armenia and Central America, and the similarity in appearance of tools and weapons from regions seemingly distant from one another in the ancient world. Donnelly extends this to folklore, comparing deluge stories from many different cultures and delving into similarities in Greek, Egyptian, South and North American mythology. Which for Donnelly all lead back to Atlantis. How could these similarities be accounted for, if not by some shared ancestral past?

Donnelly helped to make these kinds of diffusionist reasoning fashionable. An anthropological idea that was gaining prevalence at the same time in the late nineteenth century, it was based upon observing similar habits and beliefs between primitive cultures all over the world. Diffusion very much rested on the notion that civilizations were homogeneous. Donnelly pushed the idea of spreading out around the world to its maximalist conclusion, saying "all the converging lines of civilization lead to Atlantis." To him, it was a training ground for civilizations and culture, because in 6,000 years the world had made no sort of advancement that had not come from Atlantis. The counterargument was that cultures independently developed the same beliefs, though many anthropologists today view both such concepts as presenting a false dichotomy, or as irrelevant to explaining the dynamics of social life. Like most things, there's a gray area where the truth lies.

All of this led to Donnelly creating a whole new version of Atlantis, one that lived well beyond him and is prominent to this day. He gave Atlantis a lasting narrative that was embedded into people's imaginations, to the point where popular discourse around Atlantis is all but wholly traceable to him. Donnelly's *Atlantis*, its popularity, and its lasting appeal show how one historical alternative narrative survives and is subsequently built upon.

Another lasting remnant of Donnelly's influence is the way he went about arguing his point. His utilizing multiple disciplines provided the sheen of being exhaustively authoritative on the subject and gave an air of authenticity to Atlantis. However, the seeming lack of discernment for the sources he was using, not questioning them, their accuracy, or their relevance, along with the flippancy with which he discards information counter to his argument, is one that still runs through this type of writing today. Donnelly helped to create the playbook for conspiracy theories, pseudo-ians (pseudoscience, pseudohistory, pseudoarchaeology), and other alternative narratives in various fields. In many ways, he was the precursor to Erich von Daniken, Zecharia Sitchin, Graham Hancock, and many, many others to this day.

Crack open von Daniken's *Chariots of the Gods* or Hancock's *Fingerprints of the Gods*, or a number of others, and you see much of the same style of arguments. There are comparisons of myths and architectural features, and the use of science, all relayed with the same kind of assuredness Donnelly displayed that helps sell their hypotheses. Interestingly, *Atlantis*, *Chariots*, and *Fingerprints* all argue that there was one ur-civilization that seeded all others. The difference is in the source of this civilization, whether it is Atlantean, or some other as yet unknown ancient civilization, or ancient aliens.

Donnelly hit upon a vein of research and argument that was very powerful and persuasive, which others who seek alternative explanations have studied and used in the century and a half after its release. He created his own cradle of esoteric research that has influenced generations of others.

ATLANTIS: THE ANTEDILUVIAN WORLD HAD DIRECT IMPLICATIONS FOR

Lemuria, most obviously by popularizing the idea that a lost world had a major role in shaping humanity. Haeckel's Lemuria as the cradle of humankind and Donnelly's Atlantis as the cradle of human civilization supplied validation that such places existed and served as humanity's incubators.

Another general link is treating this lost world as a paradise. A special place where most anything could happen. To Haeckel, Lemuria was a paradise in that it only needed to have the perfect conditions for fostering humans to develop evolutionarily. But Donnelly treated his paradisiacal Atlantis as a more spiritual land. It was where all the stories from civilizations came together: Garden of Eden, Elysian Fields, Asgard, Gardens of the Hesperides, Gardens of Alcinous, and Olympus all in one place. *Atlantis* manages to marry history and the ethereal, a notion for Lemuria that will not go away.

For his part, Donnelly does make some nods to Lemuria: "There can be no question that the Australian Archipelago is simply the mountain-tops of a drowned continent, which once reached from India to South America. Science has gone so far as to even give it a name, it is called 'Lemuria,' and here, it is claimed, the human race originated." This shows Donnelly's familiarity with Haeckel's *The History of Creation,* as it was the only work out there at the time that put forth the idea that the human race originated on Lemuria. The German's ideas helped to inspire the American's.

Dig a little deeper and this further dislocates Lemuria from its Sclaterian origins as a band stretching from South America, Africa, Madagascar, and India. Now Lemuria can be found near Australia too. Lemuria started to have the feel that it can be wherever it needs to be. Floating across oceans, to deposit humans where there need to be humans. And now that Donnelly said it, that makes it a reference for others to use and gives them free rein to put Lemuria wherever they need it to be.

Not content with keeping Lemuria in and around Australia, later in the book Donnelly pushes the continent out farther—the original first notion that it became a part of America: "But it may be said these animals and plants may have passed from Asia to America across the Pacific by the continent of Lemuria." And a decade later there would be those writing that Lemuria was a part of California, a further demonstration that Lemuria had no set location.

Haeckel began the journey of Lemuria. He pushed it out into the Indian Ocean and ever so close to Southeast Asia. Donnelly continued that subtle displacement. He pushed it out into the Pacific. He linked it to Australia. He connected it to America. He did so with no provocation or prior works doing so. It is cases such as this that probably harm the overall argument of the book. While he is adept at backing up his claims with sources, no matter how wrongheaded it looks now, there is at least precedence and a reader then could follow the path Donnelly is building. But it is those deviances, like Lemuria being near Australia and America with no sourcing, that play as an opportunistic fabrication to throw Lemuria out there wherever needed to further the point he was making in that section. Death by a thousand paper cuts.

With *Atlantis*, Donnelly brought legitimacy to a real Atlantis and in the process created a cottage Atlantis research complex—one that is still thriving to this day, with dozens of new books researching and speculating on Plato's place. Some Atlantean believers have sided with Donnelly on the location of Atlantis. Many, though, have not. And Atlantis has been proposed to have been all over the world, including many locations around the Mediterranean such as mainland Greece, Cyprus, Sardinia, Malta, Turkey, Troy, Thera, Morocco, Andalusia; also in the Black Sea and around Great Britain, Finland, and Denmark, up and down and all around the Americas, to even Antarctica and the North Pole. Countless documentaries have been made on Atlantis and air regularly on the Discovery Channel or can be streamed on a number of different platforms.

Fiction loves Atlantis. Books, comic books, and movies all do their part to keep the Atlantis story alive for future generations. Even Donovan wrote a catchy song, "Atlantis," that mentions "the antediluvian kings," which shows some familiarity with Donnelly's work or at least works inspired by him—although the single cover art, brandishing a swastika (of the spiritual sort) and a cross, may show he had familiarity with Helena Petrovna Blavatsky and Theosophy.

So many sunken continents and so many cradles. Atlantis and Lemuria supplied easy means to promote the ideas of humankind spreading throughout, and subsequently human civilization to spread its wings and fly forth from Atlantis. What Donnelly managed to create was a brand-new Atlantis—one that exists today. In his attempt to make Atlantis a living, breathing past, he somehow gave it even more of a mythology, which in turn made it more palatable to subsequent generations. Along with Lemuria, Atlantis would turn into a mystical place fast on the heels of Donnelly's work. Plato had already set it up as a land ruled by gods who expressed a certain level of spirituality, but that will get ramped up in later works.

Donnelly's *Atlantis* would have even more consequences for Lemuria. The manner with which he argued for Atlantis would be copied by future Lemurian researchers, but he also had a more direct impact on further dislocating Lemuria, pushing it out into the Pacific. This act of mythologizing a long-lost island would prove popular, as we shall see; the same will happen when Madame Blavatsky sets her eye on Lemuria and Atlantis as their own different kinds of cradles.

CHAPTER 4:

Madame of the Occult

NOW ARRIVES THE MOMENT AND PERSON WHO TAKES LEMURIA DOWN a different path. A divergence where there will be no reconciliation with what came before and what is to come. It is fitting that Helena Petrovna Blavatsky is the one to form this fissure. Through her works and teachings, she has done much to mold spirituality in her time and ours, in the process bringing Eastern ideas to Western audiences while creating a hybrid alternative to traditional religions. What she did to change those attitudes was also directed toward myriad topics in her two popular tomes, *Isis Unveiled* and *The Secret Doctrine*, and through the writings in Theosophical organs. In addition to approaching religion, she would investigate the paranormal, history, the universe, and the whole of the scientific world, with the likes of Ernst Haeckel being antagonists in her eyes.

And for Lemuria, it would be forever changed. Before the publication of *The Secret Doctrine*, there was scientific debate around Lemuria, but afterward, Blavatsky opened Lemuria to new possibilities, a new future. A future of UFOs and underground devilry. Of alternative religions and government conspiracies.

She is one of the most influential people of the nineteenth century. Like thunderbolts that lit up the night sky, her teachings still rumble throughout the world. Much of modern popular esoteric thought can be traced back to her. Long gone but not forgotten, her influence remains, securing her ascension to become one of the Masters that directed her throughout her life. After Blavatsky, the notion of Lemuria became dislodged from a geographic location and became more abstract, more mystical. More of a state of mind than anything else. One that represented a state of wholeness, superior wisdom, and harmony, which humans can strive toward as part of a New Age of personal and psychic transformation. So many who seek alternative spiritual guidance have her to thank. She sought and found a different path. A hidden one. A secret doctrine. One that changed Lemuria forever.

BLAVATSKY WAS NOT BUILT IN A VACUUM. NO, SHE HAD A LIFETIME OF influences to help shape her esoteric thinking, starting with her mother's interests, followed by the extensive occult library of her grandparents where she spent much of her formative years, and augmented by her years of travels and studies. She accumulated a wealth of occult knowledge from an impressive number of sources. A common thread throughout would be secret teachings and those who have access to them, and those who are worthy to teach them—an idea that stretches back millennia and continues today. The number of those influences is large and expansive, but here are a few to help appreciate the world from which Blavatsky would rise up.

VAJRAYANA BUDDHISM

Vajrayana was the popular form of Buddhism practiced in Tibet. Blavatsky claimed to have learned it from her Masters when she snuck into Tibet, which is one important aspect of Vajrayana. Adherents place a great deal of importance on a teacher-student relationship, and it is through this relationship that esoteric knowledge gets transmitted. This is done by relaying tantras (from which Vajrayana gets its other name, Tantrism) and other secret sacred texts that record the flow of ignorance to enlightenment. It should be noted that sex plays a key role in this tradition and is part of the enlightenment attainment process, a.k.a. tantric sex. This would be a glaring omission of the celibate views of Blavatsky and Theosophy in general.

KABBALAH

The Kabbalah is the word used to describe Jewish mystical beliefs rooted in visionary interpretation of the Tanakh (the three collected holy books that comprise the Jewish 'bible'). Only a select few were allowed to participate in these secret spiritual traditions, which are said to have been first taught to Adam by angels; others were initiated over the succeeding generations such as Noah, Abraham, and Moses. Rabbi Simeon ben Jochai is said to have been the first to write down the basic concepts of Kabbalah in *Sepher ha Zohar* in the second century AD. However, the work remained largely unheard of and uncommented until the thirteenth century. Kabbalah explores the inner relationships between the divine and man, and lays out the understanding of the sacred tree that links heaven and earth. This is seen in the concept of the sephirot, which includes ten holy structures that joined together to bring the world into being by God's essence, and in a series of stages this led to multiple layers to reality.

PYTHAGORAS (570ish BC–475 BC)

Not only a man of mathematics, Pythagoras seemingly held many mystical beliefs, the primary of which is the secret power in numbers and their ability to

PYTHAGORAS.

Drawing of influential ancient Greek philosopher Pythagoras.

order the universe through use in different disciplines such as music, astrology, philosophy, et cetera. As a younger man, he traveled extensively throughout the East and is said to have studied under a powerful mage in Egypt, where he became an initiate to ancient mysteries. He went on to establish his own school of philosophy, where secrecy became central to life, and imparting these secret teachings, one of which was the transmigration of souls, which remain alive despite the fragile nature of the body and pass on to another body as a kind of animating force.

HERMES TRISMEGISTUS AND HERMETICISM

Hermes Trismegistus was a Greco-Egyptian god—an Egyptianized version of the Greek god Hermes, with Hermes Trismegistus ("Hermes the Thrice Greatest") being the representative for messages, magic, technology, and death. The *Hermetica* texts were ascribed to Hermes and written in Greek in Hellenized Egypt, with many of the writings being produced in the second and third century AD. They cover astrological, alchemical, and magical matters, with the main aim being salvation and what is needed to be saved. They were positioned as secret teachings that disclosed the secrets to anthropology, cosmology, theology, and the metaphysical to help discover redemption. The writings were rediscovered and became very influential during the Renaissance. From these, we get the term *hermetic*.

ROSICRUCIANS

Rosicrucians are an influential occult secret society. Its murky beginnings date back to the fifteenth century and its founder Christian Rosencreuz. The movement lay dormant for a couple of centuries before being rediscovered in the seventeenth century and becoming a model for other secret societies. While on a pilgrimage to the Holy Land, Rosencreuz befriended Arabic alchemists who opened his mind to a whole new world. Afterward, he wanted to combine these occult teachings with Christianity to forge an ideal religion. Returning home to Germany, he founded the "European Fraternity of the Rosy Cross" to "study nature in her hidden forces" and spread the word of this idealized religion. The Fraternity traveled the land, healing people. It proved to be such a good secret society that it was all but forgotten until someone raided Rosencreuz's crypt, stole the parchment from his hands, and published it as the Rosicrucian Manifestos in the seventeenth century. This created a whole new interest in Rosicrucianism, and groups began forming throughout Europe dedicating themselves to studying alchemy, mysticism, and theology. Popularity would wane but pick back up again in later centuries.

FRANZ ANTON MESMER (1734–1815)

Mesmer was an amateur physician who married into wealth that allowed him to pursue his passion, which consisted mostly of pumping people full of an iron solution, then running magnets over them to cure them of their ailments. Soon, though, he realized actual magnets were no longer needed when he discovered his own innate "animal magnetism" and the power that it held. Mesmer was a firm believer in vitalism—that there was a "vital force of life" that coursed through us, and disease arose when this flow was blocked. Animal magnetism was then used to dislodge the blockages, leading to cures. His cures turned out to be popular; however, scientists repeatedly rejected his claims. A study done shortly after his death found that most of the success came as a result of the power of suggestion, which would give rise to hypnotism.

CAGLIOSTRO (1743–1795)

The definition of an Italian charlatan, Cagliostro was born Giuseppe Balsamo, but he took on the regal name Alesandro Conte di Cagliostro and traveled about Greece, Arabic, Persia, and Egypt, ostensibly learning secret occult teachings, and received the rights of the *Arcana Arcanorum*, a mysterious Hermetic order. When he came back to Europe he made his way as a wandering magician, alchemist, and serial Egyptian Mason lodge organizer. Claiming to hold the Philosopher's Stone and peddling magical potions, Cagliostro's *modus operandi* would include ingratiating himself with the powerful people of a locale until he overstayed his welcome, then moving on. The lifestyle eventually caught up to him and he would die in an Italian prison.

ELIPHAS LEVI (1810–1875)

A highly influential French author and occultist, Levi's real name was Alphonse Louis Constant. Much of his writing would pave the way for Blavatsky's works and teachings. Levi put forth most of his ideas in his most influential work, *Transcendental Magic: Its Doctrine and Ritual* (1854), which melded together principles of secret teachings such as Western magic, the Kabbalah, and tarot. In it, he writes how there had been an undercurrent of magic and secret ideas throughout world history, which led him to try to synthesize all of those occult philosophies into one.

EDWARD BULWER-LYTTON (1803–1873)

Edward Bulwer-Lytton was another infinitely fascinating character who was a member of the British Parliament for nearly a quarter of a century and served as the Secretary of State for the Colonies. He was also an author of varying talent, writing in a diverse mix of genres from detective fiction, science fiction, fantasy, thriller to domestic tales, gaining notoriety for penning the opening line "It was a dark and stormy night." It was through this fiction that he explored several supernatural and esoteric topics, including mesmerism, esoteric takes on current science, and hollow Earth, helping to bring them to the public consciousness. His popularity extended to Russia, where Blavatsky's mother's first foray into the literary world was to translate Bulwer-Lytton's work. Blavatsky herself would also translate him to earn some cash during her travels.

SPIRITUALISM

For much of Blavatsky's public life, she remained spiritualism-adjacent. Spiritualism was a popular nineteenth-century and early twentieth-century fad/movement/quasi-religion that centered around the belief that the living could communicate with the spirits of the dead. This was accomplished by table rapping and other such means. It can trace its beginnings to 1848, when the Fox sisters in New York began their table-rapping communications with spirits. Communications usually took place during séances and were done through a medium. These practices helped to popularize séances to communicate with the dead. Spiritualism diversified into other areas such as spirit photography, automatic writing, and channeling.

JUST HOW BLAVATSKY MANAGED TO WILL HERSELF INTO A SAGE IS A DRAMA

unto itself—another of those wandering spirits dotting the Lemurian landscape. She was born in what is now Ukraine but was then part of Tsarist Russia in the year 1831 to a Russian artillery brigade cavalryman father, Colonel Peter von Hahn. The decidedly German name came from the von Hahns emigrating to Russia the previous century. Blavatsky came from a long line of Helenas: her mother, Helena (Helena Andreyevna Fadeyev) was the daughter of another Helena (Princess Helena Pavlovna) and a provincial councilor, Andrei Fadeyev.

Early in Blavatsky's life, her mother took up a literary career that began with translating occultish British novelist Edward Bulwer-Lytton. Soon after, Helena Andreyevna began writing her own works—a career that unlocked a passion in her, leading Blavatsky's mother to leave her family for a while to pursue her writing.

This further displaced Blavatsky, who as a result of her father's military career had spent her childhood moving around, being stationed at one posting or another and splitting time with her maternal grandparents. Her grandmother, Helena Pavlovna, took a keen interest in her education, particularly after the death of Blavatsky's mother when she was eleven.

During this time with her grandmother, Blavatsky first started exhibiting some of her trademark psychic abilities when a guardian angel, or spiritual protector,

A younger Helena Petrovna Blavatsky, most likely from her traveling days.

manifested to protect her from getting injured in falls around the house and even protecting her from a fall off of a horse. It also helped that her grandparents' library housed an impressive esoteric collection full of works on magic, the occult, and other such topics, all of which Blavatsky eagerly consumed prior to her sixteenth birthday.

Certain themes begin to emerge in her biography: the wandering nature of her existence, being from a family of writers, studying the occult from an early age. And finally, the paranormal phenomena that rained down in her presence would remain with Blavatsky to the end of her life.

Blavatsky spent much of her teenage years buried in those mystical books of her grandparents, where she gained an appreciation and intimate understanding of the occult. This left her withdrawn from her family, so it came as a surprise when she announced her engagement at the age of seventeen to the much, much older Nikifor Blavatsky, an official from the border region of Erivan, now Yerevan in Armenia. How they even met is a mystery. There seemed to be no pressure to wed from her father and grandparents. She showed second thoughts quickly after the engagement and tried to find a way out of it, leading her to try to induce a Kurdish guide to smuggle her to Iran immediately after the nuptials.

This did not bode well for the marriage, and their actual time together was short and apparently unconsummated. This would be a lingering topic of interest among people, mostly men, of the day and to scholars of this day. Speculation about her sexuality would follow her for the rest of her life. This was due to her being a woman and being sexualized as such, and for befriending and traveling with quite a few men during her life—though women made up just as many of her traveling companions, which also led to claims of homosexuality. The debate surrounding her sexuality appeared to bemuse Blavatsky.

The marriage to Nikifor was fraught, with Blavatsky's actions not helping what relationship there was by running away back home by herself on horseback across the frontier. She was determined. All parties were in agreement that things were not working out, so it was decided that she would go spend some time with her father in Odessa. While en route she got her first taste of freedom and it was liberating, so upon reaching Constantinople she got off the boat and never looked back. At just eighteen she found herself on her own, thus beginning a mysterious middle period of her life, that of a world traveler.

For the next twenty-five years, Blavatsky more or less wandered the world, circumnavigating it multiple times: Egypt, Turkey, Greece, France, England, Canada, America, Mexico, South America, Java, Japan, all over India, Kashmir, Ladakh, Burma, Tibet, Germany, Syria, Italy, the Balkans, Lebanon, Palestine, and finally ending up in New York in the summer of 1873.

Now all of these comings and goings are for the most part speculation pieced together from her voluminous writings and letters—all written after the fact, and very little of which can be verified. This seems to be purposefully done on her part: an act of keeping her past a myth, probably inspired by some of the occult mystics she had studied early such as Pythagoras, Cagliostro, and many others. The mysteriousness of it aided her allure. To her credit, Blavatsky comes off as a worldly person who accumulated a massive amount of knowledge. Nonetheless, it probably matters less that she did all this traveling than people believed that she did.

It was not all travel, travel, travel for her during this time. There were a few longer stretches where she did settle, such as showing up suddenly at her sister's house on Christmas night and staying there a while. During this extended stay, her sister would note a strange air around Blavatsky, accompanied by many paranormal phenomena. Raps and whisperings, other mysterious sounds which showed intelligence, penetrating the souls of those who experienced them. Blavatsky would claim that she honed and took full control over these abilities during this time.

It was shortly after this time back in the Caucasus region that Blavatsky would make a return journey to the Himalayan highlands in her third and, according to her, successful attempt to enter Tibet, which at the time was closed off to Westerners and dangerous not only due to the terrain but the presence of bandits. There have been some corroborating accounts of encountering her, or someone like her, along the Kashmir frontier close to Tibet. To bolster her claims, she had more knowledge of Tibetan Buddhism than really any other Westerner at that time. Beyond being in Tibet, allegedly, this was a life-altering period where she trained under her master/teacher who helped nurture Blavatsky's natural ability through studies of ancient, secret texts. The end product is an occult superhero.

In the home of Mahatma (Master) Koot Hoomi, she underwent extensive training. There she learned Senzar, the sacred, mysterious language of initiated adepts, which formed the basis of *The Book of Dzyan*.

I have lived at different periods in Little Tibet as in Great Tibet, and that these combined periods form more than seven years. Yet, I have never stated either verbally or over my signature that I had passed seven consecutive years in a convent. What I have said, and repeat now, is, that I have stopped in Lamaistic convents; that I have visited Tzi-gadze, the Tashi-Lhünpo territory and its neighbourhood, and that I have been further in, and in such places of Tibet as have never been visited by any other European.

She spent a couple of years in Tibet, or near Tibet, learning from Koot Hoomi. Afterward, she headed to Paris with all intent of settling there until a master appeared, instructing her to head to America. She promptly did so, arriving in New York City in the summer of 1873, finally ready to be on the world stage at the age of forty-two.

The remaining eighteen years of her life would be spent more or less in the public eye as she gradually became more well-known—first in America, then after the formation of the Theosophical Society, the world. Inauspicious was her rise, though, that started with her participating in the *en vogue* spiritualist movement

Drawing done of Koot Hoomi by the German Theosophist Hermann Schmiechen.

in the city. Not until Colonel Henry Steel Olcott appeared in her life did the transformation truly begin.

An equally fascinating character as Blavatsky, Olcott was one of the leading scientific agriculturalists in the world. He covered the hanging of John Brown, and during the Civil War, served under General Burnside and then in the War Department fighting corruption and graft. Immediately following the war he was one of the investigators into Lincoln's assassination; afterwards, he became a lawyer who did some paranormal news journalism on the side. This deep interest in spiritualist matters drew him to Chittenden, Vermont, where there were reports of a series of strange occurrences like raps and other "manifestations" of an alleged medium, William Eddy.

These strange occurrences drew Blavatsky there as well. The two met and it was kismet, with him championing her in the press and in books, helping to raise her profile. They quickly became "chums" that would be beside one another for most of the next two decades—so much so that Olcott abandoned his family to move in with Blavatsky, which allowed him to dedicate himself fully to the occult. Along with a few other like-minded people they founded the Theosophical Society in the fall of 1875 as a means to explore and study esoteric occult matters. For better or worse, the Society would play a major role in expanding esoteric thought and alternative religion. And Lemuria.

Knowing that a movement is nothing without a bible, Blavatsky set out to rectify that with the publication of *Isis Unveiled* (1877), which proved to be a huge success for her, though not so much the Theosophical Society. *Isis Unveiled* called for the revival of the ancient Hermetic philosophy, one that is steeped in Western esoteric and occult traditions, whilst strongly condemning Christianity and praising Hinduism and Buddhism, arguing that all of the world's religions came from a common source, an ancient religion, which acted as a cradle for all other religions and spiritual thought. *Isis Unveiled* presented the idea of the Akashic record, an ethereal recording of all that was and will be. The Memory of the Gods. The book showed her talent for connecting ideas and facts which might have been overlooked by others, much like Donnelly did in *Atlantis: The Antediluvian World*.

Science played an important part, in particular Darwin, evolution, and his supporters who push a materialistic viewpoint that completely neglects purpose. Evolution as Darwin and his supporters posit leaves out what happens before and after the physical aspect, focused but on a tiny piece of the puzzle, not explaining the evolutionary journey that the soul or spirit takes. It gets created by no one, floats onward from nowhere. In general, the world to Blavatsky was a weirder, more fascinating place than scientists were willing to admit. The ancient masters knew this and forged their own kind of science to help explain it all. Blavatsky's job was to bring it back to life.

Isis Unveiled set the template for all future Blavatsky and Theosophical writings by placing a strong emphasis on the teachings of secret ancient masters that only certain special persons can communicate with. Ideas for the Society all flowed out of and through her, the tone too. While it is not fair to say she *was* the Theosophical Society, she was definitely the brains behind it. These themes of secret knowledge, combating science, and the oneness of spiritual religions would get explored more in depth and evolve in her next major work, *The Secret Doctrine*, eleven years later.

Despite the success of *Isis Unveiled*, the Theosophical Society stagnated in the States. Blavatsky and Olcott thought it best to relocate to India, the heart of where most of her teachings were centered—a fruitful decision, as the Theosophical Society blossomed in the new locale.

While in India she made the acquaintance of British newspaperman A.P. Sinnett, who quickly fell under the Theosophical sway. People have a tendency to demand proof of paranormal claims. Maybe there is something in us that needs that verification. We have hang-ups over faith, the ability to hand blindly over belief. Sinnett was no different. He pestered her for access to the Masters, with whom only she communicated, though Olcott did claim to have met one once.

The idea of adepts or Masters or Mahatmas or Ascended Masters was an important one for Blavatsky, and one that would be passed down through the years. Blavatsky's masters, Koot Hoomi and El Morya, were her sources for secret knowledge, and maybe conveniently she had a near-monopoly on communication with them. They controlled the knowledge going to her. She controlled which parts of that knowledge got shared. It is quite a powerful position to be in, which is probably why so many who followed her path established the same kind of relationships with their Masters. Having that very personal conversation with the Masters helps to elevate and broadcast the messages, whatever they may be. What started with Koot Hoomi and Morya would grow and grow. Later many would have their encounters with the two, with Koot Hoomi being gregarious and visiting others years and decades after Blavatsky, but others start to show up, many from Tibet. Jesus became a Master, the mysterious Comte Saint Germain, and even a Lemurian, Ra-Mu, reached master status.

Sinnett's badgering paid off and Blavatsky arranged for him to communicate with them, thus beginning a long bizarre correspondence where Sinnett would write and the Masters would deliver their response in any number of mysterious ways, such as floating down out of the ether. Over one hundred total letters between the years 1880 and 1884 appeared that way. Sinnett would use them as the basis of his book *Esoteric Buddhism*. In those letters, Koot Hoomi says Lemuria and Atlantis will rise again as the culmination of humanity's ascension. The letters would also act as a rough draft of Blavatsky's *The Secret Doctrine*.

Following a couple of strange occurrences involving buried tea cups and brooches in pillows, Blavatsky received a major blow to her credibility. A disgruntled former employee, Emma Coulomb, spoke out to the press that most, if not all, of Blavatsky's miracles were manufactured. The letters to Sinnett were dropped through slots in the ceiling; knocks and other noises were created in hidden rooms. This was followed up and confirmed by the Society for Psychical Research's investigation into the matter, in what is known as the Hodgson Report. To people who wanted to see Blavatsky fail, this was perfect ammunition with which to write her off.

Never one to shrink away, the whole affair did not topple Blavatsky, though it did mean leaving India for good, and she spent her twilight years in spots around Europe, where work progressed on *The Secret Doctrine* as her health deteriorated rapidly.

The Theosophical Society created a publishing company to specifically print and distribute *The Secret Doctrine*, which was published in two volumes in 1888 and 1889. The massive tome was a commentary on the secretive *Book of Dzyan*, written in an even more secretive language, Senzar. It was the culmination of all her ideas and writing, an attempt at a cosmic history of humanity and the universe.

Her remaining few years were spent writing and establishing the European branch of the Theosophical Society in London. She died on May 8, 1891, a day that Theosophists celebrate as White Lotus Day.

THE SECRET DOCTRINE IS WHERE WE GET THE FULL, UNABRIDGED SCOPE of Blavatsky's vision and teachings. And because of that, it provided the vision for the Theosophical Society going forward, long after her death.

The book is a confusing bramble that meanders all over the place, all over the universe and all over esoteric thought. She did not dumb her writing down or make it easily accessible to casual readers. It requires full attention. Its intellectual abstruseness seems to be the point. As her biographer, Gary Lachman, says, "I profited from it most by seeing it as Blavatsky's attempt to create a new myth for the modern age." Her choice was the obscure world-building kind of mythmaking.

She goes deep into a wide variety of topics in the book. All of it comes from Blavatsky's memory as she quotes stanzas, with some psychic assistance from her Masters, who act as reference librarians, and she quotes from a wide range of earthly texts as well. The secretive nature of the *Book of Dzyan*, Senzar, and the Masters get at the heart of the occult.

Blavatsky fills two volumes of over 1,500 pages accompanied by copious footnotes spread over an ocean of esoteric matters and spiritual ones, and a whole lot of science from the time period. Large swaths of the book comment on evolution and how it is out of sync with the cosmic universe, almost too much information to wrap your head around. Michael Gomes does an excellent job of distilling down to the core of her argument, stripping away much of her scientific debate and leaving the essential tenets in his abridged and annotated version of *The Secret Doctrine: The Synthesis of Science, Religion, and Philosophy*. The work puts forth three fundamental propositions:

1. There exists one absolute reality that is outside of our ability to comprehend it.
2. The universe is an eternal space based upon the foundation of creation and destruction happening simultaneously, with new worlds generating and blinking out all the time.
3. There is an evolutionary journey that humanity is on and has been on, with the final stage ending with ascendance through becoming an enlightened spirit.

All of that worked toward a universal ancient truth that provided the spring for all religion, science, and philosophy.

Volume I, *Cosmogenesis*, concerns itself with the creation of the universe. The universe (our universe) traveled through seven stages, the end product being

An older Helena Petrovna Blavatsky.

the universe we occupy now. Monads get discussed as the building blocks of the Theosophist universe—the original matter. How the Earth came into being, with each planet and every soul processing through seven stages of evolution. It goes from a spiritual state to a material state in the fourth stage and back to the spiritual over millions of years.

Volume II, *Anthropogenesis*, focuses on the genesis and evolution of humans. Much like the planets, humanity is undergoing a seven-step evolutionary process, with each step being a different "Root Race," with seven sub-races nested within each Root Race. They follow the same pattern of going from spiritual to material and back to spiritual.

The First Root Race were pure spirit beings, mere images or astral figures that lived on an "Imperishable Sacred Land" and began developing 1.5 billion years ago. Earth at the time was primordial and when it became ready to support human life two groups, the Lords of the Moon and the Lords of the Flame, came together to assist in creating humanity. These groups provided the spirit of humanity, with astral bodies to use as a model to slowly build into a physical form. The Second Root Race was still spirit beings and ethereal in nature, but they slowly began to increase in density. They were nicknamed "the boneless," were semi-human, and gigantic. Known as Hyperboreans, they inhabited Hyperborea, a land stretching around the North Pole and into Northern Asia.

Then came the Third Root Race who spawned from a drop of "sweat" from the Second Root Race. Very much an act of creation, as it was the result of will acting on phenomenal matter, the calling forth out of it the primordial divine Light and eternal Life. They were the "holy seed grain of the future Saviors of humanity." The Third Root Race were physical beings, sexless, but physical nonetheless. Through a long and speculative evolutionary period the Third Root Race began to separate into the opposite sexes and finally gave birth to men and women. And they lived on Lemuria.

The Fourth Root Race were the Atlanteans of Atlantis. In the beginning, they were giants and gradually evolved into smaller and smaller beings until finally reaching human size toward the end of their stage. Possessing psychic powers and technological mastery, Atlanteans had a proclivity for bestiality, which spawned gorillas and chimps. And like in Plato's telling they abused their power, succumbing to decadence, leading Atlantis to be swallowed by the ocean.

They led to the Fifth Root Race, the coming of Aryans, and the age that we currently live in. The Fifth Root Race emerged roughly 1,000,000 years ago from Atlantis, migrating, and surviving the great flood. Dispersed across the globe, the process of sub-races began to form. However, there are some "degenerate" offshoots that are not quite worthy of being the Fifth Root Race. These degenerates are mostly indigenous peoples from all over the world. The Sixth Root Race is on the horizon and it is close to rising up in America. This American-led race will combine the best intelligence of the Fifth Root Race with the emotional stability of the Fourth (forgetting and overlooking that they succumbed to decadence) to usher mankind through to a new spiritual awakening, ending with the Seventh Root Race, which will be located on a new continent out in the Pacific, Lemuria arisen, and will be the last race on Earth. The circle having been completed:

The whole Kosmos is guided, controlled, and animated by almost endless series of Hierarchies of sentient Beings, each having a mission to perform, and who—whether we give to them one name or another—are "messengers" in the sense only that they are the agents of Karmic and Cosmic Law.

The whole order of nature evinces a progressive march toward a higher life. *There is design in the action of the seemingly blindest forces. The whole process of evolution with its endless adaptations is a proof of this. The immutable laws that weed out the weak and feeble species, to make room for the strong, and which ensure the "survival of the fittest," though so cruel in their immediate action—all are working toward the grand end. The very* fact *that adaptations* do *occur, that the fittest* do *survive in the struggle for existence, shows that what is called "unconscious Nature" is in reality an aggregate of forces manipulated by semi-intelligent beings (Elementals) guided by High Planetary Spirits.*

That is the thumbnail sketch of *The Secret Doctrine*. A certain period in time, with its arguments against specific scientific advancements that were being discussed, particularly the creation and disappearance of landmasses, bridges, or continents, and the burgeoning theory of evolution. It is something that could not have been written twenty years earlier, for many of the arguments had not been articulated, or twenty years after, as science veered away in other directions. This is most evident when Blavatsky discusses Lemuria, for it sits in the middle of her particular brand of Theosophical evolution, and the Lemurians have a huge role to play in her commentary.

Blavatsky wrote during the "age of science" when more and more people believed in natural laws governing the cosmos and not supernatural ones. And, as we have seen in earlier chapters, a diverse range of scientific topics was being brought under new laws such as physics, chemistry, physiology, and psychology. This, combined with a drastic increase in public education throughout most of the Western world, and a rise in enrollment in higher education, brought with it increased critical thinking and thought. Also at this crucial point, other societal changes followed with the rise of the press as a form of mass communication, the laying of multiple trans-Atlantic cables facilitating the spread of information across the Western world, advancements in steamship travel which helped cut down significantly the travel time of people and information, and the industrial advancements that brought forth a more educated middle class with some disposable cash and time to devote to matters such as following the latest in whatever topic interested them.

This precise and critical time period of the 1880s was a moment when science and the metaphysical were swirling around one another. A time when people were trying to understand, wanting to understand, thinking they understood, and using that to push their agendas. With this debate around trying to harmonize the spiritual and the scientific, evolution was a huge, thorny subject that rearranged all previous knowledge. And in wanders Blavatsky to provide an alternative. Incorporating physics and biological science, she used contemporary sources to synthesize varying scientific, philosophical, and historical ideas to forge her versions of all three. She spent much of *The Secret Doctrine* responding to specific scientists. Ernst Haeckel receives a great amount of scorn from Blavatsky; she tears him down in order to build up her argument of a spiritual evolution of man and the universe.

While her Lemuria gets turned into a spiritual cradle in Blavatsky's stages of cosmic transformation, she quickly points out from the beginning that she is using the name "Lemuria" because that is how others labeled it. She provides a good summation of the semantic history of Lemuria, tracing it back to Sclater and including Wallace's opposition to the idea which appears in *Island Life*, but falls upon Haeckel's use of Lemuria to facilitate the dispersion of humans. For this Blavatsky used a collection of translated essays and lectures by Haeckel, *The Pedigree of Man*, which acts as a demo version of *The History of Creation*. But it still makes the same allusion to Lemuria being a lost continent. Maybe if she did have and study *The History of Creation* (whatever volume was available then), with its more expansive explanation of his argument and providing more nuance than the mentions of it in *The Pedigree of Man*, her disagreements with Haeckel would not be so violent.

We have seen Donnelly use science, and occultists such as Blavatsky and the Theosophical Society were no different. Blavatsky spent no time going through the scientific process to prove her theories. To service her ideas, she was content with interpreting what others have done. Science provided a means to legitimacy but also a straw man that she can define her ideas against. The hard work was necessary. She was not Haeckel in the Mediterranean studying radiolarians, tracing their biological evolution, nor was she Wallace in the Amazon collecting tens of thousands of insects. But she felt no compunction to use that scientific terminology or theories posited from such studies to prop up her claims, with none of science's stamps of approval, either through approved methods or acceptance via peer-reviewed publications. This was fundamental to not only *The Secret Doctrine* but other future alternative works that established science as another tool and data point to be used in discourse.

Blavatsky was defining our place in the universe in response to challenges brought forth by Darwinism and the scientific

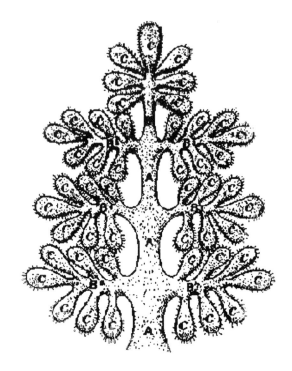

Image showing a Root Race tree diagram taken from **The Secret Doctrine.**

materialism which Haeckel embodies, opposing him mightily throughout *The Secret Doctrine*. He's a "moral murderer," "a crass materialist," literally pooh-poohing his work. The vehement opposition all boiled down to Haeckel's promotion of materialism via his monism—that matter is all that exists and that life can be reduced to these basic materials, everything united in a single substance.

Blavatsky takes Haeckel to task over and over again, claiming that his materialism denied the soul, the spirit, and the life force that propels living things. Matter was not only matter, it was alive. And this is the fact from which she builds out her cosmic evolution. In many ways, it remains similar to the basics of Haeckel's monistic evolution, the big difference being what matter is guided by. For Blavatsky, it is a monad, while for Haeckel it is a monera. Even the names are similar. In fact, *The Secret Doctrine* could be seen as a spiritual monist treatise.

Blavatsky and Haeckel shared similar views on organized religions and theology. Both were inspired and influenced by *Naturphilosophie*. She even cherry-picked certain Haeckelian ideas to use in *The Secret Doctrine* such as reproduction through asexual budding, which is how her Lemurians reproduced, and recapitulation and general embryotics. Language and the development of speech also played important factors for both. Maybe she opposed Haeckel so vehemently because she borrowed many of his ideas. The most important thing that she borrowed from Haeckel is the idea of Lemuria as a real place that served as a cradle.

FIFTY-SOME MILLION YEARS AGO ON EARTH, THERE WAS ONLY A SINGLE continent, Lemuria. Although no humans were present, you would see semi-physical large beings prowling about. The first Lemurians developed from a drop of sweat from the prior root race. The early iterations were born from eggs and were hermaphroditic. It took millions of years but these beings finally obtained physical permanence and looked somewhat similar to the humans that we are now, except they were giants, and early forms may have been cyclops. That one eye, which gave them telepathic communication between one another over long distances and also allowed them to be connected with nature and all that is divine, evolved into three eyes and then into two eyes, as they grew into the shape of humans but were giant-sized by the end of their evolutionary journey. This all came about thanks to their spiritual awakening and gaining self-consciousness, obtained over millions of years with the guidance and teachings of celestial beings, who would in turn become gods to us but also our collective souls. They coded their essence into ours, melding with us. However, they got lazy and decided on a wait-and-see approach with some other Lemurians, and these offshoots became "narrow-brained" and a degenerate race. Those who received guidance from the Masters were located in the Pacific portion of Lemuria and taught how to survive in the material world, gaining mastery of the sciences and the arts, and led the Lemurians to build the first cities out of stones and lava. Over time, these cities would be made out of metal, marble, and black stones, with the very first one appearing in Madagascar. Their civilization became undone by volcanoes and earthquakes.

Blavatsky had a whole lot to say about Lemuria. The Third Root Race, the Lemurians get more page time than any of the other Races. Lemurians came at the critical moment when humanity first began developing away from ethereal beings and transforming into more recognizably human forms through the many different permutations of Lemurians.

An important feature that Blavatsky brought up time and time again was that Lemuria was a construct of Sclater and that she only used the name because it is what others called it. While she believed and agreed that Lemuria was a real place that existed, you could step all over it, camp out, and do what you please there. However, she made a point, multiple times, that she was only using the name that others gave it. The name was not as important as the idea. She went as far as putting it in quotes and calling it an invention, saying the only reason she uses Lemuria, and for that matter Atlantis too, is for clarity:

The third Continent, we propose to call 'Lemuria.' The name is an invention, or an idea, of Mr. P.L. Sclater, who asserted, between 1850 and 1860, on zoological grounds the actual existence, in prehistoric times, of a continent which he showed to have extended, from Madagascar to Ceylon and Sumatra. It included some portions of what is now Africa, but otherwise this gigantic Continent, which stretched from the Indian Ocean to Australia, has now wholly disappeared beneath the waters of the Pacific, leaving here and there only some of its highland tops which are now islands.

She even gets into the debate surrounding Lemuria, bringing up Wallace's objections to the necessity of it, to explain it for animal migratory reasons. But she brushes off the objections: "Yet the land did exist, and was of course *pre-tertiary*, for 'Lemuria,' accepting this name for the continent, had perished before Atlantis had fully developed."

This alludes to another aspect of Lemuria: that it keeps growing and growing in size for Blavatsky. She turns it into a genuinely gigantic world that runs from the Himalayas and Gobi Desert, Mongolia to Ceylon and Sumatra, Madagascar to Australia down close to the Antarctic Circle, and juts far out into the Pacific to include Easter Island. There was also a large Atlantic portion, which included a landmass right in the center of the Atlantic Ocean, near where Donnelly placed his Atlantis and Blavatsky added a large portion that jutted up into the North Atlantic. It covered much of the entire world. It could even be seen as a precursor of Pangaea, but it definitively severs the link of Lemuria to one place, and even puts it more squarely in the Pacific than anywhere else. And it is also important that Lemuria included America—not only for later iterations of Lemuria, but for the later root races to be settled in America and for the rising of Lemuria again in the Pacific.

Blavatsky placed her Lemuria roughly in the Thanetian Stage at the end of the Paleocene Epoch, which was pushing the bounds of acceptable time for when she was writing that. And she links the destruction of Lemuria to that of the dinosaurs and makes multiple references to Lemuria breaking apart in a preview to what is theorized to have happened: "when the gigantic continent of Lemuria began separating into smaller continents," also "the continent of 'Lemuria' had broken asunder in many places and formed new separate continents." She was predicting, intentionally or not, the continental shift theory of Wegener, though she had all of this happening dozens of millions of years too late.

Lemuria was a pivotal time for Earth: when the continents formed as we know them, and a time when humans began to take shape as well. She refers to the human-leaning peoples as Lemurians and brings them into existence.

They start off as a drop of sweat of the Second Root Race that transformed and grew into giants, and then eventually back into humans, which will then make up the Fourth Root Race. This transformation takes place over the many different sub-races of the Third Root Race. Blavatsky goes into dizzying detail to explain how a "drop of sweat" turns into a living breathing thing, never really making it clear why we should care about the minutiae. Haeckelian arguments get hijacked and added to, with a sprinkling of her terminology to make them seem different.

She agrees with Haeckel's logic: "First the moneron-like procreation by self-division (*vide Haeckel*); then, after a few stages, the oviparous, as in the case of the reptiles, which are followed by the birds; then, finally, the mammals with their *ovoviviparous* modes of producing their young ones." She gets ovum-level deep into the weeds. Fission and budding, spores, intermediate, and her personal favorite, hermaphroditism. Blavatsky enjoys discussing and explaining the hermaphroditic nature of Lemurians, all playing a part in their evolution. It is important for her to get into such detail, because this Lemuria, her Lemuria, is the same as Haeckel's, but with radically different evolutionary behaviors and processes taking place which provide the means to distinguish the two Lemurias.

> Now the point most insisted upon at present is that, whatever origin be claimed for man, his evolution took place in this order: (1) sexless, as all the earlier forms are; (2) then, by a natural transition, he became a "solitary hermaphrodite," a bi-sexual being; and (3) finally separated and became what he is now. Science teaches us that all the primitive forms, though sexless, "still retained the power of under-going the processes of a-sexual multiplication"; why, then, should man be excluded from that law of Nature? Bi-sexual reproduction is an evolution, a specialized and perfected form on the scale of Matter of the fissiparous act of reproduction. Occult teachings are preeminently panspermic, and the early history of humanity is hidden only "from ordinary mortals"; nor is the history of the primitive Races buried for the Initiates in the tomb of time, as it is for profane Science. Therefore, supported on the one hand by that Science which shows us progressive development and an internal cause for every external modification, as a law in Nature; and, on the other hand, by an implicit faith in the Wisdom—we may say Pansophia even—of the universal traditions gathered and preserved by the Initiates, who have perfected them into an almost faultless system—thus supported, we venture to state the doctrine clearly.

Blavatsky goes on to use Haeckel's research on the reproduction cycle of medusae to argue the same for Lemurians, explaining how they shifted from being unisexual to very much men and women. She makes these points time and again, going out of her way to say this and picking and choosing from Haeckel's work. She wanted to differentiate her idea from Darwinism because there was nothing naturally selective about her way; it was all "absolutely divine," the creation and transformation of Lemurians all driven by higher authorities. She sees and exploits cracks in the disagreements between Darwinists to pave her way forward.

Lemuria was "the Golden Age" when gods walked the Earth and mixed freely with mortals, though Blavatsky gives a bunch of conflicting information concerning the Lemurians. At one moment, they are gods. Another paragraph, they are animals. This dichotomy of godly and animal delves into what else but racism. A particularly spiritual racism on Blavatsky's part, all unprovoked, and for no other reason than that it was something that Haeckel devoted a considerable amount of time to, as we have seen. She paid particular negative attention to native Australians and other native peoples of the South Pacific, calling them "semi-animal latter-day Lemurians," helping to perpetuate the connection between Lemuria and racism. Like her predecessor, she too was creating a racial hierarchy, and like everything else, this too would be passed down iteration after iteration. When Lemuria fell and was destroyed (the main Pacific portion, not all of it), the survivors became a part of the native tribes of Australians.

So these "animal-like" native peoples harken back to Haeckel's ape-men who inhabited his version of Lemuria. She even recognizes it as such: "If we regard the Second portion of the Third Race as the first representation of the *really human race*, with solid bones. Haeckel's surmise that 'the evolution of the primitive men took place... in *either* Southern Asia or Lemuria.'"

Lemuria was a big place, so while it can be home to primitive forms of life, it could also house the enlightened ones as well. That enlightenment was obtained through the acquisition of immortality: reincarnation. These spiritual races of Lemurians also are the origins of the Aryan nations. For her, this version was decidedly more focused on the Indian subcontinent and not around a bunch of white nationalists. Lemuria was the true cradle of the Aryan nation, all of human civilization and human religion and human spirituality.

Lemurians were not just spiritual, they were holy. The pinnacle. Towering giants, they were of godly strength. Beautiful. They had it all, which made their fall more bitter and tragic. How Donnelly made the claim that the Atlanteans were the basis for the later gods, Blavatsky said the same about the Lemurians, who were deified and worshipped.

Of this presently. The only thing now to be noted of these is, that the chief Gods and Heroes of the Fourth and Fifth Races, as of later antiquity, are the deified images of these Men of the Third. *The days of their physiological purity, and those of their so-called Fall, have equally survived in the hearts and memories of their descendants. Hence, the dual nature shown in these Gods, both virtue and sin being exalted to their highest degree, in the biographies composed by posterity. They were the Pre-Adamite and the Divine Races, with which even Theology, in whose sight they are all the "accursed Cainite races," now begins to busy itself.*

Divinity ran in their blood which fueled the lands and their descendants. And it still does, because humanity is cycling back around to the Lemurians. One day our reincarnated selves will land upon that mystical Lemurian plane and become pure spiritual beings once again. She does not rectify this vision of the Lemurian with the other ape-man version. It is of a dual nature. Virtue and sin. Combating one another. Maybe sin wins the battle, but the war is virtue's to lose.

This type of thinking is still prevalent today. The racism too. The ranking of races, and particularly disparaging indigenous peoples, would be appealing to whites seeking confirmation of their status above all others. But for Lemuria's future, this spiritual cradle and paradise proved to be an alluring draw for the next generation of Theosophists and their offspring who would go on to create and promulgate the New Age movement. All done through the words and teachings of their very own masters. Maybe Blavatsky's Lemuria was one of her only true innovations, since she borrowed so much from so many others. What she managed to do was kick off a new era for Lemuria that takes many dramatic twists and turns.

CHAPTER 5:

Moon Baskets Over Mu

WITH BLAVATSKY DEAD AND GONE, THE THEOSOPHICAL SOCIETY underwent an upheaval typical of any group that loses their charismatic leader. This turmoil impacted the existence of Lemuria. Blavatsky single-handedly pulled Lemuria out from under the ocean's waves and breathed spiritual life into it, creating a land of myths and mysticism that the scientists who came before her never imagined. Putting it into words, and from those words, Lemuria became a reality. She turned it into a real place populated by real beings who went through many permutations to eventually evolve into humans.

A small but crucial thing that Blavatsky did was cite her sources. And in those citations, she quotes all the figures that we have already seen, Sclater and Wallace and Haeckel and Donnelly. She takes that extra added step of saying she is only using the name for this place that all these others had given to it. The name Lemuria does not matter all that much; it was the name that others gave to it, so it is the name that Blavatsky used. She did not make it up. She even provided the intellectual trail that led to its creation up to her writing about it in *The Secret Doctrine*.

Those who came after her, students and followers, could not be bothered by such trivialities. Blavatsky had already done the legwork of defining the Theosophical version of Lemuria, so they did not feel the need to go about citing all of that same literature again—or even citing Blavatsky herself. Maybe at the time, when everything flowed from her, citing her was not necessary, but years, decades, and a century-plus later, things have a way of getting lost in the cushions of time. Second-generation Theosophists completely severed Lemuria from its scientific past. This allowed future followers and readers of their works to be unaware and fully divorce it from its beginnings in the process of creating a new Lemuria.

This happened piecemeal in the dying decade of the nineteenth century and the opening two decades of the twentieth century. The next wave of Theosophists would devise their own takes on Lemuria, pushing it further into the esoteric breach, while at the same time, pseudo-archaeologists tried to prove the existence of Lemuria through the historical record—both working in weird tandem to prove the existence of Lemuria to those wanting to see it proved.

Occultists flock to drama like moths to flame, and with the power void left by Blavatsky at the top of the Theosophical Society, that is exactly what happened. The Society schismatized into different branches and groups in a period rife with bureaucratic infighting and a surprising amount of internal reviews, inquiries, resignations, unresignations, expulsions, drawing-back-ins, and death, although of the natural kind. When the dust settled late in the 1890s, Annie Besant had entrenched herself as the major force of the Theosophical Society (Adyar) in India, the largest group, and earned the distinction as the "grandmother of the New Age movement."

Prior to her theosophical ascension, Besant had already lived a full, prominent life. Born in 1847 and married to an Anglican clergyman, she started to have doubts about her own faith, which led her to abandon the Church of England and leave her husband. This freed her to pursue a wide variety of liberal causes. She attacked the Church of England, became a columnist for the *National Reformer* where she advocated for a secular society, and dedicated much time and effort to promoting birth control and contraceptives. She published the pro-birth-control book *Fruits of Philosophy* by American Charles Knowlton, which was met with great outrage from the church. Enough so that Besant was arrested, put on trial, and found guilty. On appeal, the charges were thrown out on a technicality. The incident boosted her profile at the expense of losing custody of her children. In addition, she supported Irish Home Rule, unions, and the Free Thought Movement, and was the leading female orator at the time.

By 1889, she was a known, if somewhat infamous, figure in British society. The editor of *Review of Reviews* had her review *The Secret Doctrine* for the publication. The transformation was almost instantaneous, as she mentions in her autobiography where she said the book served as a "flash of illumination . . . [I] knew that the weary search was over and the very Truth was found." Her long days of wandering and questioning were over and she had found it in the arms of Theosophy.

She quickly became a member of the Society, serving as Blavatsky's pupil for the remainder of the Madame's days. Besant soon became president of the Blavatsky Lodge, the London-based group that formed around Blavatsky in the latter years of her life, co-edited their magazine, *Lucifer*, and played a big role in the Esoteric Section, a group within a group of the Lodge hyper-focused on learning as much about the occult as possible.

After Blavatsky's death, Besant moved to India and became affiliated with the largest Theosophical Society lodge, situated in Adyar, becoming its president in

Theosophical Society President and friend and enabler of C.W. Leadbeater, Annie Besant.

1907. One thing she managed to do that Blavatsky had not was to communicate in a clear and effective manner, which helped her ingratiate herself into Indian society. In India, Besant again became intently dedicated to a number of causes, such as education, where she founded the Central Hindu College that later became Banaras Hindu University, revitalizing the teaching of Hindu and Hindu scholarship, and Indian women's rights. However, her biggest contribution would be in the Indian Home Rule and independence movements; she was at the forefront of both for a number of years.

WWI was spent pressuring and hounding British authorities through a newspaper she purchased, *New India*, and built up to be the largest Anglo-Indian paper in the country—the pages of which she dedicated to criticizing British rule. This landed her under house arrest for her harsh criticisms, but would lead her to being made president of the Indian National Congress in 1917. Her Home Rule Bill of 1925 would serve as a model for Indian independence. However, her political influence among Indians began to fade after the Jallianwala Bagh Massacre (1919). She called for not inflaming the situation any further and provided a lukewarm defense of the actual event. The massacre prompted Gandhi to organize his first large-scale nonviolent protest in the struggle for Indian independence. This event would catapult Gandhi to become the leader, both physically and spiritually, of the Indian independence movement, and push Besant to more of a background figure until her death in 1933.

Early in Besant's time in Theosophy, she made the acquaintance of Charles W. Leadbeater, a strange and controversial figure whom Besant really could not or would not excise from her life, no matter how many times he stepped outside the bounds of the law, Theosophical doctrine, and plain human morality. Their partnership would go on to create some of the most influential Theosophical writings during this pre-WWI era.

Leadbeater possesses little redeeming value. Born in 1854, educated at Oxford, entered the clergy of the Church of England in 1878. A keen interest in spiritualism led him to the doorstep of Theosophy in 1883, and he would travel with Blavatsky to India. On the trip, he became the first Christian minister to proclaim himself a Buddhist, spending a number of years in Ceylon leading Theosophical educational Buddhist efforts there.

On his return to England in the mid-1890s, he made the acquaintance of Besant, and they became fast friends. Never one to shy away from showing off his clairvoyance, he ingratiated himself with his fellow London Theosophists by connecting past incarnations of people to famous historical figures—a precursor to future twentieth-century channelers. Besant helped him write and publish these occult quasi-oral histories of the past lives of members of the Society. This ability

The controversial Charles W. Leadbeater, who had many allegations leveled against him for inappropriate contact and conduct with underage boys under his care.

to project himself back to the past was one that he would use time and again.

Because Theosophy did not pay the bills, Leadbeater continued working as a tutor for several years, as he had since before his Theosophy days. That is when the rumors started. Lots of them. They were commonly referred to as "irregular practices" between him and the boys under his care. It all came to a head in 1906 with a fourteen-year-old boy, a son of a fellow Theosophical member, whom he took along with him on a speaking tour of Canada. After the tour, the boy let his parents know that Leadbeater led him in occult training sessions, which consisted of the fifty-year-old man encouraging the boy to masturbate. A coded message found in the apartment the two shared in Toronto offers insight into the child abuse that was going on . . . allegedly:

> *Twice a week is permissible, but you will soon discover what brings the best effect . . . Spontaneous manifestations are undesirable, and should be discouraged. If it comes without help, he needs rubbing more often, but not too often or he will not come well. Does that happen when you are asleep? Tell me fully. Glad sensation is so pleasant. Thousand kisses darling.*

One can see why it was written in code.

The Theosophical Society opened an inquiry on Leadbeater. And during that internal inquest, he admitted to advising adolescent boys to masturbate, and he may have touched them and demonstrated to them the proper ways to masturbate. He was subsequently forced to resign from the Theosophical Society. But many, including

Besant, were appalled at how Leadbeater was treated during this whole ordeal, which became a major platform piece of Besant in her campaign to become President of the Theosophical Society following the death of Olcott in 1907. She would reinstate Leadbeater in 1907 after winning the Presidency, but only after the Masters had to step in and explicitly instruct Leadbeater to stop telling underage boys to masturbate.

Not taking the Masters' instructions to heart, the allegations kept piling up on Leadbeater after his reinstatement. Because Leadbeater traveled all over, he serially abused boys on multiple continents, where there were reports of him sleeping in the same bed with boys, bathing in the same tub with multiple boys, reciprocal masturbation, and spiritual group masturbation sessions. All with underage boys. He kept on telling boys to masturbate, saying it was the only way to overcome their sexual desire for women. Theosophy encouraged celibacy. Then, when these boys became men, they started to come forward to claim that Leadbeater engaged in sexual intercourse with them.

Despite all of this Besant remained loyal to Leadbeater. She became enamored with the idea of a World Teacher arising to help usher humanity along the spiritual evolutionary path. None other than C.W. Leadbeater found one such potential World Teacher in the form of fourteen-year-old Jiddu Krishnamurti, a Brahmin child who was the son of one of the workers at the Theosophical Adyar estate. Just another underage boy that he had his eye on. Besant and Leadbeater all but stole Krishnamurti away from his father, after the father claimed improper contact between Leadbeater and his son. One of Besant's servants claimed to have seen Krishnamurti alone and naked with Leadbeater. Besant used the British courts to gain custody. This began an intense grooming period of Krishnamurti by Leadbeater, Besant, and other Theosophists. The aftermath forced Leadbeater from India to Australia, where he would create his own Catholic Church, the Liberal Catholic Church—and where he would spend the remainder of his life. Krishnamurti would reject the mantle of World Teacher, break with the Theosophical Society, and become a religious teacher, speaker, and philosopher for much of the twentieth century. Krishnamurti remained fairly tight-lipped on his and Leadbeater's time together, with some reporting that he called him evil, which is an apt description.

Leadbeater's scholarly relationship with Besant was a fruitful one. Beyond some past-life biographies, the two teamed up for occult chemistry experiments, where they astrally projected themselves into molecules and elements and provided a report on what they saw. Other times they experimented with the idea of what thoughts look like, writing the book *Thought-Forms*.

It is in the spirit of this science-spiritual inquiry that they turned their attention to how humans came to be. In a clairvoyant investigation titled *Man: Whence,*

Annie Besant, Charles Leadbeater, and Jiddhu Krishnamurti, along with Krishnamurti's brother Jiddu Nityananda and other Theosopical Society members. Nityananda was "discovered" at the same time as his brother and also was separated from his father.

How and Whither, they go back in time to speak with the ancients and bring back how humanity had evolved. *The Secret Doctrine* very much provides a road map for the two, but they use it in the most general of senses.

Published in 1913, *Man* continues in the same manner as Blavatsky and manages to be even more confusing and incomprehensible than *The Secret Doctrine*. It follows the belief that there are seven stages to humans' development cycle and to Earth's cycle. They use multiple references that Blavatsky makes throughout her book and expand on them greatly. In *The Secret Doctrine*, Blavatsky makes vague assertions of there being life on other planets, more like spirits, and they, in the form of spirits or angels, may have come down to aid the evolution of humanity. A proto-version of the ancient alien theory. It is all sourced out and tied together with the Bible, Kabbalists, science, and other occult matters.

Besant and Leadbeater, not having to rely on Earthly sources, pull instead from otherworldly sources and give a more detailed version of what Blavatsky provided. They get specific, involving the Moon and Mars, traveling from there to Earth in "basket-works" during the "Third Round," the time of the Lemurians:

> *Mars, at the end of its seventh Root Race, had a very considerable population to pour into the Earth, and these came streaming in for the third Root Race,*

to head it until the more advanced egos from the Moon Chain should come in to take over the leadership.

This is at a time when the idea of life on Mars was very much believed and debated, thanks to Italian astronomer Giovanni Schiaparelli's discovery of canals there. The pair astrally projected themselves back to the ancient Martian civilization to supply first-hand accounts of what life was like on the Moon, Mars, and Earth.

Beings on the Moon and Mars evolved on different trajectories, gaining ascension to physical and human forms before those on Earth did. They traveled down to Earth: "the new arrivals, the pioneers on our Earth Chain, were pursuing their long journey of the first and second Rounds and part of the third." Like Blavatsky said, that third round of the Earth Chain would equate to Lemuria.

Basket-works from the Moon traveled to Mars, and then basket-works from the Moon and Mars traveled to Earth during their third Round:

The third Round on the Earth much resembled that on Mars, the people being smaller and denser, but, from our present standpoint still huge and gorilla-like. The bulk of the Basket-works from glove D of the lunar Chain arrived on our Earth in this Round, and led the human evolution; the Basket-works from Mars fell in behind them, and the whole resembled fairly intelligent gorillas. The animals were very scaly, and even the creatures we must call birds were covered with scales rather than feathers; they all seemed to be made of a job lot of fragments stuck together, half bird, half reptile, and wholly unattractive.

This involved taking known elements at the time like Dubois' man-ape *Pithecanthropus erectus* and fitting them into their version of evolution, which adds astronomical elements from the Moon and Mars.

It is these Martian colonists who would then come down to Earth and help shepherd along the next race of humanity, primarily the Lemurians. They shared the same types of sexual reproduction, budding and oviparous, that Blavatsky ascribed to them. It was not only people living on Mars and dropping down to Earth, but beasts as well. The Martian seventh root race became Earth's third root race, Lemurians. They had to battle the second root race on Earth, which were beasts. Huge crocodile-like things and scaly birds. "Savage reptilian creatures" they battled with. Humans at this time were gorilla-like, with egg-shaped heads, and standing between twenty-four and twenty-seven feet tall. And they were black. They were also cyclops; this is something that Blavatsky claimed as well, with a central eye toward the top of the forehead. This eventually receded into the head, becoming the pineal gland, and the other two eyes slowly traveled their way across the brow. These beings from outer space taught much to the Lemurians so that they developed a mind of their own and an ego all theirs.

There were three boat-loads of these; more than two million orange people from globe A, rather less than three million golden-yellow from globe B, and rather more than three million pink from globe C - about nine millions in all; they were guided to different areas of the world's surface, with the view that they should form tribes.

These would go on to form the fourth sub-race of Lemurians which were black, "egg-headed" and around twenty-five feet tall and quite clumsy. But they began the embryonic stages of civilization, forming clans, and building cyclopean cities, with a large one found on Madagascar. They also thought it important to get into the skin color of the different sub-races, and they only became Atlanteans through selective breeding of the best of the best Lemurians, which absolutely did not involve any Lemurians with black skin. The masses of Lemurians were black at the end of the "Third Round" but by "mixing in the blue-white of the seventh Lemurian sub-race, He obtained the first sub-race which seemed to be fully human, and that we could imagine as living among ourselves." A lot of emphasis is placed on skin color.

The best of these Lemurians would be chosen to go on and become Atlanteans. As Atlanteans, their skin color would change and the next root race would go about its evolutionary journey, along the way dabbling in black magic which would get them in hot water, and the rise of the Aryan Race, the fifth root race. It is at the end of this root race that the seeds of the next one start to grow in America, California to be exact, in the twenty-eighth century. Blavatsky had spoken of America being the breeding ground for the sixth root race but did not specify California. How they came to settle in California is a bit of a mystery. Its proximity to the Pacific Ocean and the possibility of there arising from the Pacific a new continent could position California as a prime location for this new world. Whatever the case may be, it would stick in the literature that California was a chosen land, destined for future great things in the evolution of humanity. This would have major consequences for the future of Lemuria as well. At the end, Lemuria will rise again from its "age-long sleep" and complete the spiritual evolution of the root races and of Earth.

This story has an appendix in the form of William Scott-Elliot's *The Lost Lemuria*. Scott-Elliot was a Scottish laird who worked mostly as an investment banker and managed to marry into the Theosophical Society, his wife being a member of the London lodge. Possessing a general fascination with anthropology, he fell into Leadbeater's circle, becoming amazed by his clairvoyant findings. Scott-Elliot took it upon himself to apply scholarly thinking and research to Leadbeater's claims of Lemuria in order to prove their worth.

This led to the slim work *The Lost Lemuria* (1904), which confounds in its stated goal of scholarly research. All he does is use the sources that Blavatsky already provided in *The Secret Doctrine* like Haeckel, Wallace, so no new ground is being trod there; the other set of research relies on the Akashic Records, which were already coming from clairvoyant means like Leadbeater himself. Proving with the proof provided.

He does supply some additional fun details concerning Lemuria and Lemurians, such as that they began with giant gelatinous bodies and slowly evolved to have bone structures. And when they first were able to stand up on their own they could walk as well backward as forward, due to the shape of their heels and the third eye helping see them better. Also, the "Chinese language" is the lone descendant of the Lemurian tongue. Venutians, beings from Venus, came here and showed the Lemurians how to cultivate grain. Lemuria existed many, many million years ago. Well over five million years ago and during the time of "the age of reptiles," seemingly meaning dinosaurs.

For Scott-Elliot, Lemurians were tall between twelve and fifteen feet tall with very dark skin, a yellowish-brown hue, and rather unique-looking:

> He had a long lower jaw, a strangely flattened face, eyes small but piercing and set curiously far apart, so that he could see sideways as well as in front, while the eye at the back of the head—on which part of the head no hair, of course, grew—enabled him to see in that direction also. He had no forehead, but there seemed to be a roll of flesh where it should have been. The head sloped backwards and upwards in a rather curious way. The arms and legs (especially the former) were longer in proportion than ours, and could not be perfectly straightened either at elbows or knees; the hands and feet were enormous, and the heels projected backwards in an ungainly way.

Scott-Elliot provides more details referring to their attire and weaponry. They would evolve in a way, gaining a forehead and normal heels, though also shrinking in size. Lemurians are still around in the form of the aboriginal peoples of Australia, and native populations around the Pacific and Africa.

THE SCHISM WITHIN THEOSOPHY TOOK MANY DIFFERENT SHAPES AND SIZES. As the Adyar faction remained and remains the largest associated with Theosophy, intriguing offshoots emerged, such as Katherine Tingley's Point Loma Project.

The founder of Anthroposophy and former Theosophist, Rudolf Steiner.

As head of the American section, Tingley began closing up shop at the lodges scattered around the country to concentrate on the compound she built outside of San Diego in Point Loma. It was an interesting experiment in communal living in a rapidly modernizing world.

Tingley was not the only one. Austrian Theosophist Rudolf Steiner broke from the society as a result of Besant and Leadbeater proclaiming Krishnamurti the one world teacher. He went on to found his own group, the Anthroposophical Society.

One of the many fascinating characters in the Lemuria saga, Rudolf Steiner's impact on society is still felt to this day. In 1861, he was born to Austrian parents in what is today Croatia but then part of the Hungarian portion of the Austro-Hungarian Empire. He began his career working at the Goethe Archives in Weimar, writing a couple of books on the German thinker-poet, as well as extensive philosophical works throughout the 1890s while working on collections on Schopenhauer, and declining an offer to establish a Nietzsche archive. Steiner even corresponded with Haeckel at one point.

It was ultimately this association with Goethe and Nietzsche that brought him into the sphere of the Theosophists, giving lectures to the society, and in 1902 he was made the head of the German contingent. However, he butted heads with the main branch of the Society by using his training and background in German and Western philosophy, stressing those and Western esoteric traditions over the more Eastern philosophy-centric approach of the Theosophical Society in Adyar. He formally left the Society in 1912. His remaining years were spent founding and growing the Anthroposophical Society which he headquartered in Dornach, Switzerland.

And he really got into a little bit of everything. This included establishing Waldorf schools around the idea of a holistic approach to educating children, focusing on their physical, emotional, social, spiritual, and cognitive well-being, tending to those qualities to let them bloom in the child. There are still over a couple of thousand Waldorf schools and kindergartens around the world. In addition to education, he pioneered biodynamic farming, which treated the farm as a living organism, and found a middle ground of applying traditional farming techniques with modern science. A way of preparing the earth to be sustainable, with each element playing an important role, it is an idea that is still influential today as many in America and around the world practice biodynamic farming. He also played a role in creating the cosmetic company Weleda, today a multinational $500 million company, using the principles of naturopathy.

Steiner's contributions to Lemuria come in the form of his 1904 book *Cosmic Memory*, which takes a look at the very question Blavatsky pondered in *The Secret Doctrine*: that of the evolution of humanity.

For his part, Steiner plays up the extraterrestrial-based origin to man, or at least an extraterrestrial guiding hand to humanity's evolution. He dedicates a healthy chunk of *Cosmic Memory* to the Lemurian problem, making no reference to the origin of the name, and leaves it vague for the reader to figure out in those "theosophical books." Placing Lemuria "south of Asia, extended approximately from Ceylon to Madagascar," relatively tiny compared to other physical descriptions of the continent, he does say the air was thicker and the water thinner and the Earth's crust was brittle, with nothing around but palm trees, amphibians, birds, and lower mammals.

While other writers concerned themselves more with the physical evolution and providing descriptions of Lemurians on their journey through the various sub-races, Steiner mostly focuses on the educational and spiritual journey. Lemurian children underwent tortuous education to toughen them up. Those who could not handle it were left for dead. Boys took physically demanding tests, were exposed to intense heat and poked by sticks, all in the service of becoming ready to act out daring deeds.

The female educational experience included some tough love, but concentrated on strengthening their imagination, which they did in part by watching men fight to build up their ability to dream and fantasize. It worked, because women developed superhuman powers like super-memory and super-morals that led them to come up with the concept of good versus evil. These Lemurians of course got help from outside beings, "highly developed entities," that showed humans the way to become new races—and chose which Lemurians to lead on to become Atlanteans.

Steiner places a lot of emphasis on these superhuman beings and the ability to become superhuman, which he equates to thinking, gaining knowledge, wisdom, and eventually clairvoyance. These leaders evolved on other planets to their maximum maturity before coming to Lemuria to assist Lemurians to achieve their goal of developing will and imagination. Steiner does bring up some more interesting aspects concerning Lemurians, like their love life. One of the evolutionary steps was to gain the power of sensual love, a.k.a. sex, and it came to be an activity of the soul. However, it was important for Steiner to stress that sex did not lead to wisdom, because while superhumans/extraterrestrials could fornicate with regular humans, that did not mean they were passing on wisdom. No, wisdom was earned and not transferred sexually.

Lemurians lived in caves, but they took pride in making their caves as nice as possible. While home was the cave, they did manage to build mystical colleges and temples so they could cultivate "divine wisdom and divine art." Whereas magicians learned to change forces of nature through their will, pulling off these architectural feats even though they had no recognizable language, Lemurians relied on "natural sounds" to show their pleasure, joy, pain, any emotions. But they did have one trick up their sleeve: their ability to communicate through the strength of their ideas or "thought reading." This power over ideas stems directly from communing with the objects surrounding them—"it flowed to him from the energy or growth of plants, from the life force of animals. In this manner, he *understood* plants and animals in their inner action and life." This Jedi-like power of the Lemurians further blossomed so that "he could lift enormous loads merely by using his will."

SHORTLY AFTER THE THEOSOPHISTS HAD THEIR SAY ON THE MATTER OF

Lemuria, others began throwing in their two cents. None was more impactful than Col. James Churchward, who would provide Lemuria with its pithy nickname, Mu, which has stuck to it ever since.

Churchward (1851–1936) earned the rank of Colonel while serving in Her Majesty's Armed Forces in India. Upon retiring from the service he ran a tea plantation there, and during that time befriended a Rishi who taught him how to read ancient tablets that told the story of Mú, a lost ancient Pacific continent. In the 1870s, he traveled around the South Pacific with his brother, a British consul, after which he then met the mystical archaeology couple, Augustus and Alice Le Plongeon. Inspired by their findings, he spent a considerable amount of time in Central America and Mexico exploring William Niven's recent discoveries in Mexico. At the dawn of the twentieth century, Churchward started dabbling in metallurgy, and with an assist from those ancient secret tablets, came up with NCV Steel (nickel, chrome, vanadium). This would later serve as the basis for much of the armor plating used on warships and other battle instruments during the Great War. However, "Big Steel" maneuvered Churchward out of lucrative war contracts. A slew of litigation followed as he sued the steel companies for copyright infringement. Settlement brought him a princely sum of $250,000 ($4.1 million today) at the age of seventy, which freed him up to pursue his passion project of Mu.

Outside of those ancient Indian tablets, Churchward found inspiration for Mu from a couple of different sources. First, the basic story of Mu comes in large part from the archaeological exploits of the Le Plongeons and William Niven, whose tablets that he "discovered" provided Churchward with the ammunition of using one to prove the other.

Augustus Le Plongeon was a semi-professional archaeologist who teamed up with his spiritualist photographer wife Alice to travel to the Yucatán Peninsula in Mexico to prove the Mayan civilization was the oldest on Earth and the cradle of all the world's civilizations. Somewhat selective and flexible with the archaeologist record in Mexico, the couple saw patterns

Col. James Churchward, the proponent of Mu, who wrote a series of books on the ancient lost continent of Mu.

in the Mayan artifacts that would lead them to proving this Mayan cradle of civilization theory. Their findings caught the attention of Donnelly and Blavatsky, both of whom cited the Le Plongeons' research in their works. They forged ahead doing major excavations at Chichén Itzá and Uxmal, the first to do so, and presented an alternative, metaphysical history of the New World.

In 1876, the pair unearthed a large stone figure that they called Chac-Mool or Prince Coh. Augustus argued that Prince Coh was the ruler of the area, and dedicated most of the remainder of his life to spin the tale of Prince Coh, his evil brother, Prince Aac, and his sister/wife, Queen Móo. From what they gathered, Aac defeated Coh in hand-to-hand combat, killing him in the process. Móo took over ruling the territory, it now becoming the Kingdom of Moo. Then, she was forced to marry Aac. Not wanting that union to happen, Móo left for Egypt, which was a Mayan colony, by way of another Mayan colony, Atlantis. While in Egypt, Móo became Isis and built the Sphinx in honor of her slain husband/brother Coh. However, Móo's territory would spread east from Central America to Atlantis and on to Africa, with no real mention of the Pacific to be found.

Augustus authored three books between 1880 and 1896 that laid out the saga of Queen Móo, and when he passed away, Alice Le Plongeon gifted his papers to Churchward in 1911. With the foundation of a story there, Churchward would find his primary sources in the form of William Niven and the tablets he discovered in the Valley of Mexico. Niven worked for many decades in Mexico discovering new minerals and new sources of minerals. He also moonlighted for the American Museum of Natural History and came across important prehistoric ruins at Omitlán. His record is less than stellar, though, as local guides enjoyed messing with the foreigner by leading him to the "lost city" of Quechmietoplican, which in reality were abandoned mine works.

Cut to 1921: Niven soon started discovering stone tablets in the Valley of Mexico, first at Azcapotzalco, followed by other sites in the valley. When all was said and done, 2,600 tablets had been unearthed. The veracity of the tablets was called into question; from the beginning, claims were made that what he dug up was the work of enterprising locals who crafted the mystery tablets and buried them for Niven to find, though it is not exactly clear how they prospered from this arrangement. Niven tried his best to profit off of his finds, selling tablets off a piece at a time. He also donated them to museums and universities in the hope they could help find out what they could mean. This is where Churchward appears in Niven's life, stepping in and offering to take a crack at deciphering them, which Churchward did throughout his books on Mu. Niven provided Churchward with loads and loads of rubbings of the tablets, which would appear in Churchward's books. Churchward used them to craft his version of the Mu story and ended up dedicating *The Lost Continent of Mu* to Niven. The tablets later met a mysterious end, lost forever while being transported from Mexico to the United States.

Perhaps the most interesting thing about Churchward's Mu is that it is Lemuria. Same location, dimensions, and descriptions, even cribbing Blavatsky's origin story of being taught a secret language while in India to be able to read Niven's tablets. What everyone else thinks is Lemuria to Churchward, it is Mu. He seemingly goes out of his way throughout multiple books to never mention or utter the name Lemuria. That does not mean it does not still play a part in Lemuria's saga. People saw the 'M' and 'U' in Lemuria, and Mu became synonymous with Lemuria and a vital part of the Lemurian myth, as Mu would be a part of Edgar Cayce's ancient mythmaking and of many in the New Age Movement. Though they borrowed Churchward's Mu name, that was about it. And they have brushed aside his in-depth analysis of Pacific Islander symbology and cultural studies.

Despite the lack of Lemuria, Churchward's Mu shared some key similarities with it, such as being the cradle of mankind, that the people from there would go on to colonize Earth, and that it was destroyed by volcanic activity. The tablets even talked about "seven periods of time" not unlike the breakdown in *The Secret Doctrine*. Mu was also a very paradisiacal place. So whatever Mu was, it shared a whole heck of a lot with Lemuria. A couple of key differences were that

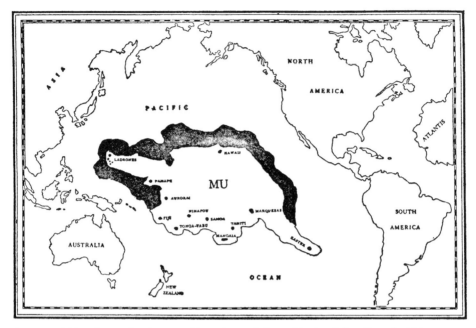

A map of Mu, drawn by James Churchward, from **The Lost Continent of Mu.**

the people of Mu were humans, of normal human size, and had normal, or near normal, abilities. Those who lived on Mu did have a quite advanced understanding of the natural sciences, but no supernatural powers like some others have bestowed on them.

In the first work, *The Lost Continent of Mu* (1926), Churchward came to a handful of conclusions such as there once having been a great continent in the Pacific, Mu, where there are now small islands—where humans first developed, the "Motherland of Man," he calls it. Those humans were a special creation and not the work of nature. This gets into the anti-evolutionary strain in Churchward's work and the divine provenance of those inhabitants of Mu.

The tablets relayed that Mu was home to 64,000,000 inhabitants—one of the many rounds of tablet interpretation that Churchward performs to prove the existence of Mu. These tablets reveal everything, the real origin of the universe and how Mu got started. The inhabitants developed an advanced civilization 50,000 years ago and disappeared 12,000 years ago. It encompassed 5,000 miles east to west, 3,000 miles north to south, and was divided into three distinct landmasses separated by narrow channels. A realm of beautiful rich grazing lands, many streams and rivers, and no mountains. A real-life Garden of Eden full of lush vegetation, bright flowers, and tall palm trees. "Gaudy" butterflies danced from flower to flower as the lively hum of crickets filled the air while herds of elephants passed the time. Overseeing this paradise were the white rulers of Mu:

The dominant race in the land of Mu was a white race *[Churchward's emphasis], exceedingly handsome people, with clear white or olive skin, large, soft, dark eyes and straight black hair. Besides this white race, there were other races, people with yellow, brown or black skins. They, however, did not dominate.*

It was important to Churchward to make these distinctions and to posit the "white race" as the dominant race, and to make them handsome in the process.

Churchward's Mu inhabitants were great navigators who used those skills to ferry passengers to various colonies that make up the bulk of all ancient civilizations: India, Egypt, Babylon, Aztec, et cetera. This is when he begins to demonstrate the cultural connections between those civilizations and Mu as presented in the tablets to tie together the lost past of Mu with what was known at the time—done with a self-assuredness that Donnelly could appreciate.

The Garden of Eden was not in Asia but on a now sunken continent in the Pacific Ocean. The Biblical story of creation - the epic of the seven days and the seven nights - came first not from the peoples of the Nile or of the Euphrates Valley but from this now submerged continent, Mu - the Motherland of Man.

These assertions can be proved by the complex records I discovered upon long-forgotten sacred tablets in India, together with records from other countries. They tell of this strange country of 64,000,000 inhabitants, who 50,000 years ago, had developed a civilization superior in many respects to our own. They described, among other things, the creation of man in the mysterious land of Mu.

By comparing this writing with records of other ancient civilizations, as revealed in written documents, prehistoric ruins and geological phenomena, I found that all these centers of civilization had drawn their culture from a common source - Mu.

Of course, certain segments treated his views with derision and certain others accepted it as confirmation.

One thing that Churchward pioneered is populating Mu/Lemuria with actual people with names. Prior to this, Lemuria was full of "pudding sacks" or beings described but really given nothing to connect with. Churchward actually discusses some of the individuals from Mu, most significantly the Emperor/High Priest, Ra-Mu, who materializes time from time as an ascended master that channelers like Elizabeth Clare Prophet and Uriel summon to spread his wisdom to their followers.

Churchward cites the Lhasa Record as the source for Ra-Mu, with the Lhasa Record being "discovered" by a "Dr. Paul Schliemann," a real "archaeologist." The quotes indicate that there is no good evidence that Schliemann ever existed beyond authoring a couple of articles of his findings in the *New York American* in 1912. Most scientists, even then, preferred to share their findings in journals, peer-reviewed journals, and not the Sunday paper. But that is how Schliemann decided to present his earth-shattering findings, and then he disappeared. His findings from the discovery of the Lhasa Record are from the article "How I Found The Lost Atlantis, The Source of All Civilization." Schliemann's article tells of Mu and the Emperor and High Priest, Ra-Mu, but Schliemann surmised Mu was Atlantis and civilization birthed from there. Reading the same newspaper article, Churchward saw Schliemann's folly and repurposed it to state that Mu, in the Pacific Ocean now, was the cradle of all civilization.

Churchward's other books, *The Children of Mu* (1931), *The Sacred Symbols of Mu* (1933), and *Cosmic Forces of Mu* (1934), further explore the symbology of the tablets and how they connect with other civilizations across the globe, and provide his own science lessons to show how in-depth was the scientific knowledge that the people of Mu possessed.

In the middle of Churchward's publishing his series of Mu books, there came the first serious study on Lemuria trying to prove its existence. Scottish writer and scholar Lewis Spence published *The Problem with Lemuria* in 1931 which relied heavily on the work of MacKenzie Brown. Spence studies the geology of the Pacific Islands, cultural ties between the peoples of the Pacific Islands, folklore of the original inhabitants, race, customs, geology, and biology. While not entirely convincing, it was an honest attempt at exploring the idea of Lemuria as an actual location. As an added bonus, Spence offers a clear, concise analysis of Blavatsky, where he is mostly positive, Steiner, and Churchward, toward whom he is very negative. If anything, it shows that Lemuria had reached a level in social consciousness that warranted such examinations.

Churchward laid the geographical and anthropological foundations for a real, existing Lemuria, and the trio of Besant, Leadbeater, and Steiner pushed it further out into a mystical landscape. Combined, it would form a very real place full of human-like beings with supernatural powers. In the worlds of those who consume such alternative narratives, these works only helped to solidify Lemuria as a place in history—never again to be put in doubt, and only to be built upon. But while every one of these placed Lemuria squarely in the Pacific, real-life Lemurians started to emerge on the slopes of Mt. Shasta in California.

CHAPTER 6:

Descent from Paradise

FREDERICK SPENCER OLIVER WROTE ONE OF THE SINGLE MOST INFLUENTIAL books in the history of Lemuria, even though he mentions it but a handful of times and sticks mostly to telling about the life of a noble in ancient Atlantis. Even still, most of the teachings and story of *A Dweller on Two Planets* have been forgotten but for one single aspect: Oliver's protagonist/reincarnated spirit whom he channeled happens upon a mysterious master near Mt. Shasta in Northern California, who travels inside the mountain to meet with other masters. This is something that Mt. Shasta has not shaken in the 120 years since its publication. However, others moved quickly to turn those masters into the lost remnants of the Lemurian civilization, deep within the mountain, where many believe they still reside.

To this day, Mt. Shasta is known as a spiritual haven, where people flock for its high vibrational states and acceptance of alternative beliefs. Communities of those seeking out different ways have settled around the mountain. It all begins with a teenage boy and the voice in his head.

Born in 1866 in Washington, D.C., Frederick Spencer Oliver's father, John Wing Oliver, a newspaperman and physician, moved the family to Bear Creek, California, in 1868. For the next twenty years, they bounced around Los Angeles, Bear Creek in Oregon, Nevada, and allegedly near Mt. Shasta in Northern California, before settling in Ballard, California, outside of Santa Barbara, which is where Oliver would spend much of the remainder of his days.

Oliver admitted to being a bit of a daydreamer as a child, referring to himself as lackadaisical and even lazy. Learning and studies were not really for him, though he claimed to have been a boy wonder at science. Despite this, his education took a backseat to his flights of fancy, with his parents never really pushing him and instead indulging his imaginative side. The first seventeen years of his life were somewhat average, or at least not traumatic, growing up in a loving, familial environment, where he developed a close relationship with his mother. Parental acceptance was pushed to the limits when, beginning in 1883, Oliver would first start hearing the voice that would lead him to compile *A Dweller on Two Planets*.

The voice, that of Phylos the Esoterist or the Thibtan, first made himself known to the teenaged Oliver while he was surveying a piece of land for his father around Yreka, California, which sits thirty miles away from Mt. Shasta. Driving stakes on the boundary of a mining claim, he took out a notebook to jot down a note, but his hand started writing something different. Under a power all its own, involuntarily, it wrote and wrote. Suitably freaked out, the boy ran the few miles all the way back to his home. Thus began Oliver's psychic relationship with Phylos.

Writer and amanuensis of A Dweller on Two Planets, *Frederick Spencer Oliver.*

For a whole year, Phylos appeared to Oliver inside of the teen's head, educating him through "mental talks" that took over the boy's life. Days would go by while he went through the cursory motions of living, not studying or reading but subsisting on the education Phylos was providing. He tried to keep it a secret, but it was becoming obvious to everyone that something was up. His father noticed and got upset at his distracted, unmotivated son, so Oliver broke down and told his parents who were a little worried but mostly curious. They wanted to meet this Phylos, but the disembodied voice would not materialize for them. Instead, only through their son would he make his presence felt as Oliver spoke directly the words that Phylos was relaying to him. This scene started attracting a small crowd and pretty soon others joined in, entranced by the lessons being channeled through the teenager. These channeled sessions became a mainstay and a way for Oliver to attract adherents, however small in number, to Phylos' teachings.

Soon Phylos instructed Oliver to start writing, transcribing what was being funneled through him, acting as amanuensis for the mystical presence. Phylos wanted to write a book and got Oliver started on the process. It turned out to be an arduous one, where at times Oliver was writing backward and all out of order, a jumbled mess. It took a couple of years, but he managed to complete a handwritten manuscript.

Now in his early twenties, Oliver stood at 5'11", with soft gray eyes and dark hair combed back to show his light complexion, and a not-quite-full mustache rested upon his upper lip. Needing a way to sustain himself, he became a newspaperman like his father. Reporting, writing, and editing in the Santa Ynez Valley, Oliver covered mostly the area around his home base in Ballard and other small farming communities, writing under the pen name Will Harrold. He focused on delivering a slice of life reporting on agriculture in the valley. For a little over a decade, he worked that beat. He would also try his hand at poetry and short stories, writing some forty stories, with little luck in seeing any of those published.

On January 2, 1894, Oliver married Edwina May Smith, the daughter of a farming family from the area, in Santa Barbara's Unity Church. The minister overseeing the proceedings, Henry G. Spaulding, was a prominent Unitarian minister from Boston on a speaking tour of California at the time. The church preached a one-world religion that God exists within you, and focused on being guided by reason and conscience to obtain religious truth, toleration of other religions, and being a generally good person. His getting married in a "Unity" Church, by a Unitarian minister, would probably mean Frederick held those same beliefs, many of which will show up in *A Dweller on Two Planets*. Frederick and Edwina would have two children, Ernon Vesler Oliver (1894–1961) and Leslie Robert Oliver (1898–1987).

Along with marriage and the birth of their first child, 1894 would be pivotal for Oliver's literary career, when he took out the first copyright on *A Dweller on Two Planets*, and the first efforts were made to see the work published. He had the manuscript manually typed out and duplicates created. All publishers rejected the book, though, and one held on to the manuscript for a year before sending it back to Oliver. Another manuscript was nearly lost in a train wreck and subsequent fire, and he became convinced "Dark Forces" were trying to thwart its publication.

Months passed. Years. Disappointments mounted. That is the writer's life, though, especially when you have a book sitting and waiting to be published, but at every turn there is a roadblock. Oliver and his agent got clever in trying to get the book published. They tried selling subscriptions to cover the costs. They spread out through Santa Barbara and surrounding towns trying to get people to commit to buying the book. And his agent traveled all over to work deals, even approaching the local government to take out ads to be placed in the book. Anything to raise the few thousand dollars needed to publish it. But all efforts were for naught; nothing worked and the schemes fell apart.

A small cadre of believers kept faith in him: his wife, his lawyer friend who was the former District Attorney, and some others who read the book and became enthralled with it and with its writer, who claimed to hold Mesmeric powers over some of them. If he were a lesser man, he told himself, he could get them to do most anything. But they failed in getting his book published. And the pain grew stronger and more bitter and more desperate.

But the years rolled by and the book, finished, lingered in publication hell, until one night while working the night editor job at the *Santa Barbara Press* putting the finishing touches on the next day's edition and reading the news from around the area, his eye gets drawn to an interview with Teresa Kerr, and something clicks inside of him.

Teresa Kerr was sitting in jail at that moment, accused of shooting and killing her estranged husband on the stairs inside of the old city hall of Los Angeles. A former sex worker who was wooed by one of her clients, George King, after being love bombed by him over several months, they had lived together and even signed a marriage agreement. But King, being a son of a scion of Los Angeles, one of the founders in the area, had political ambitions beyond working in the city engineer's office, and friends and family had finally convinced him to drop Kerr because she was a liability. So the day after Christmas in 1898 he kissed her goodbye, intending to never see her again. A couple of anxiety-ridden days passed and she decided to head down to where he worked, in City Hall, a pistol in her hand.

After waiting hours in the building, George appeared and Kerr confronted him on the steps, pulling the gun, pushing the barrel into her breast, and asking why. Why did you leave? Don't you love me? Don't you know the pain and torment you caused? Don't you care? All said with the intention of killing herself right there in front of him. To let him know what he had done to her. He grabbed the gun and in the struggle it went off, the bullet tearing a deadly path through his intestines.

King died a couple of days later while Kerr would be tried for his murder. It was a sensational crime that drew the whole city out to observe, even the outlying areas of Santa Barbara, where Oliver took notice. He was compelled by Kerr's story and its similarity to *A Dweller on Two Planets*, which features a plot point centered around a Californian man, born in Washington, D.C., who helps a "public woman" with a drinking and gambling problem rise above and live out her dream to be a painter. Like God himself was tapping Oliver on the shoulder to help this woman out. But he managed to do it in the worst possible way.

First, Oliver's friend, lawyer, and literary agent stopped by the law offices of Kerr's attorneys trying to either join the defense team or take it over completely. All for naught. This was followed by Edwina, his wife, writing a letter to a local newspaper directed to Kerr, proclaiming her desire to see Kerr come live with the Olivers.

"I want her, I need her, and she needs me! Los Angeles, so fair to many, must be a vista of Hades to this poor soul-sick girl."

She pours her heart out pleading for Teresa to come live with her and her husband, "shall we not go down the Stream of Time together, both our lives the better for our companionships, and together go to One who bids all the weary to come to Him? I have found Him and to Him would I take her."

AND THIS WAS FOLLOWED BY OLIVER'S MOTHER TRYING TO ADOPT THE twenty-five-year-old Kerr, ending with Oliver coming to Los Angeles to have a meeting with her attorneys. During these many encounters, it surfaced that he considered Kerr to be his "affinity," Phylos-speak for soulmate.

All of these advances were rebuffed, and Kerr went on to be acquitted while Oliver had a miserable rest of 1899. In the summer, he suffered a hemorrhage of his stomach and would spend the fall recuperating in Los Angeles, but his condition deteriorated, and he died on November 15, 1899, at the age of thirty-three from cirrhosis of the liver.

After his death, his mother became his literary executor and worked hard over the next few years to see her son's book be published. The story goes that a mysterious woman came forward to give the money needed to cover the costs of publishing. In 1904, Baumgardt Publishing Co. released *A Dweller on Two Planets* for the first time. Though it received little to no attention upon its publication, through word of mouth and California being a hotbed at the time of alternative and esoteric thinking, the book gained something of a cult following, leading to additional editions being published in the 1920s prior to the first stories of Lemurians on Mt. Shasta.

The book tells an interesting story of a mixture of Christian esotericism by way of Atlantis, Mt. Shasta, and Venus. It begins with Zalim, an Atlantean, and his rise to prominence in Atlantean society and the pitfalls that come along with it. Zalim becomes entangled in a love triangle with two Atlantean women, one of whom tries to kill Zalim but ends up turning into a statue. At the time of Zalim's death, he lived a luxurious life that included trips in his personal aerial submarine vessel, called a veilx.

After his death, Zalim's soul gets reincarnated into that of Walter Pierson, who bears some resemblance to Oliver's father. Both Pierson and John Oliver were born in Washington, D.C., and moved to California shortly after the Civil War. The differences end there: Pierson meets a mystical Chinese man, Quong, near Mt. Shasta, who proceeds to take Pierson on a magical, mystical tour inside Mt. Shasta. Along the way, he would teach Pierson the core of a mystical Christian philosophy that included Pierson transforming into Phylos and being astrally projected to Venus to meet with other ascended masters. Once returned to his worldly form of Pierson, he meets a former alcoholic prostitute that he helps to get out of the life

AERIAL-SUBMARINE VESSEL, ENTERING THE WATER.

Above: A drawing of an Atlantean aerial submarine, veilx, emerging from the water. Taken from A Dweller on Two Planets.

Below: A drawing of Mt. Shasta and the surrounding region taken from A Dweller on Two Planets.

MOUNT SHASTA—IN NORTHERN CALIFORNIA—14,444 FEET HIGH.

and the two of them get married. Pierson dedicates his life to the Christian occult arts while his wife kindly indulges this passion. The two die going down with a ship that Pierson decided to crew when he grew bored with life.

And that is it plot-wise for the book. While traveling to Atlantis and riding around in airship submarines and being astrally projected to Venus sounds exciting, it is all secondary and plays a small role in the main theme, which is passing along a mystical version of Christianity. The book is a winding road of lessons for the protagonists to learn and for the reader to take to heart and ingest as well. They are quasi-parables. In a world wanting for entertainment, it would make sense that a man claiming connections to Atlantis while espousing Christian beliefs would be appealing, and help explain why certain people would congregate around Oliver, listen to him, and connect with these stories and lessons.

Outside of making that connection to a hollowed-out Mt. Shasta full of ascended masters, *A Dweller on Two Planets* is important as an early version of channeled material. And the story of suddenly being inundated by a spirit directly contacting your brain gets replayed over and over again throughout the twentieth century. As well as him providing sessions of directly channeling Phylos while others gathered around and gave witness, Oliver's biggest impact would be on Mt. Shasta, hollowing it out, creating tunnels, creating masters:

What secrets perchance are about us! We do not know as we lie there, our bodies resting, our souls filled with peace, nor do we know until many years are passed out through the back door of time that that tall basalt cliff conceals a door-way. We do not suspect this, nor that a long tunnel stretches away, far into the interior of majestic Shasta. Wholly un-thought is it that there lie at the tunnel's far end vast apart-ments—the home of a mystic brotherhood, whose occult arts hollowed that tunnel and mysterious dwelling:— "Sach" the name is. Are you incredulous as to these things? Go there, or suffer yourself to be taken as I was, once! See, as I saw, not with the vision of flesh, the walls, polished as by jewelers, though excavated as by giants; floors carpeted with long, fleecy gray fabric that looked like fur, but was a mineral product; ledges intersected by the builders, and in their wonderful polish exhibiting veinings of gold, of silver, of green copper ores, and maculations of precious stones. Verily, a mystic temple, made afar from the madding crowd, a refuge whereof those who,

"Seeing, see not," can truly say:

"And no man knows * * ***

"And no man saw it e'er."

Once I was there, friend, casting pebbles in the stream's deep pools; yet it was then hid, for only a few are privileged. And departing, the spot was forgotten, and today, unable as any one who reads this, I cannot tell its place. Curiosity will never unlock that secret. Does it truly exist? Seek and ye shall find; knock and it shall be opened unto you. Shasta is a true guardian and silently towers, giving no sign of that within his breast. But there is a key. The one who first conquers self, Shasta will not deny.

This is the last scene. You have viewed the proud peak both near and far; by day, by night; in the smoke, and in the clear mountain air; seen its interior, and from its apex gazed upon it and the globe stretched away 'neath your feet. 'Tis a sight of God's handiwork, sublime, awful, never-to-be-for-gotten; and as thy soul hath sated itself with admiration thereof, in that measure be now filled with His Peace.

Before Oliver, Mt. Shasta really was like any other mountain in California. Travel stories in the newspapers before and after the publication of *A Dweller on Two Planets* mention nothing about any sort of mysterious or mythical beings living up there, or any kind of folklore that alludes to such. Nor is there any kind of paranormal activity mentioned. Majestic and beautiful, yes. But nothing particularly supernatural about it.

It rises to a peak of 14,162 feet above the northernmost region of California, the southernmost peak of the Cascade Mountains and one of the highest peaks in the U.S. "Majestic" might not do it much justice. Mt. Shasta cuts a godly physique and portent. Nineteenth-century poet and explorer Joaquin Miller calls it "the most perfect snow peak in America . . . White and flashing like a pyramid of silver . . . lonely as a God and white as a winter moon."

With a base girth of seventy miles, the mountain takes up a lot of territory being the source of many local tributaries and rivers. An inactive volcano that erupted on average once every 800 years over the past 10,000 years, the last known eruption occurred sometime in the eighteenth century. That eruption may also be the first time a European observed Mt. Shasta, when in 1786 French explorer Jean de la Perouse was sailing along the northern California coast and described what could have been an eruption taking place at Mt. Shasta.

These eruptions led to Mt. Shasta not having a singular peak but multiple structures, the most prominent sub-peak being the 12,330-foot Shastina, a craterous peak attached to the shoulder of Mt. Shasta. The mountain is referred to as Mt. Shasta to differentiate it from the town of Mount Shasta located at the base.

The north face of Mt. Shasta as seen from Siskiyou County Route A12 at sunset taken by Frank Schulenburg. (© Frank Schulenburg / CC BY-SA 4.0)

A number of American Indian tribes resided around the base of the mountain and remained there until the first arrival of European explorers and settlers in the middle of the nineteenth century, residing in the vicinity for nearly 5,000 years. The tribe directly nearest the mountain at the time of European contact was known as the Shasta, but referred to themselves as "Kahosadi" or "plain speakers." They primarily lived off the land, hunting, gathering, fishing, and living somewhat nomadic lifestyles. That way of life became dramatically upended by the Gold Rush as their people would die from disease and be forcibly removed from the area. Today several tribes live near Mt. Shasta and the surrounding area.

The name Shasta remains a bit of a mystery. There are a few possible sources for it coming from the name of a prominent local native chief called Shasti; the name of local indigenous tribe Shas-ti'ka; or the native word *tsadi*, meaning "three" and referring to the triple-peaked mountain, or the Russian word *tchastal*, meaning "white and pure mountain." By the mid-nineteenth century, the mountain was referred to on maps and in journals as Sasty, Shasta, Shasty, Shatasla, Chastise, Castice, and Sistise, with the current spelling first appearing in 1850.

But in reality, the background of Mt. Shasta means little in the Lemurian story. There are second- and even third-hand stories reportedly from American Indian sources that relate to invisible people living on the mountain. Some of these stories say that, if the wind blows just right, you can hear the playing of children and strains of music wafting down the slopes. And there are further claims that American Indians never ventured up the mountain for veneration of the Great Spirit, which dwells within the mountain. While there may be some veracity to these stories, they veer a little too close to later stories about the mountain to be given much credence. So its ascendance as a place of mystical power could have begun in 1883 or 1894 or 1899 or 1905, but most likely in the 1920s, when *A Dweller on Two Planets* received a reprinting. Mt. Shasta was just another mountain, beautiful and serene, yes, but nothing so out of the ordinary. Then along came Frederick Spencer Oliver to create a safe space for others to tell their weird Mt. Shasta encounters—and they did.

ALTERNATIVE RELIGIONS LOVE TO BLOSSOM IN CALIFORNIA. IT IS A MAGNET

for them. The tradition goes back to the nineteenth century, as more traditional forms of belief were sparse or became intermingled with the influx of so many types of cultures there. That helped to attract people to California. It called to Theosophists. It summoned spiritualists. It hearkened back to the Rosicrucians. And it is with them the story of Lemurians on Mt. Shasta picks up.

Being a European phenomenon, Rosicrucianism traces its origins back to ancient Egypt, through ancient Greece by way of Pythagoras and then Hermes Trismegistus and Hermeticism. These traditions were carried forward generation after generation by more mystically-minded folks like Kabbalists, or alchemists like Albertus Magnus and Nicholas Flamel. And Rosicrucian thought made its way to the New World with Johannes Kelpius establishing a Rosicrucian settlement in Pennsylvania. Rosicrucians have claimed that they played important roles for the likes of Ben Franklin, Thomas Jefferson, and Thomas Paine, but the society lay dormant for much of the nineteenth century. Not until the beginning of the twentieth century with New York businessman Harvey Spencer Lewis did it see a resurgence in America.

Lewis began his esoteric life as the president of the New York-based Institute for Physical Research, where he formed a group within a group, The Rosicrucian Research Society, that included I.K. Funk, the Funk in Funk and Wagnalls. This foray into Rosicrucianism inspired him to travel to France to be initiated in the rites of European Rosicrucianism. Lewis came back to America where he began assembling a like-minded group of individuals, culminating in 1915 when he formed the Ancient and Mystical Order of the Rosae Crucis (AMORC). In its early years AMORC bounced around the country from New York to San Francisco to Tampa, then to San Jose, where it is located to this day.

Lewis had a background as a commercial artist and used those artistic skills to help sell the slick magazines and journals AMORC produced, which is where their first forays into the Lemuria saga appeared. He utilized the latest technology available to him, making it a part of the fabric of AMORC, and crafted a much-needed organization to get the ideas of Rosicrucianism in front of more people in order to sustain it. To this end, he initiated a correspondence school to allow

Photograph of AMORC founder Henry Spencer Lewis. (Los Angeles Times Photographic Archive, Library Special Collections, Charles E. Young Research Library, UCLA)

people to develop their spiritual selves at home, which was met with scorn by other esoteric groups, to whom the whole point was to be initiated into a secret society by your peers, face to face—not to read a packet of materials you get in the mail. What started as a correspondence school would grow into radio stations, TV production elements, and even their own university. All of which propelled AMORC to be one of the largest occult organizations in the world.

Through Lewis' writings in AMORC publications, some attributed to him, some not, he helped to create and spread the idea of Lemurians at Mt. Shasta. The beginnings of his and AMORC's fascination with Lemuria appeared with a 1925 article in their in-house magazine titled "Descendants of Lemuria" by someone named Selvius, thought to be Lewis. The article established a lot of firsts, primary of which is Lemurians on Mt. Shasta and all of the peculiar activities they were up to out there. The first telling of the Edgar Lucien Larkin story of him seeing mysterious buildings on Mt. Shasta appears in the article. Larkin, who had just passed away at that time, was the former director of the Mount Lowe Observatory, which was more tourist attraction than scientific observatory; it was part of a railroad company's resort, with the telescope there not being all that powerful. Larkin wrote a popular column centered around mystical and science topics for a San Francisco newspaper, and published a couple of books based on those columns. He also played a big role in bringing *A Dweller on Two Planets* more popularity, writing about the book in his column and working with Oliver's mother to get a new edition published, for which he wrote a brochure publicizing the book. His being dead and being a friend of the mystical world might have made him a good tool for presenting credible "proof" of Lemurians on Mt. Shasta.

What that proof boiled down to is a story that got retold time and time again, about Larkin relaying in some second-hand manner that he was testing out a new long-range telescope, presumably at Mount Lowe Observatory, located outside of Pasadena some 600 miles from Mt. Shasta. (One version has him in the foothills around Shasta.) Wherever he was, he spotted golden domes and marble buildings and silhouettes of ceremonies taking place among the trees on the slopes of Mt. Shasta. He explained how there seemed to be an invisible barrier around the village, like an American version of Birnin Zana. He spent a whole week observing the place, jotting down notes about this strange mysterious town. Larkin never related these findings in his column or any of his books, nor did he leave these notes behind to be studied. How Selvius heard about this is as mysterious as those structures on Mt. Shasta.

Another original story is that of a strange older, regal-looking man appearing seemingly out of nowhere in San Francisco, who receives a royal welcome from city officials. There's a luncheon held in his honor. He meets with them, though nothing is known about what was discussed. And he vanishes as quickly as he appeared. It was decided that he was a Shasta Lemurian, and the story has some similarities to Quong from *A Dweller on Two Planets*. Selvius then relates some "airboat" sightings—cigar-shaped airships that sailed on the water or in the ocean, much like the veilx from *A Dweller on Two Planets*. The piece set the tone for the rest of the Rosicrucian fascination with Lemuria.

This came in the form of Wishar Spenle Cervé and the most influential AMORC work, *Lemuria: The Lost Continent of the Pacific*. It appears Harvey Spencer Lewis used a clever near-anagram of his name to come up with Wishar Spenle Cervé.

Lemuria: The Lost Continent of the Pacific (1931) echoes many of the same points as Selvius (possibly because they were written by the same person), but in manuscript length, Cervé has the freedom to expand on themes and provide more details.

A big thrust of the Rosicrucian argument lies in putting forward California as a cradle of civilization: "the state of California actually represents the oldest habited, cultivated, civilized land on the face of the Earth that is still in practically the same physical form, and in the same environment, as when God first created it." The place where remnants of lost ancient cultures survived cataclysms and spread forth is a story we have heard before, only the locations have changed, and Cervé wastes no time in hammering that idea because it is central to their belief that Lemuria survived in America and Lemurians live in Mt. Shasta.

Cervé does a good job of relying on all that came before him, touching on Le Plongeon's Mayans and Atlanteans and Churchward's Mu. Also, when Lemuria sinks, its peoples travel to Atlantis and then on to Africa. He even claims that native Lemurians derived from the proto-lemurs of Sclater and they were also proto-humans, so in the process, Cervé in a clever pirouette crosses the streams of the two paths of Lemuria and Lemurians into one. They were both actual lemurs and the mystical Lemurians of Blavatsky and the other Theosophists.

Much like everyone else's Lemuria, Cervé's sank, though its rocky eastern shoreline survived and now makes up California and Oregon. And he provides ample descriptions of these Lemurians, starting with their heads, which were much larger in proportion to the body than regular humans, and exceptionally high foreheads, with a six- to seven-inch gap between their eyebrows and hairline. They wore their hair as a golden-colored mullet braided in the back. About an inch and a half above the nose was a large, walnut-size protrusion, a soft mass of tissue that acted as an extrasensory organ allowing them to communicate over great distances and to develop a sixth perception sense of the fourth dimension. This organ is primarily what allowed their culture to survive. Beyond all of that, they were taller than average humans, with many reaching seven feet tall aided by having long slender necks.

These Lemurians loved hygiene and lived healthy lives. Working. Exercising. And resting. For the most part, they were vegetarians and transitioned into death by announcing it was their time to go. Their society was, as you might imagine, rather utopian, with elected officials and no need of money. Low to no crime whatsoever, they were not into phallic worship, and wore loose-flowing garments. They were also huge proponents of natural energy like solar power, and had universal child care.

Their marriage rituals were more like a reality show that had prospective couples travel off into the wilderness together for a couple of moon cycles. The two had to prove they could support one another, offer care and support under difficult circumstances. Only when they came back and still cared for one another—and did not despise each other—would they get married. Otherwise, they would go their separate ways. Like Oliver's Atlanteans, Cervé's Lemurians rode around in airships that had search beams powered by special minerals.

Cervé then details some of the strange goings-on around California, like the Sierras having their own peculiar Rip Van Winkle character who, if you got too close to him, would wake up and cuss you out. But there were also a large number of strange light sightings and relics of ancient people. This all leads him to Mt. Shasta and a bunch of stories that he relates to having happened around the mountain.

Bizarre people were sighted popping out of the forests, scurrying back into the woods if they would happen to be seen. These same shy introverts would show up in the towns around Shasta and trade gold nuggets and gold dust for goods, where the townsfolk described them as tall, graceful, agile, and virile, but also old. Like real-life Tolkien elves. He tells more tales of people in pure white and sandals, tall and majestic in appearance who had a knack for disappearing into the twilight when attempts were made to photograph them. When in town buying supplies they spoke English with a hint of a British accent. And they refused to talk about themselves or answer any questions. Just throw down their gold and head out, not waiting around for change.

Other reports said there were great fires seen through the trees in the forest. Figures could be seen moving around the bright light, sounds of chanting and singing accompanied by beautiful weird music. Some have claimed to have seen upward of 400–500 of those figures moving around the lights in some kind of ceremony. A supernatural fire made of a brilliant white light verging on blue. The story goes that a stone was discovered near where one of these ceremonies took place with hieroglyphs etched in it, but also on it written in English was "Ceremony of Adoration to Guatama," with Guatama meaning America. This would lead to people going in to investigate, when they would stumble into a "concealed person of large size" or peculiar vibrations. Then, an invisible energy force field would halt anybody trying to go any further and make them turn around.

With all these stories, Cervé is rather vague, never going into details, just throwing them out there to prove the weirdness around the mountain. No attribution. No names. No anything. By the time he gets around to telling/re-telling the Larkin telescope story, it is conspicuous due to the sheer amount of details that he provides for this one incident. It begins by saying that Larkin was at his observatory on Mount Lowe, trying out a new telescope, and picked out Mt. Shasta as a guide and reference point, which would be all well and good if we lived on a flat Earth, where a telescope that can observe the Moon may not have any issues picking out details on a rather large mountain like Mt. Shasta. However, we live on a round globe, which makes viewing objects 600-plus miles away impossible, thanks to the curvature of the Earth and the terrain that lies within those 600 miles.

Nonetheless, Cervé pushes onward and has Larkin seeing a gold-tinted dome among the trees—like it was some "Oriental building." Two more domes appear. And another. Then there is a marble building. As night blanketed the mountain, great and powerful lights illuminated these buildings. Larkin watched these incredible scenes furiously taking precise notes, spending an entire week watching all of this unfold. Larkin never wrote about this. Though he did write about viewing Mt. Shasta while passing by on the train and being taken by its majesty and beauty, at no point does it spark the memory of spending an entire week watching the mountain.

Cervé wraps it up by saying it should be taken with a grain of salt. Then he relays even more mystical occurrences, like how forest fires were stopped by mysterious fog and bizarre-looking cattle walking along the highway. And how there is another "village" of Lemurians in Santa Barbara (near where Frederick Spencer Oliver lived and worked) connected to Mt. Shasta through a series of tunnels—not the last time tunnels will connect places over long distances.

There are also a couple of UFO-like sightings and encounters. The first is the story of a car driving around or near Mt. Shasta being invaded by a bright light, causing it to lose all power. The occupants of the car had to get out and push it back whence they came before it would start for them again. Cars stalling out is a classic UFO scenario seen in the Barney and Betty Hill abduction, along with many other encounters—and with this one by Cervé being one of the first appearances of "white lights," UFOs, and car troubles.

There is more. A lot more, with hundreds of sightings of "peculiarly shaped boats which have flown out of this region high in the air over the hills and valleys of California and have been seen by others to come on to the waters of the Pacific

A drawing of an Atlantean aerial submarine, veilx, lit up and soaring through the sky. Taken from A Dweller on Two Planets.

Ocean at the shore and then to continue out on the seas as a vessel." Plenty of sailors have witnessed this in the reverse, seeing boats take off from the sea to fly away, and have been seen as far north as the Aleutian Islands. Golfers in the Sierra Nevadas saw a silvery vessel rise in the air before them and float away soundlessly. Tying Lemurians with UFOs had a long-lasting impact, as they vaguely share many physical characteristics and downright odd behavior, with early contactee beings described by the likes of George Adamski and Antônio Vilas-Boas in their encounters. And all from the outer space origins of Lemurians that the likes of Steiner had already established. A Lemurian morphs into a Venusian morphs into a Zeta Reticulan.

Cervé's book proved to be popular, or as popular as a book on Lemuria can be at any time. And it brought with it the unintended consequence of drawing a lot of attention to the slopes of Mt. Shasta. People started to search for the Lemurian colony within. Many souls made the trek to see the mountain for themselves. More than a few had experiences. The United States Forest Service, who oversaw Mt. Shasta at the time, received a flood of letters asking about the Lemurians. They let everyone know the entire mountain had been searched, the flats around it had been explored, everything had been photographed from the air, and they did not see anything nor had they ever met anyone who had met a Lemurian.

What helped to promulgate the Cervé vision of Mt. Shasta was a story that ran in the *Los Angeles Times* a few months after the book's publication. "A People of Mystery: Are They Remnants of a Lost Race? Do They Possess a Fabulous Gold Treasure?" by Edward Lanser appeared on May 22, 1932, and it did much to amplify the idea that there were Lemurians on Mt. Shasta and that strange occurrences were going on there.

Lanser did not present much in the way of unique information. Most of the article was repeated claims already made by Selvius/Lewis/Cervé without even mentioning *Lemuria: The Lost Continent of the Pacific*. The only new aspect was his own encounter of seeing a weird red glow on Mt. Shasta while passing by on a train and the conductor telling him that it was Lemurians. Being a major newspaper, it did help to increase belief of Lemurians on Mt. Shasta. However, the seriousness of Lanser's intent is called into question by the snarky final part of the story:

> *The really incredible thing is that these staunch descendants of that vanished race have succeeded in secluding themselves in the midst of our teeming state and that they have managed through some marvelous sorcery to keep hi-ways, hot-dog establishments, filling stations and the other ugly counterparts of our tourist system out of their sacred precincts.*

This rather tongue-in-cheek closer may out Lanser's sincerity. That the article is almost entirely derivative of Selvius' story and the Cervé book has led some to speculate that maybe Lewis wrote this one too—that he is Edward Lanser as well. But there was a real Edward Lanser who lived in Los Angeles at the time and he was also a writer, who even traveled by train through northern California.

The heat was getting turned up on Mt. Shasta, Lemurians, and also on Lewis and the Rosicrucians, who may have felt the pressure to start producing actual Lemurians. So Lewis did what many would do in his situation: he blamed all of the people who read his book and took it seriously enough to go and try to find the Lemurians themselves. He was not without some *mea culpa*: "We, the chief executives of AMORC, voluntarily assume some blame in this regard." He genuinely seemed to rue bringing Mt. Shasta to the forefront, but mostly because a bunch of true believers started calling him out on his own writings. So instead of issuing a retraction, five short years after the book appeared, in 1936, in the pages of the *Rosicrucian Digest*, he went one better and said that due to the encroaching on their space, the bulk of the Lemurians had left Mt. Shasta to move down south toward Mexico. He would not be providing their new address. All the chief Lemurian officers and advanced directors moved the center of activities and residencies from their traditional home in Mt. Shasta. The intrusion upon their privacy and their spiritual progress by annoying new mystics on the mountain became too much. The few left on Mt. Shasta would be keeping a low profile: "By this move of the colony from the old location to a new secret place, which will not be revealed, thousands of foolish followers of such matters will have a sad awakening." These Lemurians, who have been there on or in Mt. Shasta for tens of thousands of years, were living a nice quiet life, and all it took to destroy it all was Cervé publicizing their existence, ruining millennia of ancient mystical tradition.

Cervé/Lewis helped usher in a weird time in and around Mt. Shasta. Perhaps because of *Lemuria: The Lost Continent of the Pacific* these events started to be reported, or maybe the stories appearing in the book gave people the confidence they needed to report their own encounters. Nevertheless, Cervé kicks off a Golden Age on Mt. Shasta, solidifying the mountain and Lemurians in the esoteric world and shaping Lemuria as a place of spiritual and technological perfection.

Abraham Mansfield, who was the Chief of the Gods of the Lemurians, a title bestowed upon him like it was to James Churchward before him, wrote in the 1970s about an encounter that his friend experienced in 1931. His friend was out deer hunting, tracking a wounded deer around the northeast side of the mountain until he became tired and lost in the process. A Lemurian pops out in front of him saying, "I am a Lemurian. What are you doing here?" The Lemurian, seeing the hunter was in a bad way, brings him inside the mountain, down tunnels made of gold, rooms lined with gold, gold slab beds, and even a special golden pillow that will make dreams come to life. Then the Lemurian told him about all the tunnels that connected Mt. Shasta with the rest of the world, "a world within worlds." He also showed off a fantastic garden with giant carrots, and the hunter was told of and shown their greater knowledge of "atom power," ESP, electronics, science, everything. They were able to pick up messages recorded in time and space from older civilizations back to the beginning of time. Then the hunter woke up back near where he had met the Lemurian and was able to make his way back. The scene bears some resemblances to later alien abduction accounts.

This led to another 1931 story from Dr. Maurice Doreal, who was in California lecturing when he heard of Lemurians on Mt. Shasta. Going to investigate, he was given the true story of how Atlanteans fled the sinking Atlantis and traveled into the California mountains. By the time of Doreal's visit, only 353 still lived on Mt. Shasta. But they had unlocked the secret of the atom. The Atlanteans and Lemurians underwent a great war, which the Atlanteans were winning so the Lemurians retreated to their "pleasure palaces" and were placed in a state of house arrest. So Atlanteans took up shop in Mt. Shasta and every three months would fly out in their cigar-shaped airships to check in on their Lemurian prisoners. In Mt. Shasta, the Atlanteans lived in an underground city with their incredibly beautiful marble

Image of Phylos taken from **A Dweller on Two Planets.**

houses, Greek-like temples, lovely parks, and gardens using "energies" to keep plants growing perfectly.

Throughout the 1930s, Nola Van Valer would travel up to Mt. Shasta with friends to camp out in the summer months; she kept coming back because she got to meet Phylos. Frederick Oliver's Phylos. On the east side of the mountain near their campsite, a large rock began to open up, revealing a door that led to a cavern where Phylos stood—in one of the seventeen underground temples found all over the world. He was looking fine and pure in long white robes. He treated Van Valer to a similar treatment found in *A Dweller on Two Planets,* showing her around the inside of Mt. Shasta while preaching mystical truths as he went, which relayed much that appears in the Bible. Year after year she would come back to meet with Phylos and other masters until one year they did not show up. Van Valer would go on to found the Radiant School of the Seekers and Servers in the 1960s near Mt. Shasta.

Then comes the story of J.C. Brown, who some think was Lord Arthur J. Cowdray in disguise. Brown was hired by Cowdray's company in the early 1900s to prospect for gold in the Cascade Mountains where he stumbled across a mysterious cave and tunnel system. He kept exploring and exploring it for miles. Along the way, he found traces of gold and copper until he discovered two rooms filled with treasure. Gold and copper objects lying about, along with a couple of dozen skeletons. All very tall. Then, he inexplicably left it all there. He came back out, concealed the entrance, and then spent the next thirty years studying the lore around what he found. Now a seventy-nine-year-old, Mr. Brown appears in Stockton, California, in 1934, telling this story and saying he is finally ready to retrieve the gold and take people to Lemuria. He claimed that he was under the influence of "Indian masters" that were jealous of the hidden continent, which kept him from going back all these years. So it created a lot of red tape about "getting them into the right mood" to go in and take the valuable treasures within. Brown spent two months in town whipping up a frenzy, giving interviews to newspapers. People quit their jobs, sold off their furniture and businesses to raise funds for the expedition. A special glass bottom boat from Argentina was ordered to transport them there. And when it was time to head out to Lemuria, Brown ghosted them, never to be seen again. A Basque sheepherder in Nevada claims the old man died in 1936 and was buried in the Black Desert.

Which leads to one of the most well-known and influential encounters to have happened on Mt. Shasta, that of Guy Ballard. While his book *Unveiled Mysteries* was published in 1934, the event in question happened in 1930 when the Midwesterner Ballard was in California for work, staying in the shadow of Mt. Shasta. He immediately fell in love with the area and spent his time taking long strolls in the woods around Mt. Shasta. On one such constitutional, he runs into a dreamy character who provides Ballard with a creamy liquid to raise his spirits. He introduces himself as Saint Germain, then begins relaying spiritual lessons to Ballard. Page after page of teachings. From Mt. Shasta, Saint Germain takes Ballard on an astral time journey to Egypt and back. He tames a panther, visits a time when the Sahara was a tropical forest, and Saint Germain starts to send dove-delivered messages to Ballard to summon him back to Mt. Shasta. Ballard's tale shares a number of similarities with *A Dweller on Two Planets*, whose protagonist also meets a mystic on Mt. Shasta who takes him on similar astral journeys and imparts the wisdom of Ascended Masters (AM). *A Dweller on Two Planets* even refers to and spells *I AM* like Ballard would do when he later founded the "I AM" Activity Movement.

Quite a few others shared similar experiences to those of Guy Ballard in the years and decades following the 1930s. After the briefest of acting careers, Earlyne Chaney became initiated in a secret temple in the woods around Mt. Shasta where one day, while camping, a mysterious stranger led her on a spiritual tour that helped her and her husband to found the New Age church and mystery school Astara.

Aurelia Louise Jones tells of how Lemurians speak a language called Solara Maru but they know English and speak it with a slight British accent. They used airships to travel to Atlantis powered by crystals, the fleet being called "the Silver Fleet." The airships also used stealth technology, while the Lemurians shifted between third, fourth, and fifth-dimension vibrational states, and live in the "Crystal City of the Seven Rays."

This is followed by William F. Hamilton in 1977 coming across a "young very pretty blonde girl with almond-shaped eyes and small perfect teeth" named Bonnie. She proceeded to tell him about being born in the Lemurian colony of Telos built inside of Mt. Shasta. Telos had an elaborate train system that ran on electromagnetic impulses and connected all the underground cities. Robots grew everyone's food. When asked about how things were destroyed, Bonnie tells an interesting tale:

The Atlanteans were taking pot shots at China and they were using a form of vibrating crystal rays off certain elements in the atmosphere and bouncing them off satellites in orbit around earth. At this time earth had two moons. One of them was taken out of its course by the Atlanteans, the smaller moon. They were vibrating the rays of the crystal higher and higher and hoping to direct the small moon as a missile aimed at China and India. The Atlanteans' major crystal was located near Bimini and they could not control it as the force went higher and higher and the moon plunged to the earth, split in two, and fell on the heads of the Atlanteans themselves bringing about their final destruction.

These experiences ushered in a new era for Mt. Shasta as a beacon of all sorts of mysterious, strange encounters that stretch forward to this day. And by the end of the 1970s, people started to believe that Lemurians were utilizing crystals for their powers to hollow out an underground city below Mt. Shasta to preserve their culture, treasures, and records.

One of the most prevalent sightings around the mountain was that of little people. On the northwestern flat area near the mountain appear tiny little mounds, which some have claimed were built by tiny moundbuilders. The earthen formations first received archaeological attention in the 1940s. They have been described as "grass-covered nipples" and cover some 600 acres. Each mound measures sixty feet in diameter, with the dirt rising in an almost perfect circle to a crest approximately two feet above the ground. Each one is surrounded by a stone path or mosaic, formed by volcanic stones from around the mountain. Investigators seem puzzled by how the rocks were set in circular trenches with smaller rocks at the bottom and larger and larger rocks on top, showing some level of purpose.

These strange mounds have led to strange accounts of little, gnomish people. One hiker in the area claimed to have been yelled at by a small, gnome-like person because he bent the branch of a fern. This led to more little people gathering around, one of whom spoke English and said that the grass-covered nipples were used for agricultural ceremonial purposes. Then they started hanging out with the hiker at his campsite, correcting the story as he was writing it down, telling him that they came from Atlantis and moved to North America when the continent sank before settling in California. They let him tour their abodes where they lived rather plainly with little wooden tables and benches, eating fruits, berries, and veggies.

Another encounter with little people said they called themselves the Koenig Race and were here to tend to nature, and the "low vibrations" sent them underground into caves around Mt. Shasta, where they lived for hundreds of years and were forgotten and remembered only in folklore. Next are the Yaktayvians, who were similarly small and reportedly the greatest bellmakers in the world. Their bells produced beautiful sounds and music, and they used the sound of the bells to hollow out Mt. Shasta and build their city within it.

Two picnickers were approached by a little person who asked if they wanted some gold, saying there was lots of it in the mountain. They skittered away, returning with a sack of coal that they said was black diamonds and contained a secret, like a coal fortune cookie. Others showed up to form a band or orchestra of sorts, singing and playing on anvils. They said they were from Lemuria, which sits in the center of the corners of the Earth. They were taught by Koot Hoomi, Blavatsky's old teacher, before going away. And not only gnomish creatures have been seen; there have also been numerous fairy sightings around Burney and McLeod Falls.

Along with the little people sightings were other mythical characters. A bespectacled Hanna Spitzer was camping around Mt. Shasta and was called upon by unknown visitors who lived nearby, but she was out of sight of their camping area. At night, these mysterious beings could be heard making noises and singing, which definitely had an impact because in the morning, her vision was a perfect 20/20 and she no longer needed glasses.

During WWII, a Japanese American escaped from an internment camp near Tule Lake in Northern California, and while heading south, he took shelter from a storm around Mt. Shasta where he was approached by what he thought were indigenous peoples. They referred to themselves as the "Clock People." They had been living there since 1906 when the great San Francisco earthquake pushed them to the safe confines of the dormant volcano. There in the center of an underground burrow, they maintained the clockworks that they believed controlled history. When the day comes that the clockworks are destroyed, it will bring about the "Eternity of Joy," a delightfully menacing prophecy.

In the 1970s, two ladies were relaxing in their living room when five vapor beings began to materialize in front of them. Between seven and eight feet tall, wearing long robes and pulsating, the vapor beings claimed to be from the mountain and originally from Lemuria. They were particularly interested in one of the women's daughters, who they said was a former Lemurian, but after hanging around for six weeks and the daughter rebuffing their advances, they evaporated away.

Not only vapor beings haunted the surroundings around Mt. Shasta; a whole host of creatures real, mythic, and robotic also made appearances. One election day, a gorilla-like being, described as being a moron of low intelligence, plopped itself down and observed the election, but when it started ogling a woman who was counting the votes, they forced it out. Someone else claimed to see a dapperly dressed reptilian walking along the highway one night.

There have been a slew of interesting Bigfoot sightings by the mountain. These include a couple of beer-drinking campers who swear that a Bigfoot strolled out of the woods to give them a crystal. In 1962, a hiker is said to have watched a female Bigfoot give birth high up on the mountain, while others have watched a female Bigfoot breastfeeding and the discovery of large footprints around the mountain, though some of those footprints were of the three-toed variety. Others claim the Shasta Bigfoots have a peaceful heart but only average intelligence; however, they can become invisible at will, which allows them to avoid confrontation, harm, and even enslavement "in the name of science"—a trait they picked up from the Lemurians, who can also go invisible at will and teleport.

Quite a few UFO sightings have been reported in the area since the airship flap in 1896, which originated in northern California, up to the present day. Mysterious flying objects are a part of the Mt. Shasta story and the Lemurian one as well. In 1955, eight to ten bright white lights buzzed a lumber yard security guard. In the 1970s, activity seemed to ramp up as multicolored spaceships were seen, police officers reported seeing disc-shaped objects in the sky, and there was a mass UFO sighting in November 1980. There were claims that Mt. Shasta was a major spaceship station, a place for UFOs to refuel while hiding in the lenticular clouds that form above the mountain. Some have even said that the UFO that first made contact with George Adamski may have come from Mt. Shasta and traveled through an underground network of tunnels from Northern to Southern California.

Which has led to several extraterrestrial abductions. Helen White had one such classic abduction experience: having a bright light engulfing the car she was in, with alien beings taking her from it. Next thing she knew there was a trio of beings around her, speaking English, telling her she would not be hurt, and then she was back in the car. There was a second abduction and an attempt at a third that was thwarted by her screaming in the alien's face, jumping in her truck, and speeding back home.

In 2010, a three-year-old boy disappeared from his family while camping. Family and authorities searched for him for five hours before locating him near a spot that had already been searched. By the time the shock wore off, he told an incredible story of being led away by a robotic clone of his grandmother to a cave littered with souvenirs taken from other people, like shoes and backpacks. The robot grandmother's head emitted a light and kept wanting the boy to poop on a piece of paper on the floor. When the boy would not, the robot grandmother led the boy back out to be found. The "real" grandmother, upon hearing this, suddenly recalled her own strange encounter that happened while camping. One night she found herself face down in the dirt outside of her tent with two puncture wounds on her neck.

What these stories represent is an increasing detachment of Lemuria from the known world and moving it into a paranormal one. The second round of Theosophical influencers had played up the mystical powers of the Lemurians, and through *A Dweller on Two Planets* and the Rosicrucians they brought not only Lemurians but also a whole host of otherworldly phenomena with them to modern America. In a way, this placed Lemurians in the same category as Bigfoot and UFOs, and brought them to the present day. This also pushed Lemurians underground, which would be the scene for Lemuria's next adventure.

CHAPTER 7:

The Ballad of Richard & Ray

NEITHER MT. SHASTA NOR MADAME BLAVATSKY REPRESENTS THE MOST penetration Lemuria obtained into popular culture. That came about through the Shaver Mysteries, a series of stories published in the pages of a pulp magazine in the 1940s. When the world was still at war, another war was being played out under the earth. A far more nefarious conflict. What started as a letter published in the back pages of *Amazing Stories* quickly exploded as more and more stories hit the press, igniting consternation among sci-fi fans and being discussed in *Life* magazine.

It came from the obsession of one man, Richard Shaver, and the editor he reached out to, Ray Palmer, and would go on to spawn nearly twenty stories in a twenty-nine-month span and push the idea of Lemuria out into public consciousness like had not been done before or really since. The hundreds of thousands of people who consumed Richard's stories or read the coverage of Lemuria gave it the most press it had enjoyed in the eighty years since it had been coined. And it all came from the tortured soul of one man and the opportunistic fellowship he forged with another. They would help push Lemuria firmly underground, into a hollow Earth, and also into the realm of conspiracy. The true mystery is how these stories ever saw the light of day to begin with.

THE MYSTERY'S NAMESAKE, RICHARD SHARPE SHAVER, WAS BORN IN 1907, a child of Pennsylvania. His father ran a restaurant in various towns across Pennsylvania, and Richard grew up a normal, All-American boy. The family was never well-off but made do, and Richard seemed more motivated by girls and fun-loving than anything else. After graduating high school, he moved to Philadelphia to live with his brother, Taylor, whom he looked up to and idolized. There he began to read more, trying his hand at writing and also drawing. When his brother moved to Detroit, his family followed, leaving Richard alone in Philadelphia, but he soon joined everyone in Detroit in 1931 at the age of twenty-four.

It was in the Motor City that he began attending the Wicker School of Fine Art, which served as a true awakening period for him. Working on his art. Supporting himself by modeling. Beginning a relationship with a part-time instructor at the school, Sophie Gurvitch. Through her, Richard got involved with Communist organizations in Detroit, such as the John Reed Society, and quickly settled into the bohemian subculture of the city. The school closed the following year, leaving Sophie out of a job and Richard in need of something to do, so they got married. Richard got a job at the Briggs Auto Body plant. And that is when life started to go downhill.

Richard's brother Taylor died in February of 1934 from a combination of heart disease and pneumonia. He was thirty and had been a constant companion to Richard. Someone Richard wanted to emulate. Taylor had had some success selling stories to boys' magazines like *Boys' Life*, with Richard wanting to follow in his footsteps but failing to dedicate himself to writing. His death was a major blow, one that Richard was unable to accept—or he just refused to accept that his brother, his star, had faded away on his own. Some months prior, Taylor, who worked for the U.S. Border Patrol, told Richard about experiencing problems along the Canadian border. With Prohibition still in full effect and organized crime smuggling bootleg liquor across the border, Richard became obsessed and convinced that something more nefarious lurked behind his brother's death.

For Shaver, the paranoia came first. Thoughts of being watched and followed crept inside of him. Next, the voices came. At first, they only began to appear at work. Being broadcast via his welding gun. Something in the wiring got crossed that allowed him to overhear the conversations of all the plant workers: Richard's a Commie. Richard's gay. Richard. Richard. Richard. Day after day these voices assaulted the inside of his head. He provides a harrowing description of the moment in one of the Shaver Mystery stories:

I looked down at the gun on the floor and I was trembling. What was going on? That voice had been no voice, or thought, of a worker in the plant… unless it was the thought of a madman!

A madman?

I sat down, white and shaken as the thought struck me. Maybe I was mad! Maybe there were no voices at all. Maybe I'd never actually heard the voices of anyone else. Maybe my own mind was cracking up, and inflicting these weird illusions upon me.

The Shaver in the Shaver Mysteries, Richard Sharpe Shaver from **The Hidden World** *(Fall 1962).*

And it started to follow him home.

Auditory hallucinations are known to be triggered by trauma and are often associated with schizophrenia and related psychotic disorders. And many writers who tackle Richard's story provide an armchair diagnosis of schizophrenia for him. While what he was describing might fall under such a diagnosis, it is presumptuous and insensitive to heap upon the man such easy labels after the fact. It does seem safe to say that Richard was experiencing some level of undiagnosed or misdiagnosed mental health issues.

The relentless torment became too great, and the voices chased him away to Pennsylvania, back to his family and away from his pregnant wife. Two years passed in this way. Sophie gave birth to their daughter whom he would visit in Detroit from time to time. Soon Sophie's family convinced her to have him committed to Ypsilanti State Hospital in 1936. While Richard was in the hospital, Sophie died by electrocution in an accident involving a space heater and the bathtub. Her family became the guardians of Richard's baby girl, with whom he would not have a relationship for the rest of his life. With Sophie's death, her parents also became the legal guardians over Richard, putting them in control of his potential discharge from the institution. Under their guardianship, Richard was not leaving that hospital any time soon, for fear of him taking his daughter away from them. He had other plans and was intent on getting out. Since the hospital was overcrowded it allowed patients like Richard to leave and stay with relatives, provided they regularly check in. Pennsylvania is quiet and Ypsilanti is cold, and this arrangement presented the opportunity to flee altogether. He took it. He started a life of bumming all over the East Coast and up into Canada.

During these roving days, he acquired a tail, Max, an evil dero that followed him from town to town harassing him. Max was not some nebulous spirit invading his mind. Nor were the deros. To Richard, they were real. Actual beings from within the Earth whom he could hear. See. Experience. Interact with. Be tortured by. And much of the next decade was spent either on the road or in psychiatric institutions.

While in these state-run facilities, primarily the Ionia State Hospital for the Criminally Insane, he may have undergone electroconvulsive therapy, which was a common treatment for schizophrenia. Scenes from his later stories showing how thought records work are eerily similar to electroconvulsive therapy treatment. The hospital provided him little contact with the outside world, so he naturally turned inward, spending his time learning as much about the deros as possible. Taking notes on any pieces of paper he could find. He learned about their advanced ray technologies. He gained more information that led him to develop his own theories, such as the existence of elaborate cavern worlds, and that gravity was a push effect and not a pull one—the result of a universal element he called *exd*. He presented his findings to Einstein, who brushed them off, but Richard would not let such setbacks stop him. He persevered, later writing, "Did insane people go insane simply because their brain functioned *too well*? Is an insane person only a person whose brain is more active than it should be?"

With all of these ideas and knowledge, secret, hidden knowledge, swirling around in his head, he was discharged in 1943 and set about trying to find someone who would listen to him, publish these ideas, and inform the world of the impending dangers.

RAYMOND ALFRED PALMER WAS BORN IN MILWAUKEE IN 1910 TO A REAL piece of work of a father. When as a young boy Ray became stuck in the spokes of a truck wheel that took off and dragged him down the street for a few terribly agonizing seconds, his father refused to seek medical attention for the boy. Instead, he laid Ray out on the kitchen table to convalesce. When that somehow did not heal young Ray, a spinal surgeon was called. This would lead to the first of many long hospital stays for Ray, and marks the beginning of his life of near-constant pain.

This spinal injury at such a young age would have a lasting physical impact on him. It caused a deterioration of his spine that stunted his growth, leaving him sickly and in and out of hospitals growing up. But it is while recuperating that he claimed to have formed special mental healing powers, lying there day after day thinking, picturing in his head, *calcium, calcium, calcium*, until the calcium started to form around his spine helping him to heal. It would serve as an entryway to the paranormal, a direct connection with it that remained with him the rest of his life.

During these stays, Ray would read anything he could get his hands on. A particular favorite for him became science fiction, a new genre that combined a love of science with fictional tales. Early science fiction stressed the science, and writers would go a long way around to include the latest in scientific developments in their stories. Kids and adults began to eat it up. In the 1920s, a string of science fiction pulp magazines started up, with titles such as *Science Wonder Stories*, *Astounding*

Amazing Stories *editor Ray Palmer.*

Stories, and *Amazing Stories* spurring on the growth of a fandom culture around the genre, the magazines, the writers, and science. In many ways, this nascent fandom was the roots of today's fan culture. The early magazines promoted participation through contests and letter sections, creating a sense of community between the content creators and consumers. Those followers started banding together to produce their own material, much of which was in response to the state of science fiction at that given time and the latest scientific news. The movement is now known as First Fandom, one that Ray was firmly entrenched in.

Science fiction enabled Ray to be a part of something for the first time. He started by entering a story contest in *Science Wonder Quarterly* and writing letters to science fiction publishing pioneer Hugo Gernsback. This led him and others to start the very first science fiction fanzine, *The Comet* (1930–1933), which they mostly passed around themselves. Ray served as the editor, writing a regular column. Though the endeavor only lasted a few issues, it gave him a taste of the publishing and writing world, and he wanted more. For the next decade, he would spearhead other fan endeavors, write his own stories for magazines, and build a reputation for himself within the science fiction community.

All this led to Ray, at the age of twenty-seven, being named editor of a major national science fiction magazine, *Amazing Stories*, in 1938. *Amazing Stories* was one of the original science fiction magazines started by Gernsbeck in 1926, though the magazine fell on hard times and had many different publishers before the Ziff-Davis Publishing Company purchased it in early 1938 and made Ray its first full-time editor. Publications and their editors are judged by their circulation, which suited Ray's capacity to be a schemer, possessing that unique knack a good editor needs to gin up interest and turn a publication into something relevant. He worked quickly to transform *Amazing Stories* from a rather stodgy publication with a dull style to something more lively and entertaining. He began publishing more and more letters from fans, including a young Philip K. Dick and Ray Bradbury. House style under Ray evolved, becoming one of derring-do and focused on keeping the story moving along—what the writers called "thud and blunder." This changed the tone and tenor of the stories toward more thrills, wonder, humor, and sex. He started writing a column called "The Observatory," which he used to introduce the stories and articles of that issue and address criticism of himself from the science fiction fan community. Forever a trickster spirit, Ray wasted no opportunity to talk or write about himself. Through these, you get the real sense of his mastery over his domain, a carnival barker trumpeting his brand.

Secured in his fifth year as editor, Ray's path would cross with Richard's when the latter wrote a letter to *Amazing Stories*.

THE SHAVER MYSTERIES, AS THEY WERE ADVERTISED, WERE NOT REAL MYSTERIES but more mystery in the mysterious sense, and got their start when Richard mailed a letter to *Amazing Stories*, pleading for someone to listen and to understand. As the story goes, Associate Editor Howard Browne read the letter and promptly threw it into the trash. Ray got up, picked it out of the trash, and printed it.

Richard's letter described the ancient Mantong alphabet, derived from a combination of "man" and "tongue," which gives a glimpse into how the alphabet goes about combining words, how it provides the basis for most modern languages, and was the language spoken by lost ancient civilizations:

Sirs:
Am sending this in hope you will insert it in an issue to keep from dying with me. It would arouse a lot of discussion.

Am sending you the language so that sometime you can have it looked at by some one in the college or a friend who is a student of antique times. The language seems to me to be definite proof of the Atlantean legend.
A – is for Animal
B – is to Be
C – means See
D – is the harmful energy generated by the Sun
E – is Energy
F – means Fecund
G – means to Generate
H – means Human
I – means I
J – is the same as G – generate
K – means Kinetic, as in motion or energy
L – is Life

M – *means Man*
N – *means child, as in 'ninny'*
O – *means Orifice, a source*
P – *is Power*
Q – *means Quest*
R – *horror; signifies a large amount of D present*
S – *means the Sun, which emits D*
T – *is the beneficial force, the opposite of D*
U – *means You*
V – *Vital; in Shaver's words, 'the stuff Mesmer calls animal magnetism.'*
W – *Will*
X – *Conflict, sometimes meaning D and T in opposition*
Y – *means Why*
Z – *means Zero, or when T and D cancel one another out.*

A great number of our English words have come down intact as romantic — or man tic — "science of man patterning by control," Trocadero — I ro see a dero — "good one see a bad one," applied now together. It is an immensely important find, suggesting the god legends have a base in some wise race than modern man, but to understand it takes a good head as it contains multi-thoughts like many puns on the same subject. It is too deep for ordinary man — who thinks it is a mistake. A little study reveals ancient words in English occurring many times. It should be saved and placed in wise hands. I can't, will you? It really has an immense significance, and will perhaps put me right in your thoughts again if you will really understand this. I need a little encouragement.

This convoluted alphabet was put to the test by Ray, who wrote:

We present this interesting letter, concerning an ancient language with no comment except to say that we applied the letter-meaning to the individual letter of many old root words and proper names and got an amazing "sense" out of them. Perhaps if readers interested were to apply his formula to more of these root words, we will be able to discover if the formula applies… is this formula the basis of one of the most ancient languages on Earth? The mystery intrigues us very much.

The letter appeared on page 206 in the January 1944 issue, sharing the space with an ad for a "Super Power Crusher Grip." The response was immediate as dozens, hundreds, thousands, maybe tens of thousands, if you believe Ray, of letters poured into the offices of *Amazing Stories* offering their opinions on the language, on Richard, on Ray, on everything really; this simple letter sparked the imagination of *Amazing Stories* readers. Impressed by this outpouring and by the breadth of Richard's claims as well as sensing the giant iceberg lying below the surface that the letter presages, Ray began a correspondence with Richard who was all but eager to tell Ray more.

This led to Richard sending a 10,000-word manuscript/letter he called "A Warning To Future Man," which by all accounts was a rambling undiluted exposition of his worldview, with the story/missive acting as a means to spread the word of humanity's imminent danger due to dero incursion and influence. Ray and *Amazing Stories* served as a means to an end. Now what exactly was in Richard's manuscript is not known. It does not appear to have made it down through history, because Ray took the manuscript and expanded upon it greatly, turning it into the 31,000-word novelette that was published in the March 1945 issue, and he gave it the title "I Remember Lemuria!"

Now Lemuria and Lemurians had been used as a backdrop and locale in a few stories during Ray's tenure as editor, most notably in Stanton A. Goblentz's "Enchantress of Lemuria" (*Amazing Stories*, September 1941) which was influenced by *A Dweller on Two Planets* and the rest of the 1930s stories revolving around Lemurians and Mt. Shasta. In the same issue that hyped the first Richard story there appeared Berkeley Livingston's "Truk Island" (*Amazing Stories*, December 1944) which centered around battling Lemurians and the Japanese. One *Amazing Stories* writer claimed Ray slapped Lemuria on to the title as a marketing tool because lost continent stories always increased sales.

What exactly Ray added or what Richard had written in this first story is hard to tell. Ray claimed he added all the "trimmings" but did not change any of the "factual" accounts that Richard provided. His one noted change was the origin story for how Richard obtained the knowledge: not from actual caves and the people in there, but from a "racial memory." This he did for reader believability. Racial memory is a turn of phrase that he came to quickly because he uses it in his editor's note to Richard's original letter, and it shows his familiarity with Blavatsky, Theosophy, and the Root Races, and with esoteric and occult topics in general. Richard never showed an awareness of such works, being more of a student of weird fiction, particularly Bulwer-Lytton's work whose book *Vril, The Power of the Coming Race* covers much of the same ground as Shaver's dero, mythology, and popular science. He was outwardly hostile to the writings of Churchward whom Ray had encouraged him to read. Ray soaked up all manner of esoteric thought, storing it away to use in some form or fashion. This rebranding as a

The cover of the March 1945 Amazing Stories in which the very first Shaver Mystery story "I Remember Lemuria!" appeared.

"racial memory" allowed him more leeway to call it a "true story," for readers to believe this all could have taken place a long time ago on a planet that is our own. By keeping certain elements like characters and locations, Ray was able to maintain its memory status while staying true to Richard's story. Also in the months-long build-up to the actual publication of "I Remember Lemuria!", Ray played up that it was fact and not science fiction, and he hedged his bets by all but stating "I believe Shaver believes this."

Ray's rewriting of the story allowed him to control the narrative and to write himself into it as well. He added extensive footnotes, excessive even, to the stories to help give them the slightest veneer of believability. For Richard's part, the early stories feel like he was happy to have someone take him seriously, allowing Ray to direct things:

First of all, he wants to point out that Shaver actually believes his own statements to be the truth and that these convictions of his are woven into an entertaining series of stories for a definite purpose. This purpose is (1) to find others who have had experiences of the same sort, get them to write, and compare their experiences with those of Mr. Shaver and of one another, so as to confirm or corroborate his statements by the only means possible at this time.

Thus, we urge every reader who has such convictions within him, who believes there is a mystery connected with his purpose here on Earth, who believes he has a work of some far-reaching scope to perform, who believes he is part of a great plan, and who is convinced that he knows things today unknown to science, to write to your editor, WHO IS ONE OF THOSE PEOPLE! TIME HAS COME FOR ACTION!

The use of "racial memory" also enabled Ray to pass Richard's stories off as channeled material. In that sense, it was not much different from *A Dweller on*

Two Planets or another work that was highly influential to Ray, *Oahspe: A New Bible*. But Richard's message was that of a warning and not one of salvation. Where *Oahspe*, Blavatsky, and *A Dweller on Two Planets* offered ancient wisdom, Richard's look back presented only the deranged remnants of society. The only lessons to be learned were beware the dero, a classic good vs. evil story, which to him was more practical than providing more sermons. Never more apparent than when the world was at war and untold atrocities were beginning to come to light, his stories could be seen as a metaphor for that descent into Hell everyone was experiencing. With the second story, Ray had to clarify that it was not actually a racial memory at all but a thought record. The title of the second story was "Thought Records of Lemuria," with a thought record being a "kind of micro-film" that the ancient giants used to record their memories. To view the records, you were plugged into a projector that beamed it into your skull, creating an intense feeling of actually being there and witnessing the events. Not so dissimilar to electroconvulsive therapy Richard received while in mental institutions.

Between March 1945 and August 1947, *Amazing Stories* published seventeen Shaver Mystery-related stories. More Richard-penned stories appeared too, but those were traditional science fiction "yarns." And Shaver Mystery stories were not exclusive to *Amazing Stories*; other mystery-related stories would run in *Fantastic Adventures* and *Other Worlds*, but the bulk of the stories were printed by *Amazing Stories* in those two and a half years, reaching a crescendo with the June 1947 issue, which was wholly dedicated to the Shaver Mystery. It became a prime focus of the magazine for those years, with nearly every story being advertised on the cover and the first story to appear in the magazine. The popularity over this time skyrocketed, with circulation topping at over 250,000 copies for a single issue—compared to other pulps, which were considered to be doing well for themselves by selling 50,000 to 60,000 copies. Ray knew a cash cow when he saw one and made sure to milk the Shaver Mystery dry.

This increased popularity brought about increased scrutiny from the vibrant and highly opinionated science fiction fans. They generally hated the stories, hated Ray for printing them, and Richard for writing them. The popularity was spurred on by those outside of organized fandom. It struck a nerve for them. The controversy surrounding the Shaver Mystery, or the Shaver Hoax as they liked to call it, helped propel it from general fan bitchiness to a cultural phenomenon. It was a controversy of Ray's own doing as he promoted so heavily science-fiction stories that had no science in them. If anything, the stories were anti-science, going against the grain of many established scientific principles like gravity. To science fiction fans for whom science was a real passion, this was a bridge too far and they lashed out against Ray and *Amazing Stories*. Fanzines lambasted them. One fan group made plans to submit *Amazing Stories* to the Society for the Suppression of Vice. A multitude of letters poured in criticizing the stories and the decision to publish them. And other science fiction magazines piled on, roasting the stories. As the loud criticism mounted, the publisher, William Ziff, began pressuring Ray to tout the stories as fiction, and it would be a struggle for him to maintain editorial independence.

But Ray's attentions were being pulled elsewhere as he became involved in the flying saucer craze that swept across America in 1947, as well as starting his own publishing endeavor, *FATE* magazine, where he was free to pursue his interest in the paranormal, UFOs, and the occult. So in 1947, the mystery began to wind down, at least in the pages of *Amazing Stories*. Ray came up with an idea to "solve" the mystery, which amounted to forming the Shaver Mystery Club, a small zine, and pawning the mystery off onto that—throwing the whole thing back into Richard's lap and saying good luck. Then in April 1948, he wrote as close to an answer on the mystery as he ever would, stating twice that it was a fiction magazine that published fictional stories, never outright saying the Shaver Mysteries were fiction while leaving the implication blowing in the wind.

Amazing Stories *is a fiction magazine. Even if we say we think something is founded on fact, that doesn't make it true—and if we insisted on something like that, we'd have people believing our fiction . . . Now we can turn the Shaver Mystery over to the Shaver Mystery Club, headed by Mr. Shaver himself, and relax. Don't think it has been an easy job to track down all the hoaxers and non-hoaxers in our effort to secure for our readers the proof they wanted. After all, it was our readers who deluged us with letters claiming Shaver's first stories were more than based on truth. We have carried the ball this far, and with next month's announcement, we complete our work for you readers who wanted proof. Editorially, we have already presented Shaver's theories twice, and we'd risk our high standard of originality if we continued. Shaver has said what he has to say—and there's no sense to saying it again. We are a fiction magazine, and fact has no real place in it, now that the fact has been proved. ALL our stories are based on fact. Didn't we invent almost everything, including the atom bomb? Well, it's time we went on to new fields of the future, to place them before the inventive minds of our scientists, so that they too, in years to come, will be realities.*

Richard clung on to his mystery stories for a few more years but they quickly fell out of favor. In the 1960s, he would discover the proof to these stories by way of hidden art found within rocks that he referred to as rock books. All stones contain records of a lost civilization through images and words found both on the surface and when cut into and sliced into thin layers. He would slice rocks in two, take photos of them, and interpret the meanings he saw into multi-material artworks that utilized household items like glue, wax, and paint applied to cardboard or plywood for canvases, creating quite evocative pieces of art that look like science fiction images by way of Milton. He called the art Rokfogo/Rogfogo, spending his remaining days working on his rock books, passing away on November 5, 1975.

Over the last remaining decades, Richard maintained a relationship with Ray, the two partnering on a few publishing ventures like *The Hidden World*, which offers more insight into the autobiography of Richard, and published parts of their voluminous correspondence during the Shaver Mystery saga. When Ray ran into some incurable writer's block while working on his memoirs he turned to Richard and turned the book, *The Secret World*, into part autobiography, part art book of the Rokfogo works.

Ray for his part stayed in publishing, though with diminishing returns remaining in the pulp magazine game, and branched out to books before retreating to putting out a newsletter. In the time since the Shaver Mystery, he was active in promoting and shaping UFO lore theories around government conspiracies and subsequent coverups, hollow Earth (more on that in a bit), and paranormal topics in general, setting much of the tone and agenda in the field, with surprising staying power.

WHAT GETS LOST IN THE DISCUSSION AROUND THE SHAVER MYSTERY ARE the stories themselves. Much attention gets paid to the controversy and the personalities surrounding it, and rightly so because the stories themselves present a rather bleak worldview in a less-than-appealing manner. A bad story poorly told. A story that is a couple dozen long stories only sort of interconnected by the world Richard is illuminating for us.

They generally take place in wild, futuristic, and exotic locales filled with daring intergalactic chases and intrigues, fetishistic sex, and quirky obsessions, presented as really happening tens of thousands of years ago but all done in the guise of hack science fiction stories.

Twelve thousand years ago Earth (a.k.a. Lemuria or Mu) was home to two races, Titans and Atlans, with a third race, Nortans, later being introduced. These two extraterrestrial races colonized Earth/Lemuria/Mu. A thought record Shaver was shown had him and his wife traveling down to Lemuria: "other spaceships drifted down into the great clearing where we had landed first of all upon this planet which we called Lemuria or Earth." They lived here for millennia, constantly growing, some up to 300 feet tall, and living for thousands of years—by far the biggest of the Lemurians there have been and described. These giants built giant machines

Cover of the June 1945 **Amazing Stories** where the second Shaver Mystery story, "Thought Records of Lemuria," was published.

that also lasted thousands of years. They were smart, forging advanced technologies perfecting speed-of-light travel, and even bioengineering new races to do all the manual labor, while also developing sophisticated ray technology. These bioengineered beings would turn into humans; others had six arms, were half-humanoid or half-serpent, and became the basis for the gods and myths of all the world's civilizations. That ray technology was used for healing, and there were rays for transmitting thoughts (telaug), rays to observe events over vast distances (penetray), and rays for sex (stimray).

However, it was a different set of rays, the sun's natural rays, that soon turned bad and poisonous to the Titans and Atlans. To evade their harmful effects, the giant races of Lemurians began tunneling underground, creating vast networks of subterranean tunnels and cities that would come to house close to 50 billion individuals in this cavernous world. Even being below ground proved not enough, and over time the destructive force of the sun's rays penetrated to their underground world. The majority of Titans and Atlans were forced off-world to go find a new planet to live on some 12,000 years ago.

Some beings were left behind, though: the bioengineered robot races, most of which moved back to the surface. Adapted to the sun. They forgot about the caves and built human civilization as we know it today. Some chose to remain underground, with most of those turning into psychotic dwarves known as deros. The etymological origins of the word come from a combination of the words "*de*trimental *ro*bot" and also from the term "abandondero," which means "the abandoned ones." Richard described them thusly: "Fearfully anemic jitterbugs, small, with pipestem arms and legs, potbellies, huge protruding eyes and wide, idiotically grinning mouths." The deros got hold of the ancient machinery of the Titans and Atlans and learned to utilize the ray technology. They promptly put it to use to antagonize everyone aboveground and had been tormenting Richard for years. This included being responsible for everything from stealing your keys to starting wars. Their depravity knew no bounds, and Richard and Ray would tell the stories of how the deros would kidnap women, bring them underground, and turn them into sex slaves whom they tortured for fun. Their antics have been attributed to secret societies. Deros have been known to impersonate FBI agents and the rich and powerful. There were some underground dwellers who were good, though, and worked toward thwarting the deros, a Sisyphean task.

That is the gist of the Shaver Mystery, or at least the portion that pertains to Lemurian mythology told in a couple of the stories. Many of the stories tell tales of spider-witches, mermaids, and a whole host of other fantastical tales—which is all well and good, but it was all being passed off as happening during Earth's ancient history. These were not just a bunch of loosely connected stories in a shared universe, but the thought records of a long lost society.

Lemuria's role was as the home of these ancient races of giants. It was Earth itself, and for the most part, it was much like what we know Earth to be today. However, what has gotten attached to Lemuria is the underground nature of the stories. Lemurians had already been pushed deep under Mt. Shasta, and now Richard was offering additional proof and an alternative narrative for how Lemurians acted there. With this, Richard helped to cement Lemuria in the realm of Hollow Earth Theory and subterranean worlds.

DIG DOWN 1,800 MILES OR SO AND YOU REACH THE EARTH'S CORE. A HOT place where molten metal churns, creating the Earth's magnetic field. Above that, you reach the mantle, the largest layer of the planet, which is mostly solid and consists of about 84% of Earth's density. Topping the mantle is the Earth's crust where rests everything we know and enjoy.

Back in antiquity, the underworld formed the common belief of the Earth's innards, a series of myths and legends from ancient Sumerians on to Orpheus and the realm of Hades in Greek lore up to Dante's *Inferno*. Devilish realms full of spirits too evil to survive on the surface so they made their home within it. In that regard, Richard's deros continue these ideas and even modernize them: evil subterranean beings creeping into our world to wreak havoc.

However, in the seventeenth century, serious scientists began looking into what was inside our planet. German scientist-philosopher Athanasius Kircher, the same one who first drew a map with Atlantis on it, published his *Mundus Subterraneus* (The Subterranean World, 1665) where he wrote on many a topic, including relating some early Fortean stories like people growing webbed fingers and extra lung capacity since they spent so much time underwater, describing dragon lairs, and the discovery of mummified remains of giants 200 cubits tall. His major focus was exploring Earth's honeycombed deep cavern system that housed dragons and giants, but its primary use was for water. Kircher theorized that a great passage ran the length of the planet from pole to pole where all the Earth's water gets cycled through. Water gets sucked in at the North Pole creating a dangerous maelstrom, then gets spit out at the South Pole, causing strong currents that push out, away from the pole. This made exploring the poles near impossible. The one true lasting impact Kircher had was this notion that there were openings at the poles, which would persist in hollow Earth theories well into the twentieth century.

The next great advancement in inner Earth theory came with the publication of Edmund Halley's (the discoverer of the comet) paper, "An account of the cause of the change of the variation of the magnetical needle, with an hypothesis of the structure of the internal parts of the earth," in *Philosophical Transactions* in 1692. To Halley, the Earth was a hollow shell whose crust was 500 miles thick, containing three smaller concentric spheres roughly the diameters of Mercury, Venus, and Mars. An atmospheric buffer of 500 miles separated each sphere, and gravity aided in keeping them apart from one another. The spheres had their own magnetic poles, which moved along the same axis but at different speeds. This helped to explain the Earth's magnetic anomalies. Within the spheres, there were many unknowns like "peculiar Luminaries" that provided mysterious light sources to sustain life in them. Later, Halley would expand on his idea to say Earth was thinner at the poles, allowing luminous materials to escape from the inner spheres and causing the aurora borealis.

Later in the eighteenth century, Leonhard Euler put forth the idea that the Earth was hollow and home to a small molten core that acted as an inner sun providing conditions to support life. This was followed by John Leslie, who said there were two suns inside the hollow Earth named Pluto and Proserpina. These would be the last legitimate scientific theories regarding the hollow Earth. With science veering off into other ideas about the Earth's core, it allowed for a bevy of alternative theories to rise up in the nineteenth and twentieth centuries.

The first and maybe the most prominent was Captain John Cleves Symmes and his Hole. The American Symmes was a veteran of the War of 1812, and upon retiring from the Army settled in St. Louis. He became interested in science and astronomy, which led him down the path of believing in a hollow Earth. For Symmes, Earth was made up of a collection of spheres that is open at the poles. Those spheres are held together by tiny particles of "aerial fluid" that pushes against all solid matter. Symmes' Earth looked a lot like a donut or a huge gaping wound. He published his theories in a series of circulars starting with *Circular No. 1* (1818), which he sent out to every college and scientific association in America and Europe, members of Congress, and newspapers, making sure to include a certificate attesting to his sanity.

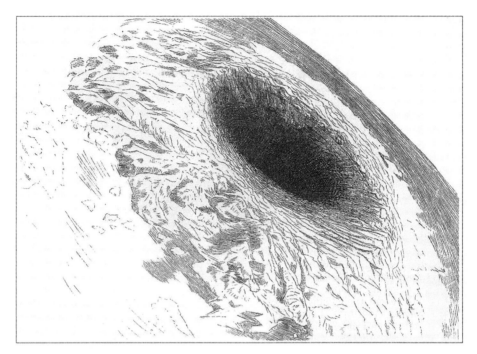

An illustration of what Symmes' Hole would look like from space.

He next went on a speaking tour despite his lack of prowess as a speaker, but he began advocating that this inner land could become U.S. territory, telling his audiences to petition Congress to send Symmes on a polar expedition. Though many petitions made their way to Washington, Congress never took Symmes' claims seriously. And the phrase "Symmes' Hole" became popular in the 1820s and 1830s, being used as a catchall for lost items. Like if your cattle wandered off, they probably went out grazing in Symmes' Hole.

Symmes would go on to partner with James McBride to publish a collection of his letters, circulars, and scraps of theories in a work called *Symmes's Theory of Concentric Spheres, Demonstrating that the Earth is Hollow, Habitable Within and Widely Open About the Poles* (1826). Ultimately, Symmes pushed himself too hard trying to spread the word about the hollow Earth and died at age forty-nine in 1829.

Next, another American, William Reed, would advance Hollow Earth Theory with the publication of his *The Phantom of the Poles* (1906). Reed was a bit of an armchair explorer who researched the accounts of polar expeditions and was struck by the abnormal phenomena reported in them. This left him convinced the poles were unreachable and there were openings at both of them. He rationalized that a hollow Earth makes good sense and good economy, and somehow objects would weigh less than on the surface.

Shortly thereafter, sewing machine magnate Marshall Blutcher Gardner threw his hat into the ring with the publication of *A Journey to the Earth's Interior, or, Have the Poles Really Been Discovered* (1913). Gardner positioned himself as an anti-Symmes, calling the Captain a crank, and promoted the old idea that there was a central sun within the Earth, because how else could something survive within there? So a 600-mile-wide sun sits inside, providing a tropical atmosphere.

What followed in the '20s, '30s, and '40s were the tales of underground Lemurians and Masters by the likes of Oliver, Cervé, and Richard. All who added stories of real-life living beings who had inhabited an inner world, though these stories did not outright say the world is hollow, only that there are extensive cave systems and cities as well as races of evil dwarves. The true last gasp of Hollow Earth Theory happened shortly after the Shaver Mysteries fizzled out, springing up thanks to the efforts of Ray Palmer.

In the December 1959 edition of *Flying Saucer,* Ray wrote about Admiral Richard E. Byrd's expeditions to the North and South Poles in 1947 and 1956. Byrd gained instant fame in 1926 for flying over the North Pole with Floyd Bennett, both of them receiving the Congressional Medal of Honor for the flight. Leaning heavily on F. Armando Giannini's *Worlds Beyond the Poles* published in 1959, Ray focused on Byrd's comment that he visited the land beyond the poles during a flight over the North Pole in 1947. What could that possibly mean if not some mysterious land within the Earth? For Ray, Giannini, and many others, that is the only plausible explanation.

However, it turned out that Byrd never actually went to the North Pole in 1947, only the South Pole, so Ray had to print a retraction two months later and blamed Giannini for the faulty information. Byrd's expeditions paved the way for establishing the scientific bases that are on Antarctica now. But coming so close to the end of WWII, many conspiracy theories have been put forth that he and the soldiers he led on that expedition were really wiping out the remainder of a super secret South Pole Nazi base. Some say it was a secret submarine base while others say it housed Nazi UFOs or the starting blocks of the Fourth Reich. While Admiral in rank, Byrd never commanded soldiers nor partook in combat or military operations in either WWI or WWII, making him a somewhat poor choice to unroot a rabid enclave of polar Nazis. It appears that Giannini misread some items from Byrd's article about his 1947 Antarctica expedition that appeared in *National Geographic,* "Our Navy Explores Antarctica" (October 1947), where what land beyond the poles there happened to be was merely the large swath of the interior of Antarctica that remained unmapped and unexplored. But no one remembers that or cares about retractions, and these erroneous claims would form the basis for Dr. Raymond Bernard's *The Hidden Earth* (1964), which has been the most popular, widely read and accessed book regarding the hollow Earth.

DR. RAYMOND BERNARD'S REAL NAME WAS WALTER SIEGMEISTER, AND HE
lived a full, weird life. An actual doctor, he earned his Ph.D. from Columbia University in 1924 writing his dissertation on Rudolf Steiner. Maybe because of his interest in Steiner, Siegmeister became fascinated with the health benefits of lecithin, a fatty substance found in egg yolks, soybeans, and wheat germ. He began selling lecithin through the mail throughout the 1920s and 1930s, promoting it as a health food, which got him into trouble with the United States Post Office who soon refused to mail anything from him. This was a catalyst to change his name— he shuffled through a string of them, Raymond Bernard being one—and to start him on a wandering existence of promoting natural living and health food while also setting up a series of failed colonies in Florida, Ecuador, and Brazil, where he attempted to found a "super race."

Once settled in Brazil, there he became acquainted with a couple of Brazilian Theosophists who claimed to have visited the Subterranean World and saw famed lost British explorer Percy Fawcett held captive there. He also discovered the book *From the Subterranean World to the Sky* (1957) by O.C. Huguenin, which leans heavily on Atlantean lore, with the Atlanteans using UFOs to escape the destruction of Atlantis by flying through holes in the poles to the inner earth where they rebuilt their civilization. The final linking source Bernard needed to connect everything was Ray's *Flying Saucer* article on the Byrd expeditions. Bernard had all the material he required.

Byrd's expedition reports were dissected, focusing primarily on word usage with intense emphasis on "beyond" and "land," which had to mean Byrd was talking about the inner earth he witnessed himself. Then, he utilized Reed's and Gardner's works to explain how this could be possible. The answer he fell upon was that there is a gentle, unrecognizable downward slope leading toward the opening at the pole. So gradual, in fact, that you do not even realize that you have traveled from Outer Earth to Inner Earth: "starting at 70 to 75 degrees north and south latitude the Earth starts to CURVE IN." As it curves in and under the surface, water still adheres to the crust at the opening, creating a carnival duck shooting game-like effect for ships traveling through. This is the "beyond" to which Byrd is referring. He claims the government was suppressing Byrd's findings, which forced the Admiral to talk so cryptically.

As a *pièce de résistance*, Bernard throws out there that "there is a large population inhabiting the inner concave surface of the Earth's crust, composing a

Walter Siegmeister, a.k.a. Dr. Raymond Bernard, author of The Hollow Earth.

civilization far in advance of our own in its scientific achievements, which probably descended from the sunken continents of Lemuria and Atlantis. Flying saucers are only one of their many achievements." Coming back to Lemurians and flying saucers all living underground together in the 1960s.

As during the decades prior, this seemed to be the main thrust of Hollow Earth Theory: some beings human-like (Lemurians), and some not so human-like (deros). Which brings us to Maurice Doreal, real name Claude Dodgin, whom we met before when he experienced Lemurians at Mt. Shasta. Doreal founded the Brotherhood of the White Temple in 1929, and he never met an idea that he could not piggyback onto. For instance, he claimed after WWI to have traveled to Tibet and spent years studying with the Dalai Lama, much like Blavatsky and Churchward, who traveled in the same area and learned from spiritual leaders there.

He would go on to utilize Richard's deros and an underground society of evil creatures. His beings used to live specifically in or under Antarctica and were more serpent-like humanoids that developed hypnotic powers, allowing them to appear human to humans. They put this ability to use acting as spies to terrorize humanity. But humanity fought back when they discovered that these Serpent People could not pronounce the word "Kininigin." Now, how humans discovered this particular devastating attribute is unknown, but the knowledge allowed the blond-haired, blue-eyed white master race to seek and destroy the Serpent People. Doreal was a frequent letter writer and advertiser in *Amazing Stories* and published little pamphlet books that promulgated his theories. Shortly before his death, he would lead his followers into the Rocky Mountains of Colorado to avoid the coming nuclear apocalypse.

This was the beginning of the rise of the Reptoids. Which might not have too much bearing on the Lemurian story, other than tales of being abducted by Lemurians and taken underground, or Shaver's deros doing similar things, or Bernard's remnants of Lemurians flying UFOs around having already been established. And who's to say that the Ultraterrestrial beings from another dimension, plane, or parallel universe, theorized by the likes of John Keel, Jacques Vallée, and Mac Tonnies, are not the same as the Mt. Shasta Lemurian sightings or the earlier tales of fairies and other mythical beings.

Richard's stories of Lemuria helped to produce the idea of underground reptilians bent on mischief and evil, an idea which has survived to this day. In "Thought Records of Lemuria," he provides a tale of an extraterrestrial race of lizard people invading Mu and doing battle with the Atlans there: "their will to live had been great, but their will to destroy was as full, thus coloring all their thoughts with vicious intent, for the will to destroy and the disintegrant electric forces are of the same."

These evil lizard men and the general reptilian nature of the underground dero helped to create and perpetuate the idea of nefarious reptilians who live below the surface and arise to harass and one day rule over the human world—thanks in most part to David Icke and his world-dominating, shape-shifting reptilians (which manages to be incredibly anti-Semitic in the process) and which today has been adopted by the alt-right QAnon crowd to accuse any and everybody in power of being a reptilian doppelgänger. And a confluence of ideas happens at a place like Dulce, New Mexico, and the alleged underground war being fought there between humans and malevolent reptilian-like alien forces, who share much in common with Richard's deros.

IT IS INTERESTING THAT OUTSIDE OF THE TITLE "I REMEMBER LEMURIA!" the first story does not mention Lemuria. Instead, Richard and Ray called the land Mu, which may be a nod to the work of James Churchward and Augustus Le Plongeon. It is not until the appearance of the second story, "Thought Records of Lemuria" (*Amazing Stories*, June 1945), that they thought to include a footnote explaining that Mu was an abbreviation for Lemuria. But one thing it definitely was was a place called Lemuria. Titans, Atlans, Nortans, et al. referred to it as Lemuria, and not Earth, which only became Earth after the godlike giants left and we humans were left to adapt and build our society here. There is a powerful message that lies within the heart of that and in the struggle between the surface dwellers and the subterranean deros.

Richard has been compared to L. Ron Hubbard, who built a religion from similar science fiction foundations, Scientology. And one can easily see a similar path Richard could have walked down if he were more focused on self-improvement or self-actualization. But no, his dero-based demons would not allow for that. It kept him and his outlook negative. He was too preoccupied with warning others of the threat they posed to offer any kind of salvation from their withering influence.

We are all screwed, in Richard's worldview, while someone like Hubbard offered means to cleanse oneself of their thetans and other negative influences, all for a price. To Richard, it was not a business but a solemn duty, and to Ray, it was a means to sell magazines.

Richard, while managing to craft a compelling new mythology for the rapidly technologized world, also offered no comfort. The best he could do was hope that his warning reached enough people, to stir them into fighting the deros, but he held no romantic notions about our chances of that succeeding. So maybe in another world Hubbard's Xenu was not the center of the mythos surrounding Scientology, and it was Lemuria forming the basis of Shaverology. But it was not meant to be, and it would be left for others to elevate Lemuria and Lemurians to new, spiritual heights.

Thanks to Richard and Ray, Lemuria became tied to a conspiracy culture that also dabbled in strong feelings of persecution. Lemuria became populated with people with names and lives; a rich world-building occurred which opened doors for spirits to be from there, promoting conspiracy and dragging Lemuria into it, and tapping into it to spread their wisdom to a new generation—a New Age.

CHAPTER 8:

Heirs to the Glimmering World

FIRST, THE CIGARETTE SMOKE. THEN, THE NOISE. IT ALL TOOK ME BACK.
The incessant chiming of the slots. Electronic ditties, thousands of them, competing with one another. A remembrance of days past from my time as a busboy in the restaurant of a dog track and casino in college. The noise seared itself into my soul and got triggered with each press of the button. It deafens you, sure, but also deafens your ability to speak or act. And here I was in a casino on the hunt not for riches but one particular item.

An attendant pointed the way to the elevators where a security guard sat on a high stool by the doors letting people on and off. Maybe they do not trust people with elevators here.

"This the way to the metaphysical expo?"

"Uh-huh." And he swiped his badge and called the elevator. The doors opened and a couple joined me in the car, while security swiped his badge again and pushed the button for the second floor. Not much one for small talk, I kept to myself until we stopped our ascent and were let out into a large conference room but not large enough by half. The amount of people browsing paralyzed me for a second. A couple of years into a pandemic and having been fairly studious in avoiding situations like this, the anxiety rose. With a tinge of loneliness as well. A whole room full of people slammed together and all I could taste was the COVID in the air.

Moving from booth to booth, I see many interesting wares: Tibetan prayer bowls, decorative shawls, artwork, jewelry, Wiccan paraphernalia, pagan items—it really does span the whole metaphysical spectrum. Psychics. Palm and tarot readings. Those supplying insight into your past lives and providing expert advice for your chakras. And someone taking photos of your aura, which does sound tempting, but I was only looking for one thing.

By far the most prevalent items available are the bins of crystals and gemstones that line many of the tables: moonstone, jade, onyx, celestite, opal, jasper, topaz, lapis lazuli, agate, garnet, turquoise, tiger's eye, peridot, howlite, malachite, feldspar, dolomite, amber, serpentine, shiva lingam, nummite, wavelite, lodolite, aragonite, scaplite, magnesite, dragon's blood, larimar, atlantisite, and quartz crystal. Table after table I eyed them all but each one let me down. Not an advertised Lemurian crystal anywhere. There were many fine examples of clear quartz, but none claimed to have been from Lemuria. A little bummed, I headed back to the elevator to be let back down. Not wanting to leave empty-handed, I bought a print from an artist that shows flying saucers over the Giza pyramids surrounded by large skeletal serpents.

Even though Shaver was not interested in creating any sort of religion or equating his version of Lemuria with spirituality, this did not stop others from utilizing the idea of Lemuria and tying it in with the next wave of alternative spirituality in America, primarily the New Age movement that rose to prominence from the 1970s to the 1990s. The term New Age eventually became a catchall for all manner of metaphysical endeavors and still today is used to describe any and everything from music to healing.

This movement harnessed many of the ideas that came before it, primarily from Theosophy and its offshoots, but also from Christian Science, New Thought and others, and influenced by the flying saucer craze that led to new UFO-centered religions, all getting mixed together in a cosmic gumbo. In this next journey, Lemuria would be the starting point for numerous spiritual ventures; whether they be channeled entities, models of government, or the land of crystals, Lemuria was there in its familiar role as a cradle, and in some instances also used as a tool. A most convenient way to get your point across.

This version of Lemuria feels settled in, comfortable in its skin. So much work had already been put into proving its reality, telling its history, what happened to its people—with those same people wandering around still, very much alive even if buried underneath oceans. Since that work has been done, Lemuria gets to be the foundation of so many other things. Many of those we have seen still play a role in the future of Lemuria. For the New Age, Lemuria offered a spiritually pure land, where they were oppressed and subjugated because of their beliefs. Persecution served as a key theme, with another key theme being tied to race and white superiority, a particularly toxic mix that has permeated to the present.

Crystals provided a means and conduit to ancient healing practices, and good commercial prospects too. New Age utilized two distinctive tools: channeling and crystals, both of which had significant involvement with Lemuria. Also, both were made more prominent by the Sleeping Prophet himself, Edgar Cayce.

Channeling offered a direct way to communicate with this elevated past and recover all of their lost wisdom. This spirit contact, which had been around for centuries, paved a new path with various popular channelers of the late twentieth century. It is important to keep in mind that the New Age was not a singular thing or organization, but individuals and the groups they formed by building around the idea that through personal transformation you can transcend this world, this realm, this plane, and ascend to another. When enough of us do so, that will initiate a new age for humanity.

Most of the ideas and concepts came from older occult traditions, as these ideas spread outward from Blavatsky, Besant, Steiner, Bailey, AMORC, et al. New people took up the call and added to it, forming their own groups and providing new energy for the latter half of the twentieth century. Not to be confused with new religious movements that were starting to spring up around the same time that were also relatively small and drew people around a singular belief, often providing a twist to a major religion, such as Hare Krishnas and Hinduism, or the Unification Church (Moonies) and Christianity. New Age typically rejected these religions and adopted Western esoteric traditions in their place, many of which derived from Eastern religious thought and practices—relying on their old practices for tools for self-understanding, or supplementing the esotericism with vague allusions to Jesus as only another ascended master, and utilizing positive messaging. New Age is this mainstreaming of Western esotericism, as more and more people were exposed to it and in the process refreshed it for a new generation.

FOR HER PART, BLAVATSKY SPEAKS OF A NEW AGE THROUGH THE COMING of the Sixth and Seventh Root Races. Along with that, she and Koot Hoomi, in the *Mahatma Letters*, call for the reappearance of Lemuria and Atlantis—itself a whole New Age.

A good place to start as any for the origins of the New Age movement is the person regarded as popularizing the term "New Age," Alice Bailey. While the phrase had been around for a while, Bailey made it her own, and it was a term her students and then their students would go on to solidify. Born in 1880 in England, Bailey was raised in the church, but as a teen, a turbaned man paid her a visit. To her, she was chatting with Christ, but others convinced her it was none other than Koot Hoomi. Twenty years later she moved to California where she became involved with the Theosophical scene, serving as the editor of *Theosophy* magazine. There, in November of 1919, Master Djwhal Khul, whom she refers to as the Tibetan, first contacted her. Khul kept appearing to Bailey, nagging her to collaborate on some books for the general public. Like Frederick Spencer Oliver, Bailey would act as amanuensis for Khul, channeling him and recording his teachings in books like *Initiation: Human and Solar*, *The Seven Rays of Life*, *Discipleship in the New Age*, and *Esoteric Healing*. Her means of channeling proved to be a bridge from old-school Theosophy masters to New Age spirit

The mother of the New Age and former Theosophist, Alice Bailey.

guides. Bailey, though, provided a twist by injecting the notion that Jesus was going to come back, upholding him as a loving, spiritual figure. This canoodling with Christianity, without ever being pro-church, caused a major fracture with the Theosophical top brass, namely Annie Besant, and they expelled her.

That proved a blessing in disguise for Bailey, who went on to found her own school around Khul's teachings, the Arcane School in 1923. The school specializes in training for discipleship in the New Age, and was founded after so many responded to her writing and Khul's teachings, demonstrating a need to know more about how to interpret it all and providing a means for new ideas like meditation to transfer into Western minds. And it was through the school and her writings that for the next quarter of a century Bailey would make her impact.

For the most part, she adhered to traditional Blavatsky doctrines such as humanity developing through stages and root races, but she expanded on the notion of "Ageless Wisdom" by pushing the idea of seven rays, or cosmic energies. And she promoted the prospect of a new world religion, believing a common thread linked all religions, in an effort to create a fusion between Buddhism and Christianity. All done in the service of humanity with emphasis placed on fellowship.

Her popularity happened at a time when people in general were seeking out new paths to spiritual fulfillment, as they fell out of alignment with old beliefs of spirituality. She was never anti-Christian, which helped to appeal to Christians who felt left out of mainline denominations. When more people started to look toward occult lore, psychic abilities, and esoteric groups to push religion toward validating these alternative identities, she was there to provide a welcoming scene:

We are now one people. The heritage of any race lies open to another; the best thought of the centuries is available for all, and ancient techniques and modern methods must meet and interchange. Each will have to modify its mode of presentation and each will have to make an effort to understand the underlying spirit which has produced a peculiar phraseology and imagery, but when these concessions are made, a structure of truth will be found to emerge which will embody the spirit of the New Age.

It is a perfect encapsulation of what will become New Age thought, which demonstrates the evolution of Blavatsky's teaching. Bailey presented a far more digestible and appealing way forward: still with the secret channeling teacher/master leading the way, but way more down to earth and open. Less negative toward others and focused on uplifting oneself and those around them. All appealing messages.

As her profile was growing in the 1930s, another surprisingly influential group would blossom too, whom Bailey kindly referred to as "prostituting and bringing down almost into the realm of cheap comedy one of the most notable happenings which has ever taken place upon our planet." She was speaking of Edna and Guy Ballard's I AM Activity Movement, which we have seen in relation to Guy Ballard's spiritual awakening that took place on the slopes of Mt. Shasta; their origins and actual teachings had a long-lasting impact on New Age thought but also right-wing political rhetoric in America.

Called ordinary but clever, the Ballards brought a rabid, pro-American pageantry to their brand of esotericism. Very much a power couple, they barnstormed across America in the second half of the 1930s holding "classes" in towns, building a following they counted in the millions (but more like tens of thousands), done in the service for Guy to self-elevate himself to the level of Blavatsky, Besant, Bailey, and others. They were an alternative spiritual force that others envied for the support they received and the monies they raked in.

For Guy Ballard that appeared to be the ultimate dream. He was a man obsessed with two things: gold mines and the occult. Both would get him into trouble. On multiple occasions, he would sell stock in oil companies and keep on selling stocks even after the projects had long since disappeared. He possessed that natural charm that little old ladies love to hand over the last of their life savings to. In the 1920s, one such woman financed a trip for Guy and Edna to live in an isolated cottage in the Sierra Nevadas. There Guy spent his days wandering the mountains in an obsessive search for gold, the inspiration for "his" book *Unveiled Mysteries* which saw him roaming Mt. Shasta much in the same way Walter Pierson did in *A Dweller on Two Planets*. There is no good proof that Guy or Edna ever visited Mt. Shasta during the 1920s or 1930s.

Not long after returning to his home in Chicago, a grand jury indicted Guy for running a con game where he sold stocks in a "Gold Lake," a California-based scheme. Two women came forward saying they invested thousands of dollars in the project. When they reached out to him to ask about the project or inquire about the money he played dumb or told them that he was powerless and penniless and could not pay them back. This led him to the Chicago District Attorney taking the case to the grand jury, who indicted Guy on March 25, 1929. An arrest warrant was issued, but he skipped town and traveled back to California, living in Los Angeles under the name Dick Gilbert. For the next couple of years he lived the good life, attending metaphysical lectures and looking for gold mines. This is the same time period when he was supposedly receiving his spiritual lessons from Saint Germain around Mt. Shasta and learning the secrets of the Ascended Masters whilst on "government business." This business appeared to be avoiding jail.

With Guy on the run, Edna worked at her sister's occult bookstore, where she immersed herself in occult literature from a wide variety of sources, from

Guy Ballard shortly before his trip to California on "government business" where he became a student of Saint Germain.

A Dweller on Two Planets to Theosophical works to the likes of Alice Bailey and Rosicrucians and Christian Science, as well as the works of Baird T. Spalding, who stayed with the Ballards at one time. She compiled the material, using the knowledge she gained to turn Guy into someone worthy of being in the presence of Saint Germain at Mt. Shasta. It all led to the manuscript of *Unveiled Mysteries*, with more than one person claiming she wrote the book and was the boss of the operation with Guy relegated to doing as he was told. Beginning in 1930, Edna held "secret classes" which appeared to be her reading from some of the latest occult works like the esoteric spiritual writings of William Dudley Pelley.

Pelley was a short-story writer turned Hollywood screenwriter turned mystical experiencer, the last of which first transpired "while studying the question of race" in his bungalow in the mountains outside of Los Angeles. In that state of mind, he was visited by a mystical being that shattered his reality and made him shift his focus to spiritual and occult matters. He started a magazine, which had AMORC as an advertiser, and focused on typical Theosophical, Rosicrucian, and other alternative topics. But he could not stay away from the racial question and politics, which led him down a metaphysical right-wing extremist road.

He became increasingly radicalized against the Jewish influence on the government while lauding the work being done by Hitler in Germany and Mussolini in Italy. In the process, he created the Silver Shirts, his own group of fascist toughs, styled after Hitler's Brown Shirts. Right around the same time the Ballards' I AM Movement was gaining traction, with the publication of *Unveiled Mysteries* providing momentum as they honed their stage show, Pelley fell into legal trouble with the government, giving his esoteric followers an opening to jump ship and join up with the Ballards, who were all too happy to pivot their message to be more patriotic and include Jesus to entice these new adherents. Guy started saying Jesus spoke through him and to let his new followers know that Saint Germain was a fellow master and every bit as real as he was. The Ballards even created their own extremist group among them, the Minute Men, who worked the crowds to make sure there was full obedience during their meetings.

Their messaging began to be fiercely patriotic, proclaiming that Saint Germain and Jesus together had a divine plan for America. They even claimed I AM was not a religion but a patriotic movement, with the announcer saying at the start of each meeting "WE MUST SAVE AMERICA!" Vicious entities within and without were attacking America, and Guy was the only one who could banish them all. America would not even be here if not for Saint Germain's maneuvering during the Revolutionary War. Le Comte de Saint Germain was American through and through. America's guardian angel, sent to purify, protect, and illuminate the people of America. Humanity began in America, and America was the key to bringing spiritual light back to the world. And they excluded Blacks from their movement. Their conservative, pro-American, white nationalism appealed to many.

Beyond that, they made sure to have a spectacle of a meeting with beautiful large-breasted women acting as ushers. Their stage was adorned with mounds of flowers, pine trees at both ends strung up with colored lights, a grand piano, and large portraits of Saint Germain and Jesus looking very Aryan-like with blond hair, blue eyes, both with lily-white skin, with Guy dressed in pastel suits and Edna in a formal gown. With success they established permanent I AM temples all over the country to serve those fully committed, the Hundred Percenters. They also had incredible merchandise, selling books, which Guy loved signing, records, pins, rings, posters, and photos of the Ballards, Jesus, and Saint Germain.

While on stage, beyond preaching their pro-American, white nationalist rhetoric, they also came out in favor of celibacy and that you should not eat anything with a face nor consume alcohol or tobacco. And that there was hope in America, for a golden age was coming. That your true self is divine and can accomplish anything it wants in this world through the power of thought. And borrowing nearly verbatim from Theosophy the notion that the Ascended Masters had all been ordinary but through reincarnation, they realized their ascension through spiritual realization, à la Phylos in *A Dweller on Two Planets*.

The Ballards created a whole new team of Ascended Masters that allowed Guy to become one himself while providing some distance from Theosophy. The ultimate goal for I AM students was bodily ascension, with Guy claiming his physical body was indestructible—so charged with light that nothing could harm him. Nothing but heart disease, of which he died in December of 1939. This was a blow to the theology of I AM. Another major blow came the following year when Edna, their son Don, and eight others were charged with eighteen counts of fraud stemming from the $3,000,000, roughly $63.5 million today, they collected over the years from their followers. The subsequent trial would find them guilty, and appeals went all the way to the Supreme Court where their conviction was ultimately overturned due to women being excluded from the jury. Part of the novel defense was arguing that Guy summoned an invisible force, K-17, to sink an undetected flotilla of Japanese subs off the coast of California. With that taking up much of the 1940s, the I AM Movement lost steam. Edna and 300 followers left for Santa Fe, with the remnants eventually migrating to Mt. Shasta, where they still keep a library and reading room and put on an annual elaborate pageant that tells the life of Jesus.

Those disillusioned by Guy's death and their legal troubles would go on to form their own groups such as the Bridge to Freedom and most notably the Summit Lighthouse, which morphed into the Church Universal and Triumphant (CUT) led by Elizabeth Clare Prophet that proved to be highly popular during the 1970s and 1980s. At a CUT retreat at Mt. Shasta in 1976, Prophet channeled the spirit of Ra-Mu, a Lemurian high priest and now an Ascended Master. These groups built upon I AM's talk of Ascended Masters, use of positive affirmations and decrees, use of simplified devotional language, and even use of colorful attire and artwork that would become synonymous with New Age culture.

It all owes a heavy debt to Oliver's (or Phylos') *A Dweller on Two Planets*, offering a modern spin with new thrills—although not all so new, seeing as Oliver's family sued the Ballards' Saint Germain Foundation for plagiarizing parts of *A Dweller on Two Planets*. But the lawsuit was thrown out because the judge agreed with the argument that, since Oliver never claimed to have been the author but only the transcriber, writing down whatever Phylos told him to, he was left with no right to the copyright. While the Ballards were borrowing whole chunks of *A Dweller on Two Planets*, the Lemurian Foundation went a step further and publish the sequel, *An Earth Dweller Returns*.

The Lemurian Fellowship arose from a collaboration between Robert Stelle and Howard John Zitko. They combined to turn the Fellowship into a mail-order citizenship-building school built around the concept that Lemuria was the first great civilization, followed by Atlantis, with America poised to be the next one. A new type of citizen was needed to inhabit and lead this next great civilization. Everything is new: "A New Race is emerging in America. A New Civilization is being born. A new kind of human being is being created for a new kind of world." Not just a New Age being born, it is a whole New Earth—where you need to get on board to gain citizenship in this "New Race of Christ-honoring, divinity-conscious" America. Lemuria is going to rise out of the Pacific and when it does, it will fulfill biblical prophecy, and the United States of America will ascend to the status of Lemuria and Atlantis, with Americans transforming into Lemurians and Atlanteans.

Seventy-eight thousand years ago on the continent of Mu/Lemuria, a select few outstanding individuals organized the first human society when they realized there was a better way to live. They acquired an understanding of universal law, taking baby steps toward social harmony through teaching those who chose to live cooperatively in abeyance with God's laws. This Lemurian society, the Mukulian Empire, grew into the ideal land, but over time as it grew and grew the proletariat increased their power, while the citizen philosopher-kings shrank because so few sought out citizen training; this led to Lemuria's downfall. Then, it sank.

The Lemurian Fellowship formed in 1936 to retrain those willing to regain the glory of Lemurian ways to become "New Age Citizens." We were Lemurians. We are Lemurians. And will always be Lemurians. Becoming a New Age Citizen will help ensure your survival during Armageddon and the collapse of the current civilization. It puts you front and center for the coming American civilization. The Lemurian Fellowship thus offers training essential to participating as a New Age Citizen, a kind of initiatory prep school teaching moral, physical, emotional, and intellectual lessons, all for the low price of $49.95.

By the time Howard John Zitko appeared on his doorstep with a manuscript, Robert D. Stelle was already on the wrong side of fifty. But he managed to jam a lot into those five-plus decades, trotting around the globe, writing cowboy stories, becoming an osteopath and homeopathic doctor, and fitting in some gold prospecting. And now he was ready for the next stage of his life, one which he thought would be as the sales manager of the Chicago-based correspondence course scheme called LaSalle Extension University. Fate would have it that when it was clear the correspondence school was going nowhere, Zitko showed up.

Howard John Zitko was some thirty years junior to Stelle. From Milwaukee, he quickly got sucked into the occult and like most who do, he devoured as much on the topics as he could. He became involved with Bailey's Arcane School and was conversant in Theosophical teachings. But his heart seemed to lie in Lemuria. He read *A Dweller on Two Planets* and all of Churchward's Mu books. Early in the 1930s, Zitko began having "Egoic memories" of Lemuria, which sounds much like Palmer's use of "racial memory" to describe Shaver's story. Zitko started seeing Lemuria as a grand civilization and began writing a novel to explore the economic, political, and social values based on his concept of socialism.

Making the rounds of Chicago publishers, one told him to get in touch with Stelle to help touch up the novel. And as the story goes, Stelle was waiting for Zitko because he had his own Lemurian premonition that 78,000 years ago he and Zitko had worked together to found the Mukulian Empire with a little help from Masters and Angels from Venus.

Taking a look at Zitko's book, Stelle suggested it would make a better lesson plan than it would a novel. So they should turn it into a series of lessons that could be sold, much like a correspondence course, like the one he was previously

The founder of the Lemurian Fellowship, Dr. Robert Stelle. (Lemurian Fellowship)

involved with. Zitko, eager to see someone interested in his work, agreed to it and the first lesson was published, followed by them forming the Lemurian Fellowship.

In a scenario reminiscent of the early Shaver story, where Shaver submitted a manuscript and Palmer greatly rewrote it, Zitko turned in his material to Stelle only to be surprised by what would be printed. Stelle used Zitko's writings on economics, politics, and social values as a base for his ideas. He tacked on extra material that had been relayed to him by the Council of Seven and the Lemurian Brotherhood. In any case, radical differences appeared from what Zitko had written, but not enough to stop Zitko from touting a form of the teachings for many decades later. It helped soothe whatever hurt feelings there were over the changes with the venture being so profitable. The Fellowship took in large amounts of cash from donations, legacies, and student fees—enough for the Fellowship to buy a dude ranch in Ramona, California, outside of San Diego, which they still own and operate.

Stelle originally sought for the ranch to be an experiment on industry in the Kingdom of God by applying Lemurian economics. What started with small industries like soap making and basket weaving were to be precursors for a large industrial Utopia that he had planned for outside of Chicago. While that plan never came to fruition, one of the lasting legacies of the Lemurian Fellowship has been their crafts. Lemurian Crafts became a mid-century aesthetic movement. Lemurian craftsmen at Ramona primarily created home goods and architectural hardware that was in demand in the 1950s and 1960s, with the Museum of Modern Art in New York acquiring a beaker for their permanent collection and the Museum of Contemporary Crafts acquiring a vase. Though demand and production have ebbed significantly in the past half-century, Lemurian Crafts create beautiful, hand-finished music stands. The level of attention to detail stands as a testament to the principles and ideals of Lemuria.

What might not be an expression of those Lemurian ideals is bank fraud, which Zitko was charged with in 1941. He was accused of selling unregistered stocks in the Lemurian Fellowship, which were drawn from the Bank of Lemuria and could be converted into bonds of the Lemurian Temple—none of which existed. Before this fraud took place, Lilian V. Bense, who went by her medium name, Beth Nimrai, approached Zitko with a manuscript, *An Earth Dweller's Return* (1940), that claimed to have been the second volume to Oliver's/Phylos' *Dweller* saga. She said she received the manuscript through an inheritance from a relative of Frederick Spencer Oliver, even though no mention of a second volume was ever made by Oliver in his life or during his struggles to get *A Dweller on Two Planets* published. Nor did his mother, who worked tirelessly to get it published after his death and oversaw further editions after it received renewed attention in the 1920s and 1930s, ever seek to get it published. No, it was the medium who came forth with this, and the Lemurian Fellowship who published this Lemurian-heavy tome.

An Earth Dweller's Return does a couple of things to *A Dweller on Two Planets*. It changes around Oliver's story quite a bit, saying that he meant to publish these changes and updates to *A Dweller on Two Planets*. But yet again, he never mentioned those changes while he was alive, at which time there was no shortage of talk about *A Dweller on Two Planets*. Phylos comes back and he has some changes he would like to make—most notably he wants to add a whole lot more details about labor laws, education, elections, and how they all interact with one another, or all the same topics that Zitko found interesting.

The book provides more information concerning Lemuria and goes into quite a lot of detail about the destruction by comet, thanks to the sinfulness of the Lemurians. They brought their demise on themselves. But seeing the comet coming some fled into great caverns, proving to be the lucky ones who survived while the others were vaporized in the blast. Oliver becomes a character in the story, and as such, Oliver's past-life problems get the blame for those of *A Dweller on Two Planets*: "the wrong Frederick Spencer Oliver did Merissa when he was Mainin, was the great reason for the retardation of his work. The two children of Frederick Spencer Oliver also retarded the work in his life . . . Thus karma tells its own story as a lesson for others to heed."

Now, why Phylos did not pick up on this the first time around is a mystery. But it continues with the negativity aimed toward Oliver, with Phylos having some choice words for his old amanuensis:

My work has been given to the world through Frederick Spencer Oliver who was greatly handicapped in so doing by his physical suffering, his uncongenial environment, and the influence of those who were dominated by adverse ruling thoughts. But those who will read my words as expressed through the revised Lemurian Edition of A Dweller on Two Planets, *the history of* An Earth Dweller's Return, *and other books I may be permitted to release will quickly perceive the differentiate between the true and the false under the influence of the spirit of truth.*

Zitko seems to have published the book without Stelle's knowledge, who was angry upon hearing about it, saying that they should have left *A Dweller on Two Planets* alone. By 1947, the partnership between the two had evaporated. Stelle would focus on the ranch and write his magnum opus, a trilogy of novels set around the Lemurian mythos he helped forge. The first book, *The Sun Rises*, was published in 1952, and shortly thereafter he died in his sleep. The Lemurian Fellowship withdrew from the world, or at least stopped actively promoting the Great Plan.

Zitko went on to be a mainstay in the New Age sphere when he founded the World University, whose curriculum focused on alternative education and was based on his Lemurian Theo-Christic Conception lesson, as well as authoring a guide on tantric sex practices.

TOWARD THE TAIL END OF THE 1940S, A TRULY MOMENTOUS THING OCCURRED over the mountains of Washington. Kenneth Arnold had an experience with UFOs, which he described as moving like a saucer skipping across the water. Thus flying saucers were born, and it seemed to be the right place and right time for the flying saucer craze to boom around the United States and the world, with the likes of Ray Palmer helping to spur it along.

Right after the Arnold sighting, people started coming forward claiming they had been visited by the occupants from those flying saucers, even being taken on interstellar trips with these beings from other planets. This first wave of experiencers have come to be known as contactees, and these contactees would position themselves as spiritual leaders hoping to bring salvation to humanity through the lessons learned by the Space Brothers. The most well-known was George Adamski. Like so many characters in this book, Adamski was involved in the esoteric occult scene in California in the 1920s and 1930s, creating the Royal Order of Tibet and scraping by as a metaphysical teacher stealing mostly from I AM. With the coming of the saucers, Adamski began lecturing on them and saying he had been visited by a Venusian named Orthon in 1952, who spouted many of the same lessons that Adamski had been saying for years now, adding an anti-nuclear test angle and fear of the spread of radiation. He teamed up with a British filmmaker and writer, Desmond Leslie, who took Adamski's encounter and spiced it up a bit to create the 1957 best-seller *Flying Saucers Have Landed*.

Pre-Arnold extraterrestrial contact was mostly of the spiritual or astral realm kind and dealt with advancing humanity, both spiritually and technologically guiding our spiritual evolution. These early contactee reports share a lot with meetings of Lemurians. They were handsome and stately and white, looking like good, tall, strong, blue-eyed blond-haired master race Aryans who held mysterious technologies, took the select few on trips across the galaxy enlightening them, who then came back with a purpose to spread this message they were imparted.

Several religions would form out of contact with flying saucers and aliens. The earliest was the Aetherius Society, founded by George King in the mid-1950s, which placed Lemuria at the heart of their creation story. For the Aetherians, Lemuria was a great ancient civilization that was in contact with other great civilizations on Venus and Mars. This contact led to Lemuria splitting into two camps. The white magicians learned advanced metaphysical sciences from the extraterrestrials on Venus and Mars, while the black magicians were hungry for power and detonated a hydrogen bomb that destroyed Lemuria. But before that happened, spaceships came and ferried away the chosen.

Another group that got their start at the same time was the Unarius Academy of Science, the brainchild of Ernest Norman and his wife, Ruth Norman. Ernest was a palm reader and psychic, but in the 1950s he graduated to channeling, being the conduit for the Venusian space brother Mal Var, and in 1956 he published his first book, *The Voice of Venus*. Ruth and Ernest met at a psychic convention in a spiritualist church in California where he gave her a past life reading, revealing to her that she was the pharaoh's daughter who had found baby Moses in the reeds. The two middle-aged spiritualist fans became a couple and married soon after, founding the Unarius Science of Life in 1954. Early on they held meetings, doing psychic readings in person and through the mail, living mostly on the proceeds of Ruth's dairy delivery business she had started with one of her ex-husbands.

For the remainder of Ernest's life, until his death in 1971, the Unarius Academy remained a rather vanilla saucer-inspired group. Where most groups lose vision, adherents, and direction when a founder dies, the Unarians blossomed when Ruth Norman took over after Ernest's passing. Ruth became reborn as the Universal Radiant Infinite Eternal Light, or Uriel for short. Her personality and charisma held the group together and brought it to the attention of the outside world. Ruth's exuberance further pushed Unarius as a flying-saucer group, and she increased the number of publications they released as the group began receiving many more messages from the Space Brothers.

An important distinction for Unarius is that they consider themselves a science and not a religion; even though they may deal with some spiritual concepts, it is important to maintain an objective and interpretive distance. Unarians were and still are in contact with these spiritual beings from a heavenly planet, whom they referred to as the Space Brothers. The Space Brothers are cosmic scientists

A bust of cosmic visionary Ruth Norman, a.k.a. Archangel Uriel, on view in an anteroom at the Unarius Academy of Science during the 28th Annual Interplanetary Conclave of Light. (© Brian Cahn/ZUMAPRESS.com/ Alamy)

who fly around the universe spreading enlightenment and it is the Unarians' goal to reunite with them—if possible, to even be reborn on these higher planets at the pinnacle of spiritual dimensions and to live among the most perfect Space Brothers, becoming masters of energy and obtaining ultimate scientific knowledge. They see the Space Brothers at work all over the place, whether in the daily news, on TV, or in the movies. They are everywhere.

Energy plays a key role. It has its own frequency which connects people to memories of past lives, other planes of existence, and even prophecies. Students of Unarius then channel their past lives and the lives of the Space Brothers in order to heal themselves as part of past-life therapy. It is through these channeled past lives where Lemuria plays a major role in their beliefs—what they call the Great Lemurian Cycle that stems from Unarian students and Uriel giving testimonials about their past lives on the planet Lemuria.

About 156,000 years ago, eleven Unarian Supermen from Lemuria crash-landed on Earth. One of the eleven, Ra-Mu, Uriel in a past life, wanted to work to enlighten the humans here on Earth but the diabolical Ta-Mu, one of the other Lemurian refugees, plotted to kill the saintly Ra-Mu because he opposed spreading their spiritual enlightenment to such peons. Ta-Mu's machinations worked, because as Ra-Mu was about to board a spaceship back to Lemuria a mob attacked and murdered him. This is what led to society's downfall. Lemuria on Earth was not a fun place. Lemurians were controlled by electronic surveillance and lived like robot zombies under the thumb of brutal overlords, in constant fear of spies ratting them out. The remaining Unarians became evil scientists who did their enslaving via implants to force compliance. They performed surgical experimentation by grafting animal parts onto human bodies, and Lemurians became cannibals creating actual Soylent Green, the movie having been released shortly before these revelations. All of this lasting nearly 100,000 years and ending with Lemuria's destruction around 68,000 years ago.

It is no coincidence that this Lemurian society mirrors much of the dero world that was postulated by Richard Shaver. Even their past life memories work a lot like Shaver's thought records. Like many others we have seen, the Unarians borrowed from Theosophy, Spiritualism, Western religions, flying saucer lore, and more to construct their mythology. But they would also mine popular culture as well: TV shows, movies, and maybe even Shaver's short stories or other science fiction works. Still around, the Unarians offer past-life therapies via Zoom on Sundays and Wednesdays.

All of this was done through channeling. Channeling dots this entire tale. Whether it is Blavatsky's communing with her ascended masters or Frederick Spencer Oliver being taken over by Phylos, it has played a major part in the Lemurian story. And channeling will keep on playing a key role in Lemuria, because in the New Age movement as a whole it has become a driving factor. Channeling enabled more philosophical teachings to enter into New Age thoughts by bringing messages from authoritative spectral entities, God, Ascended Masters, and ETs, via superior wisdom and communicating through the channeler.

Edgar Cayce served as an inspiration for many that followed him. He was not traditionally a channeler, as his communications came through the trance-like state he put himself into and not handed down from anyone in particular, or at least he never claimed them to be. But the going into a trance-like state, which Cayce did along with popular spiritualists of his day, preceded many of the popular New Age channelers like J.Z. Knight and Jane Roberts. Many people from all over the world wrote to Cayce. His readings began as a means to provide health-related answers to those writing in seeking his help. Cayce would often delve into the past lives of that person in order to diagnose their ailments and offer up alternative health advice, which he did for nearly half a century.

And those past lives are where all the lore lies, such as his digging into life in Atlantis, which he started referencing out of the blue twenty years into his forty-year career. He began bringing up lost civilizations, and spent a considerable amount of time talking about that lost continent, and not much concerning our Lemuria. He also went into all sorts of detail on other historical and biblical events. While the readings themselves are interesting, what is more remarkable is that Cayce never wrote anything himself. Most of the readings were taken down by a secretary in shorthand. He amassed a huge archive of written material. During his life, he received much attention for these readings, but little was released by him or the organization that grew up around him to support his work. When

Edgar Cayce from whose readings and the books derived from them helped to popularize the healing power found within crystals and other rocks and minerals. (Chronicle/Alamy Stock Photo)

Cayce died in 1945, his popularity skyrocketed in the following decades through the efforts of his son, Hugh Lynn Cayce, and the Association for Research and Enlightenment (A.R.E.) as they began an aggressive publishing campaign that disseminated Cayce's readings, some 16,000 of them. In these readings, there were bits and pieces: a little Atlantis here, a little biblical talk there, some mentions of auras, and so on. Thanks to the A.R.E., the Edgar Cayce Foundation, and Hugh, thousands of volunteers mobilized to cross-index these pieces against each other, pulling together coherent views from the disparate parts. Books were released around a theme like Atlantis and relevant readings compiled together, commented on, and interpreted. Some of those books stick closely to the text and others go heavy on commentary and interpretation. From the 1960s onward, they would prove to be a major influence on the New Age.

Of particular interest to Cayce was that specific health problems stemmed from negative residue carried over from previous lives. Since Atlanteans were particularly sinful during their time on Earth, many people's current problems stemmed from them. This bad karma passed through many incarnations, making its way through the generations, and showed up as physical and emotional reactions to this ancient spiritual pain. It needed to be set right before they could be healed.

Where the Atlanteans were naughty, the Lemurians were more virtuous, so they accrued less karmic debt and therefore caused fewer problems for people today. So, fewer readings dug into Lemuria, but there are some tantalizing details that give some life to Cayce's Lemuria. Unlike their Atlantean counterparts, Lemurians were not materialistic and were more peaceful. They held great paranormal powers and were spiritually attuned. Lemurians had built a forgotten civilization in the Gobi Desert, the extreme eastern portion of which made up the western shores of North and South America. This shared some characteristics with Churchward's Mu, with Cayce's readings coming out after Churchward's books. And those books might have proved to be inspiration for his going into detail about some specific Lemurians who were spiritual leaders, such as Amululu, a priestess who helped civilize her people and establish the Incal civilization.

One of the first and most influential New Age channelers was Jane Roberts and her channeled entity, Seth. Seth provided their thoughts and teaching through the New York-based Roberts beginning in 1963 and broadcasted through her for the next twenty years until her death in 1984. She began writing down Seth's messages, resulting in what is known as the Seth Material. It came at the right time, as many were looking for alternative means of spirituality when along came the Seth Material to open up brave new worlds for them. Study groups across the world formed to discuss Seth's teachings, the core of which centers around a person's ability to create their own reality.

In discussing their earlier iterations, Seth tells of there being three Pre-Atlantean Civilizations, the second of which was Lumania, a decidedly Lemurian-like place with the only difference being a couple of letters. Lumania was an advanced superior society full of telepathic beings, whose thoughts existed in a multi-dimensional realm. They used sound for healing and power. They shied away from violence and aggression, using energy blockages that acted as a kind of psychological deterrent to war. They did not expand from their strongholds in Africa and Australia but were physically weak and frail, so they started to "breed" with primitive cultures to try to make up for their physical condition. It was too little, too late, as they died out but in physical form only. Those who survived lived underground, where they coexist in time with us. Some of their ephemeral selves appear from time to time from an alternate universe.

Lumania and Lumanians did not catch on and become the new Lemuria. Still, Roberts' success inspired and encouraged many who had channeled experiences to take them seriously, and to share those with the world. One such person was Judith Darlene Hampton, or Judy Zebra Knight, or J.Z. Knight, who began channeling the spirit Ramtha starting in 1977. In the 1980s, she broke through to be the most successful channeler around, appearing on TV and radio, with her Ramtha books becoming best-sellers. Knight was a star and quite wealthy, which caused much criticism of her and her motivations.

Ramtha was an ancient Atlantian. Slight spelling differences serve as the main distinguishing feature of Ramtha's Atlantis, a warrior from 35,000 years ago who returned to teach all that he learned through Knight. The bulk of the teachings revolved around the belief that a person is a god, a master, who forgot that, but in remembering their true self they can then turn into a creator themselves to have whatever they desire. All sunshine and positivity in the beginning, but as the years passed Ramtha became darker and darker, providing more apocalyptic warnings.

Ramtha spends a good deal of time telling what life was like while he was on Earth. From the slums of Onai, a port city in Atlatia, a.k.a. Atlantis, Ramtha was born to exiles from Lemuria, who were oppressed and treated like slaves. The Atlatians were responsible for Lemuria's destruction, as they misused technology that created the disaster which destroyed Lemuria. The survivors moved south to find a new home in Atlantis, in the process becoming serfs to the Atlatians. This imparted a socio-economic dynamic to Lemuria in the New Age. Lots of talk of oppression and differences in societies between them and the Atlatians.

Lemurian culture was built on communication through their thoughts, with no technological acumen but highly developed spiritual understanding. Believing in something they called the "Unknown God," an essence and power that could not be identified, the Atlatians hated them for this because they did not view it as progressive. Because of this, the Atlatians treated them horribly, as Ramtha put it: "we were considered stinking, wretched things. We were the no-things, the soulless, mindless wastes of intellect because we were without the scientific understanding of such things as gasses and light." With this prevailing sentiment toward Lemurians, Ramtha witnessed his mother raped in the streets and then her and the baby die. This traumatized the teenaged Ramtha, who fled into the mountains and at fourteen amassed an army of Lemurian slaves around him and marched on Onai seizing the city, opening the granaries to feed the poor, and burning the city to the ground. As his army grew, he went on a campaign to fight more Atlatians, but an assassin stabbed him in the back. Though he survived, he spent his convalescence having a spiritual awakening, the revelations from which he would reveal to Knight 35,000 years later.

Knight and Ramtha are still around, and the Ramtha's School of Enlightenment in Washington, where Knight resides and is surrounded by a loyal following, still operates, though not with its controversies like claims that residents at the school were forced to drink lye.

Though not a channeler, but an experiencer, believer, and definitely a popularizer, Academy Award-winning actor Shirley MacLaine authored a series of best-selling books including *Out on a Limb* and *The Camino*, where she documented her spiritual journey to New Age topics, including reincarnation, channeling, and Lemurian culture. In the TV movie version of *Out on a Limb*, she gives a plug to *A Dweller on Two Planets* as the book falls into her hands in a Singapore bookstore and provides her introduction to channeling and mediumship. In *The Camino*, MacLaine goes in depth into her reincarnated past life in Lemuria. She describes it as the biblical Garden of Eden and treats Lemuria much like Ramtha's version, which was a civilization at odds with Atlantis. Its capital city was Rama, located where Hawaii lies now. Lemuria was divided into seven states or counties and united under the worship of one god. Their home was a lush, tropical, rolling landscape, where Lemurians, thanks to their harmonious existence, would live an incalculable number of years and then decide to dissolve away.

The other distinctive feature about the New Age is its elevation of crystals for healing and other uses. There is a long history of using crystals and gemstones for a number of different purposes—some for healing, and some for religious practices. But the most well-known occult application would be for prophecy, the proverbial crystal ball, or like Elizabethan magician John Dee's seer crystal used by him to peer into the future. But by the nineteenth century, these aspects had fallen by the wayside, and esotericists like Blavatsky and her subsequent influences focused, if at all, on the clairvoyant powers and not much else when it came to crystals and gems, only alluding to some secret values of precious stones.

Edgar Cayce later slipped in mentions of crystals and gems and their health benefits, and those tidbits were scattered across multiple readings spanning decades—which were not known until the A.R.E. published in the early 1960s a tiny book, *Scientific Properties and Occult Aspects of Twenty-Two Gems, Stones, and Metals: A Comparative Study Based Upon the Edgar Cayce Readings*. The editors put forth a wide range of uses for gems, stones, and metals to influence a wide variety of physical, mental, and spiritual conditions. Certain of these minerals contain vibratory forces that can be attuned to similar forces in a person to have the desired effects by harmonizing with the creative forces of the universe. All of those negative universal influences stifling our normal body, mind, and soul functions can be "counteracted" by wearing in some cases certain gemstones, or metals. The book was influential in setting the tone and belief in alternative healing practices. Time and time again these materials and others would be lauded for vibratory forces and harmonizing yourself.

About twenty years later, Dr. Frank Alper of the Arizona Metaphysical Society released a trio of books, the *Exploring Atlantis* (1980) series, that helped to firmly establish crystals as being important to the lost ancient worlds of ours, Lemuria and Atlantis. While Atlantis receives the lion's share of attention in the work, Lemuria's past gets briefly told. One hundred thousand years ago, Lemuria was split between two factions: one of love and one of war, who both employed mutants to do manual labor for them and considered them slaves. About 20,000 years later Atlantis was settled, by mostly lightfaring people. Those Lemurians who did not appreciate the negative vibrations on Mu reincarnated themselves on Atlantis. This culminated in a major war between Mu and Atlantis, a 50,000-year-long war by Alper's estimation, that took place in the tunnels connecting the two and ultimately destroyed both civilizations.

During that war in 85,000 B.C., Earth's vibrations shifted, causing the sinking of both continents. Then in 77,777 B.C. aliens landed in Florida and began resettling Atlantis, and they are the ones who manufactured crystals for power and healing. Examples of how to use these crystals include:

The most common system is to encircle the individual, who is in a prone position, with twelve crystals. One by the head, one by the feet, and five evenly spaced on each side of the body. You will use your thirteenth or control crystal, in your hand, passing it over the twelve crystals will create a unified magnetic field around the individual. Have him lie in this position for five to ten minutes, and the healing will be accomplished. This type of formation is utilized for full body, full energy system healings.

Alper's books were enough to tie Lemuria and crystals together, and since the 1980s the idea of Lemurian seed crystals has permeated New Age and metaphysical circles, in the process becoming one of the most defining features of Lemuria today.

Your typical Lemurian seed is a larger quartz crystal with horizontal striations running through it, with each groove representing a different era and some believe holding records of that time, not so dissimilar to Shaver's rock books. Most come from Brazil, which so far has been absent in most Lemurian myths. On the side of a crystal, there is an indentation,

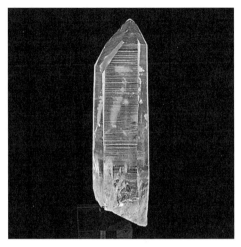

A brilliant example of a Lemurian Crystal with striations running through it and a "key" or notch at the bottom ready to be unlocked. (Crystalarium)

which is known as a key. Unlocking the crystal will unlock your consciousness. Shelley Kaehr, Ph.D., provides the details on how to do so:

I take my index finger on my right hand and put it in the key and hold it there. You will feel a rush of energy run through you that you won't believe! Again, just use the hand and finger you feel most comfortable with.

My giant keyed crystal seems to like to be held firmly in my left hand with my left thumb in the key. I have another one though that needs my index finger in it just a certain way. If I don't have it exactly that way, it won't download properly.

The Lemuria from the Lemurian seed myth existed prior to the time of the dinosaurs. The Lemurians were peaceful and telepathic interdimensional beings from another space and time who slipped through the fabric of space to find a planet in order to plant the seeds to fuel their galactic colonies. Finding Earth a suitable space for their seed farms and being a spirit form, they located a gentle animal to merge with and found one in the lemur.

These lemur-Lemurians started planting outer space crystal seeds all over the planet, so they could be used to fuel spaceships, transmit data to the future, and maintain good vibrational states. Then, the dinosaurs came, created by masculine energy, and the little lemur-Lemurians were no match, and most disappeared or spirited away. Those with the willpower stayed and lived underground creating a vast network of caves and tunnels. The preponderance of masculine energy over time shifted the balance of the Earth, and a chunk of something fell from space and wiped out the dinosaurs, leaving only those lemur-Lemurians living underground.

And that is when the aliens came. First to rebuild after the destruction that wiped out the dinosaurs, then to exploit all of our natural resources like crystals and gold. Humanity grew from these aliens, the ignorant, inbred offspring. Millions of years of devolution.

That is where Lemuria sat at the end of the twentieth century: a land of alien crystals seeded by other alien-possessed lemurs and a people who were oppressed and enslaved for their spiritual beliefs. Much how New Agers felt at the time, and to this day, persecuted for the audacity to believe in things out of the mainstream. A long way from the days of simple land bridges. What started as one kind of tool turned into another completely different kind of one. Over the decades Lemuria quickly lost focus and became as ethereal as some of the Lemurians, able to do and become whatever it needed to be. Animal migration, human evolution, continental drift, spiritual enlightenment, races, evil forces, ascended masters, healing, socio-spiritual awakening, and whatever new can be thought up for Lemuria to represent.

Toward the end, it picked up this idea that Lemurians were persecuted for who they were and what they dared to believe in. In some ways, this continues the theme of there being an adversary. Always in need of one, like Haeckel was for Blavatsky, or the deros were for Shaver, always a need to combat something. But it was also something new and potentially dangerous, because believers started to broadcast these persecuted thoughts, and to connect with others who felt persecuted—underscoring the New Age story of Lemuria as a land of peace, love, and harmony that pursued individual perfection, finding the balance between spirituality and technology. This is what happens when you allow science to guide your lives: spirituality gets destroyed. It is an appealing concept in a rapidly technologizing world. Lemurians knew how to cope. If only we could remember to do the same and coexist in a modern world. But like in Lemuria, there are negative forces out to get us and bring us down.

CONCLUSION:

If You Don't Know Where You're Going,
Any Lost Continent Will Take You There

And now we arrive in the present and what is being said about Lemuria today, mostly online on places like 8kun:

We are living in a world of mad scientists that think they are God, the same people from Atlantis and Lemuria. End times man, end times.

Atlantis/Lemuria, I read somewhere they were experimenting with mankind and that is why God destroyed them.

When they protect scientists and idolize them as truth, means that God is dead in their hearts and we are in the last days of Atlantis and Lemuria... Any noble scientist will know this is the reason Atlantis and Lemuria were destroyed, don't mess with the genome of God or else. The mad scientist got too big for their britches.

Mu variant of COVID-19 was named after Lemuria.

If you're new to 'conspiracies,' this is what's going on. Firstly everything is fake...Democracy is fake...News isn't really news...History is almost completely false. Atlantis, and before that Lemuria, existed.

Efforts are being made to help Earth clean the evil, re-join this union and restore the glory known during the times prior to the fall of Atlantis and Lemuria before the demonic Cabal took control by manipulating the desires of the weak.

26,000 years ago the Cabal was formed with the goal the enslaving the entire planet. The major superpowers at that time on the planet were Atlantis and Lemuria, akin to US and Russia today, so the Cabal engineered a war. Since mis-using advanced tech for wars isn't exactly going to end well, it culminated around 11,500 years ago when the Atlantean fleet glassed the Lemurians (located either at today's Gobi desert or in the Pacific depending on the source; more likely Pacific) and the Lemurians pulled an asteroid from the belt between Mars and Jupiter (ironically also a remnant of past wars) and smashed it into the Atlantic ocean. This is why you have things like Ring of Fire and tectonic plates acting up all the time. This event is described in the Bible as the Great Flood.

Have heard this somewhere before (Spirit Science?), Jews per their story told, came from Mars and fucked up Atlantis, Lemuria, or both.

The Cabal carry thousands of years in this world, From Atlantis and Lemuria. For to avoid the New World, first must to die the old world of the cabal. Since are people isn't ready yet.

The true Aryan has convinced the descendants of Lemuria, the original Germanies, that they too are Aryan. You are not of the Aryan nation. This is a lie. You are a Lemurian. You may have olive skin and a round face. You do not have high cheek bones and deeper white complexion. Look around it is obvious. Don't you see all the pretty people? They are more beautiful than the us. They can fuck themselves. I don't care if they are pretty and got shapes of geometry. I got Jesus and stuff. They can piss out my faith and genetics. The ancient Atlantians are enslaving the ancient Lemurians.

Dolphins are Lemurians/atlantians? Idk

In times of Atlantis it was called Flaturn but being so close to us Earth took on its properties and went flat too. The Lemurians didn't like this and fucked Flaturn off past Jupiter where it's stayed ever since. It's all recorded in the picture NASA doesn't want us to see.

The Atlantis was destroyed 12380 years ago by a rock strike from orbit when unspiritual Lemurians avenged the glassing of their Pacific continent (of which only Hawaii remains) by hauling an asteroid from the asteroid field between Mars and Jupiter (which itself was a planet in the past also *destroyed by other, even more ancient hypermassive faggots) and slamming it into Earth.*

The Atlanteans (and Lemurians) sure made a complete shitshow 11,200 years ago

Lemurians were active this morning on Shasta

Something similar to Wakanda already exists under Mt. Shasta in California. Surviving Lemurians (after the Great Flood) live there.

they fucking black ET
some black people are kinda red like an insect
and some black people are real black like an african
and some blak people are light skinned casue their slave master was
spicing and dicing
alll i am saying
you are part of the galactic federation now
i do have <earth blood>
okay
you all attack me
but you dont realize that the ancient Lemurians are insects
who populated the earth after atlantis sank
anyway.
adamic man is more important than the lemur
because it is <source> some how

This sort of discourse is what happens when you allow the promulgation of a myth or alternative narrative. It evolves to be an omen of the dangers of all kinds of unsavory things. What you do not see in these posts are rational arguments over the etymological origins of the term Lemuria, or reasoned debates on the authenticity of such a landmass even existing. Who has time for such frivolities when there is real evil out there to smite?

So Lemuria gets taken as historical fact, another cog in the New World Order—a perfect culmination of all of Lemuria from Haeckelian race dynamics to New Age subjugation politics, with a sprinkling of demonic cabals, anti-Semitism, anti-science, anti-vaxx, and a few other modern predicaments that have left us kicking against the pricks. Lemuria as a tool lives on today in a QAnon world. And why wouldn't it? We have already seen that there existed on Lemuria's curious road up to this moment all sorts of alternatives and conspiracies. Lemuria is pliable, malleable, and easy to shape to any ideology, and throughout its history it has been attached to many popular conspiratorial themes like anti-government or anti-science.

The New Age never materialized. But the adherents still stuck around and the narrative shifted from the coming age to emphasizing the spiritual journey and the transformative importance that it had. After the realization sunk in around the turn of the century of there being no new age on the horizon, there began a melding of New Age spiritual beliefs with conspiracy theory paranoia (what Ward and Voas termed "conspirituality") that grew up on the web and expresses two primary convictions, both of which we have witnessed in the history of Lemuria: 1) a secret group is controlling or trying to control society, and 2) a paradigm shift in our consciousness is taking place. All creating a general feeling that society has lost its way. For the New Age, this was a shift, because many in the movement had rejected politics or were anti-political, though they were fundamentally opposed to capitalism, environmental destruction, and political corruption, and predisposed to conspiracy beliefs like being anti-fluoride and anti-vaccine.

That this new form of New Age belief exists online and among a generation who grew up online means there is little by way of leadership and structure, and a constant bouncing around from topic to topic. While 9/11 helped expose many to new conspiracy theories and conspirituality, the psychic toll of the COVID-19 pandemic along with a healthy dose of Trumpian conspiracy rhetoric has seen more people denying the pandemic's existence, and becoming frustrated and angered by the implementation of lockdowns, business closings, and vaccine mandates. This anger and frustration have moved the opponents of such measures to seek out avenues.

New Agers were already suspicious of mainstream beliefs and hold to more natural healing practices rather than medical vaccines, and were already convinced that those with dark or low vibrations, or events causing low vibrations such as chemtrails, 5G, or vaccinations, were impeding ascension, and now those wicked actions have a new source in the deep state.

This denial of the pandemic's existence is shared between New Agers and QAnoners, and thanks to shared online platforms and hashtags they have managed to come together. As the posts from 8kun show, they brought Lemuria along with them and a critique of society that this modern world is void of meaning and has sapped the power from the people.

Reinforcing this bond between the two groups would be the shared whiteness. Conspiracy theorists tend to be white males while New Agers lean more toward white and female. The alternative, conservative nature of QAnon also leans heavily toward supporting white nationalist ideals, and as we have seen, the New

Age antecedents veered toward outright Nazism and white supremacy, with nearly the entire history of Lemuria being shrouded in racism. Every iteration and step has been accompanied by either racist claims or carried on by racists like Haeckel, Pelley, and Ballard. All of them supported or elevated the notion of the white race's superiority either in coded Aryan rhetoric or by disparaging native or non-white races. Lemuria for all of them was a means to prop up the idea of the greatness of the white race, either through the excellent blond blue-eyedness of Lemurians or the opposite, making Lemuria the cradle for subhumans and where all the "other" races originated from. For New Age and QAnon believers that would be right in their wheelhouse. So it is with little surprise that both camps promote whiteness with blatant privilege. This would lead to shared support for Trump. MAGA platitudes are from the same lineage as those spouted by William Dudley Pelley and Guy Ballard, only louder, more far-reaching, and more consequential. In 2021, Michael Flynn, Trump's initial pick for National Security Advisor, was caught plagiarizing from a direct Ballard offshoot, Elizabeth Clare Prophet, with one of the only changes being switching out "I AM" for "WE WILL."

This New Age and conspiratorial right-wing combination mostly keeps itself to various online forums and social media, but it does lift its head out into the real world, manifesting in the form of groups like Love Has Won—a cult/influencer phenomenon thought up by Amy Carlson, who claimed to have been the reincarnation of figures such as Jesus, Cleopatra, and Marilyn Monroe, the daughter of Donald Trump, and the former queen of Lemuria. She crafted a whole theology that mimicked old tropes of becoming awakened and having our energies ascend, but with the added wrinkle of "there's an evil cabal of global elites that eat children and are keeping the world in a low vibrational state." Love Has Won's followers are soldiers fighting all of this. Though the fighting took the form of video streams and Telegram posts, with only about a few dozen core members who lived together, a couple of hundred remote ambassadors and a few thousand followers online were comforted by Carlson's erratic videos where she would berate her followers for not giving her tequila quickly enough, calling them "dick whores." That drinking problem ultimately led to increasing health problems for Carlson, who exacerbated them through use of alternative medical treatments like colloidal silver, which in her latter days gave her skin a distinct blue hue. In addition, her paranoid proclamations of the elite evil cabal trying to constantly kill her would harm her. As her health was declining and her adherents were forced to carry her around everywhere, she kept asking to be taken to the hospital, but her followers denied her, for fear the cabal would kill her there. She was left to perish in April 2021, and her followers kept her remains around, draping Christmas lights on them as a makeshift shrine until authorities were able to retrieve them.

Maybe that is the true American evolution of Ascended Masters: from the peaceful, spiritual path leading Lemurians around Mt. Shasta to the "dick whore"-spouting, tequila-swigging streamers of the twenty-first century. And what does that spell for Lemuria's future? What kind of tool will it become, if at all?

Lemuria has never really broken through to mainstream culture. It was truly a lost continent that you had to go looking for and was not put in front of you like Atlantis. Shaver's "I Remember Lemuria!" remains the single most popular occurrence of Lemuria that brought the idea to the most people, but that was short-lived and soon forgotten by the populace at large. And Lemuria is brought up every now and then by the more esoteric creators like H.P. Lovecraft, Jack Kirby, and Thomas Pynchon, or lore borrowed for a video game. There does not seem to be much excitement for continuing the legacy of Lemuria or even trying to prove its existence anymore. For the believers, that has already been done beyond a shadow of a doubt, and for the rest it is another example of weird things that crazy people say and move on. Maybe Lemuria will be moved on from. But I doubt that. Ever since its inception, Lemuria has provided mystery and hope. A means to explain and express.

This remains a human story, with humans doing the innovating and creating and believing. Believers in Lemuria have stopped striving toward an idealized Lemuria, probably because it already exists here in America. Violent, racist America. Lemuria arisen. Maybe it never sank in the first place and we are the Lemurians and the deros being persecuted and doing the persecuting. Maybe we're carrying on the legacy of Lemuria for the next hundred millennia, or until we finally do ascend and return to be with our Lemurian sisters and brothers, completing the circle.

I have tried to steer away from proving or disproving Lemuria's existence. Whether Lemuria did or did not exist seems rather beyond the point. Lemuria seems to exist to prove something else and not itself, so those like Churchward, who try to prove a real-life Mu or Lemuria, seem lost themselves. Lemuria is not meant to be real or to have actually existed. That would zap the power and meaning from the place. Lemuria needs to exist in the beyond, out past our ability to comprehend; otherwise, it is only a highway for ancient lemurs. And while we should put the lemur back in Lemuria, it should not be forgotten that it was a made-up name to begin with. Maybe if anything, this journey proves how we have evolved to consume and accept such alternatives.

A NOTE ON REFERENCES

A work of history is nothing without its sources. While I have used a number of different sources, there is one I would like to call out—Sumathi Ramaswamy's *The Lost Land of Lemuria: Fabulous Geographies, Catastrophic Histories*. It is an excellent academic work that lays out the history of Lemuria, and in the early days of my research, it provided gateways to different topics, in particular when dealing with the scientific debate around Lemuria. In addition, Ramaswamy provides a great overview of Kumarikkantam, or Kumari Kandam, the name the Tamil people gave to Lemuria. Having no knowledge of the Tamil language or background in the Tamil people's culture, I would have ended up copying whatever Ramaswamy has written about it anyway. So please do check out her work, for it is an interesting story about how the Tamil people claimed ownership of the idea of Lemuria for their own myth-making purposes from the late nineteenth century and well into the twentieth century.

REFERENCES

"70 Followers To Promised Land Stranded." *Stockton Independent.* June 20, 1934. www.newspapers.com/image/legacy/608138793

Abouzelof, Julie. "Ancient Origin of Healing Crystals." *Moonrise Crystals*, March 7, 2022. moonrisecrystals.com/ancient-origin-of-healing-crystals/Abrahams, Edward H. "Ignatius Donnelly and the Apocalyptic Style." *Minnesota History* 46, no. 3 (Fall 1978): 102–11.

Albers, Paulinus Cornelis Hendricus, and John de Vos. *Through Eugène Dubois' Eyes: Stills of a Turbulent Life*. Leiden: Brill, 2010.

Ali, Jason R., and Miguel Vences. "Mammals and Long-Distance over-Water Colonization: The Case for Rafting Dispersal; the Case against Phantom Causeways." *Journal of Biogeography* 46 (2019): 2632–36.

Alper, Frank. *Exploring Atlantis*. Vol. 1. 3 vols. Irvine, California: Quantum Productions, 1981.

Anderson, David D. *Ignatius Donnelly*. Boston: Twayne Publishers, 1980. archive.org/details/ignatiusdonnelly0362ande

Ashwal, Lewis D., Michael Wiedenbeck, and Trond H. Torsvik. "Archaean Zircons in Miocene Oceanic Hotspot Rocks Establish Ancient Continental Crust beneath Mauritius." *Nature Communications* 8, no. 1 (January 31, 2017). doi.org/10.1038/ncomms14086

Bailey, Alice. *Discipleship in the New Age*. New York: Lucis Publishing Co., 1976. archive.org/details/discipleshipinne0001bail

——. *Esoteric Healing*. New York: Lucis Publishing Co., 1953. archive.org/details/esoterichealing0004bail

——. *From Intellect to Intuition*. New York: Lucis Publishing Co., 1969. archive.org/details/fromintellecttoi0000unse_n5n0

——. *Initiation, Human and Solar*. New York: Lucis Publishing Co., 1951. archive.org/details/initiationhumans00bail

——. *Telepathy and the Etheric Vehicle*. New York: Lucis Publishing Co., 1971. archive.org/details/telepathyetheric0000bail

——. *The Seven Rays of Life*. New York: Lucis Publishing Co., 1995. archive.org/details/sevenraysoflife0000bail

Barker, A.T. (ed.). *The Mahatma Letters to A.P. Sinnett from the Mahatmas M. & K.H.* Adyar, Madras: Theosophical Pub. House, 1962. archive.org/details/mahatmalettersto0000unse

Barkun, Michael. *A Culture of Conspiracy: Apocalyptic Visions in Contemporary America.* 2nd ed. Berkeley, California: University of California Press, 2013.

Bassias, Yannis. "Was the Mozambique Channel Once Scattered with Islands?" *GEO ExPro*, October 2016, 58–62. www.geoexpro.com/articles/2016/12/was-the-mozambique-channel-once-scattered-with-islands

Baxter, Stephen. *Ages in Chaos: James Hutton and the Discovery of Deep Time.* New York: Forge, 2003. archive.org/details/agesinchaosjames0000unse

Beckley, Timothy Green. *Timothy Green Beckley's Subterranean Worlds inside Earth.* New Brunswick, NJ: Inner Light Publications, 1992. archive.org/details/subterraneanworl00timo

Beekman, Scott M. "Silver Shirts: The Life of William Dudley Pelley." Dissertation, Ohio University, 2003.

Bernard, Raymond. *The Hollow Earth.* Kempton, Illinois: Adventures Unlimited Press, 1964.

Besant, Annie. *Annie Besant: An Autobiography.* London: T. Fisher Unwin, 1893. archive.org/details/anniebesantautob00besaiala

Besant, Annie, and C.W. Leadbeater. *Man: Whence How And Whither.* Wheaton, Illinois: The Theosophical Press, 1947. archive.org/details/manwhencehowandw031919mbp

Bindon, Peter R. "The Ancient Mystical Order Rosae Crucis, AMORC: Its Origins, Organisation and Some Notes on Ceremonies." *Goulburn Research Seminar*, 2006. linfordresearch.info/fordownload/Research%20Papers/Bindon%20AMORC%20Glbn2006.pdf

Bitto, Robert. "The Lost Continent of Mu & the Mexican Mother Civilization." *Mexico Unexplained*, June 25, 2018. mexicounexplained.com/lost-continent-mu-mexican-mother-civilization/

Blavatsky, Helena Petrovna. *The Complete Works of H.P. Blavatsky.* London: Rider & Co., 1933. archive.org/details/completeworksofh0001blav

——.*H.P. Blavatsky Collected Writings, 1882–1883 (Vol. 4).* Wheaton, Illinois: The Theosophical Publishing House, 1969.

——.*Isis Unveiled: A Master Key to the Mysteries of Ancient and Modern Science and Theology.* Los Angeles: The Theosophy Co., 1931. archive.org/details/in.ernet.dli.2015.90215/page/n5/mode/2up

——.*The Secret Doctrine: The Synthesis of Science, Religion, and Philosophy.* Point Loma, CA: The Aryan Theosophical Press, 1905. archive.org/details/secretdoctrine01unkngoog/page/n6/mode/2up

Blavatsky, Helena Petrovna, and Michael Gomes. *The Secret Doctrine.* New York: Jeremy P. Tarcher/Penguin, 2009.

Bonesteel, Michael. "Gods of the Cavern World." *Raw Vision*, Winter 2014. rawvision.com/blogs/articles/articles-gods-cavern-world

Borsos, David. "The Esoteric Philosophy of Alice A. Bailey: Ageless Wisdom for a New Age." Dissertation, California Institute of Integral Studies, 2012. www.proquest.com/docview/1030968328/abstract/16EFE2B919FB4BF5PQ/1

Bradby, Ruth. "Channeling - The Cinderella of the New Age? A Course in Miracles, the Seth Texts, and Definition in New Age Spiritualities." In *Handbook of Spiritualism and Channeling.* Leiden: Brill, 2015.

Bruce Walton (ed.). *Mount Shasta: Home of the Ancients.* Mokelumne Hill, CA: Health Research, 1985.

Bryan, Gerald. *Psychic Dictatorship in America.* Los Angeles: Truth Research Publications, 1940.

Byrd, Richard E. "Our Navy Explores Antarctica." *National Geographic*, October 1947.

"California Is Said to Be a Part of the Ancient Continent of Lemuria, and the Center of Civilization That Antedates the Fabled Continent of Atlantis by Thousands of Years." *San Francisco Call.* September 13, 1896.

Campbell, Bruce F. *Ancient Wisdom Revived: A History of the Theosophical Movement.* Berkeley: University of California Press, 1980.

Cande, Steven C., and Dave R. Stegman. "Indian and African Plate Motions Driven by the Push Force of the Reunion Plume Head." *Nature* 475 (July 7, 2011): 47–52.

Carlos, Kristine D. "Crystal Healing Practices in the Western World and Beyond." Thesis, University of Central Florida, 2018. stars.library.ucf.edu/cgi/viewcontent.cgi?article=1283&context=honorstheses

Castleden, Rodney. *Atlantis Destroyed*. London: Taylor & Francis Group, 1998.

Cayce, Edgar. *Edgar Cayce on Atlantis*. New York: Hawthorn Books, 1968. archive.org/details/edgarcayceonatla00cayc

——. *Scientific Properties and Occult Aspects of Twenty-Two Gems, Stones, and Metals : A Comparative Study Based upon the Edgar Cayce Readings*. Virginia Beach, VA: A.R.E. Press, 1979. archive.org/details/scientificproper00cayc

Censky, Ellen J., Karim Hodge, and Judy Dudley. "Over-Water Dispersal of Lizards Due to Hurricanes." *Nature* 395 (October 8, 1998): 556.

Cervé, Wishar Spenle. *Lemuria: The Lost Continent of the Pacific*. San Jose: Supreme Grand Lodge of AMORC, 1982. archive.org/details/lemurialostconti0000cerv

Chajes, Julie. "Blavatsky and the Lives Sciences." *Aries - Journal for the Study of Western Esotericism* 18 (2018): 258–286.

Chia, Aleena, Jonathan Corpus Ong, Hugh Davies, and Mack Hagood. "'Everything is Connected': Networked Conspirituality in New Age Media." *AoIR Selected Papers of Internet Research*, September 15, 2021. doi.org/10.5210/spir.v2021i0.12093

Childress, David. "Lemurian Fellowship-Stelle Connection." *The Ultimate Frontier*, December 14, 1986. the-ultimate-frontier.org/communities/Ramona/Stelle%20Connection.htm

Churchward, Jack. "Did Churchward Give Niven A Bad Name in 1926?" *James Churchward's Mu*, January 20, 2012. jameschurchwardsmu.blogspot.com/2012/01/did-churchward-give-niven-bad-name-in.html

Churchward, James. *The Children Of Mu*. New York: Ives Washburn, 1931. archive.org/details/in.ernet.dli.2015.77375

——. *Cosmic Forces of Mu*. New York: Ives Washburn, 1934. archive.org/details/cosmicforcesofmu00chur_2

——. "James Churchward: 1931 Lecture." *bibliotecapleyades.net*. n.d. www.bibliotecapleyades.net/arqueologia/esp_churchward07.htm

——. *The Lost Continent of Mu*. New York: Crown Publishers, 1931.

——. *The Sacred Symbols of Mu*. New York: Ives Washburn, 1933. archive.org/details/sacredsymbolsofm0000chur

Cope, John C.W., and Geraint Owen. "Continental Drift." In *Encyclopedia of Environmental Change*. London: Sage, 2014.

Cranston, Sylvia, and Carey Williams. *HPB: The Extraordinary Life and Influence of Helena Blavatsky, Founder of the Modern Theosophical Movement*. Santa Barbara: Path Publishing House, 1993.

Crockford, Susannah. "The Power of Belief in Conspiracy Theories." *The University of Chicago Divinity School*, December 17, 2021. divinity.uchicago.edu/sightings/articles/power-belief-conspiracy-theories

——. "Where the Path of Denial Leads." *Contending Modernities*, February 11, 2022. contendingmodernities.nd.edu/theorizing-modernities/where-the-path-of-denial-leads/

David King. *Finding Atlantis*. New York: Harmony, 2005. archive.org/details/findingatlantist00king

de Camp, L. Sprague. *Lost Continents: The Atlantis Theme in History, Science, and Literature*. New York: Dover Publications, Inc., 1954. archive.org/details/lostcontinentsat0000lspr

Deveney, Pat. "Lemurian Ambassador (IAPSOP)." *International Association for the Preservation of Spiritualist and Occult Periodicals*, August 3, 1921. iapsop.com/archive/materials/lemurian_ambassador/

Donnelly, Ignatius. *Atlantis: The Antediluvian World*. New York: Harper & Brothers, 1882. archive.org/details/atlantisantedilu00donnuoft

"Dr. Robert D. Stelle: Founder of the Lemurian Fellowship," *The Ultimate Frontier*. n.d. the-ultimate-frontier.org/communities/Ramona/Robert%20Stelle.htm

Duns, Pamela. "Nothing Higher than the Truth: Modern Theosophy, Buddhism, and the Making of Cultural Nationalism in India." Thesis, McGill University.

Dusanic, Slobodan. "Plato's Atlantis." *L'antiquite Classique* 51 (1982): 25–52.

——."The Unity of the Timaeus-Critias and the Inter-Greek Wars of the Mid 350's." *Illinois Classical Studies* 27–28 (2002/2003): 63–75.

Engelbrecht, Gavin. "Durham University Experts Believe They Have Uncovered Sunken Continent 'Icelandia'." *The Northern Echo*, June 29, 2021. www.thenorthernecho.co.uk/news/19406579.durham-university-experts-believe-uncovered-sunken-continent-icelandia/

Farber. "Ignatius Donnelly: Paranoid Progressive in the Gilded Age." *Minnesota Lawyer*, May 30, 2018. minnlawyer.com/2018/05/30/ignatius-donnelly-paranoid-progressive-in-the-gilded-age/

Feder, Kenneth L. *Encyclopedia of Dubious Archaeology: From Atlantis to the Walam Olum*. Santa Barbara: Greenwood, 2010. archive.org/details/encyclopediaofdu0000fede

"Finder of Lost Continent Gone; Followers Puzzled." *Oakland Tribune*. June 19, 1934. www.newspapers.com/image/legacy/106272921

Forbes, Edward. "On the Connexion between the Distribution of the Existing Fauna and Flora of the British Isles, and the Geological Changes Which Have Affected Their Area, Especially during the Epoch of the Northern Drift." In *Memoirs of the Geological Survey of Great Britain and of the Museum of Economic Geology in London*, 1:336–403. London: Longman, Brown, Green, and Longmans, 1866. pubs.bgs.ac.uk/publications.html?pubID=B07010

Galbreath, Robert. "The History of Modern Occultism: A Bibliographical Survey." *Journal of Popular Culture* 5, no. 3 (Winter 1971): 98–126.

Gardner, Charlie J., and Louise D. Jasper. "Discovery of an Island Population of Dwarf Lemurs (Cheirogaleidae: Cheirogaleus) on Nosy Hara, Far Northern Madagascar." *Primates* 56 (2015): 307–10.

Gardner, J. Starkie. "The Permanence of Continents." *The Popular Science Review* 20 (1881): 117–127. people.wku.edu/charles.smith/wallace/zGardner1881PopSciRev.pdf

Gardner, Marshall B. *A Journey to the Earth's Interior; or, Have the Poles Really Been Discovered*. Aurora, IL: Marshall B. Gardner, 1913. archive.org/details/journeytoearthsi00gard

Gasman, Daniel E. "Social Darwinism in Ernst Haeckel and the German Monist League. a Study of the Scientific Origins of National Socialism." Dissertation, The University of Chicago.

Gill, Christopher. "The Genre of the Atlantis Story." *Classical Philology* 72, no. 4 (October 1977): 287–304.

Gliboff, Sander Joel. "The Pebble and the Planet: Paul Kammerer, Ernst Haeckel, and the Meaning of Darwinism." Dissertation. Johns Hopkins University, 2001.

"Glimpses of Atlantis." *American Scientific Review* 37, no. 4 (1877): 48–49. www.jstor.org/stable/e26064171

Grafton, Anthony, Glenn W. Most, and Salvatore Settis. "Hermes Trismegistus and Hermeticism." In *The Classical Tradition*. Boston: Harvard University Press, 2010.

Green, Nile. "The Global Occult: An Introduction." *History of Religions* 54, no. 4 (May 2015): 383–93.

Griffith, Joan T. "James Churchward and His Lost Pacific Continent." *Biblioteca Pleyades*. n.d. www.bibliotecapleyades.net/arqueologia/esp_churchward02.htm

Guimont, Edward. "Hunting Dinosaurs in Central Africa." *Contingent*, March 18, 2019. contingentmagazine.org/2019/03/18/hunting-dinosaurs-africa/Gutierrez, Cathy. *Occult in Nineteenth-Century America*. Aurora, CO: The Davies Group Publishers, 2005.

Haeckel, Ernst. *The History of Creation: Or the Development of the Earth and Its Inhabitants by the Action of Natural Causes*. New York: D. Appleton and Company, 1887. archive.org/details/dli.ministry.14031/E03776_The_History_of_Creation_Vol_1/

——.*The Last Link: Our Present Knowledge of the Descent of Man*. London: Adam and Charles Black, 1898. www.gutenberg.org/files/44541/44541-h/44541-h.htm

Hall, Manly P. *The Secret Teachings of All Ages*. New York: Jeremy P. Tarcher/Penguin, 2003.

Halley, Edmond. "An Account of the Cause of the Change of the Variation of the Magnetical Needle, with an Hypothesis of the Structure of the Internal Parts of the Earth: As It Was Proposed to the Royal Society in One of Their Late Meetings." *Philosophical Transactions of the Royal Society of London* 17, no. 195 (October 19, 1692): 563–78. doi.org/10.1098/rstl.1686.0107

Hammer, Olav. *Claiming Knowledge: Strategies of Epistemology from Theosophy to the New Age*. Leiden: Brill, 2003.

Hammer, Olav, and Mikael Rothstein. *Handbook of the Theosophical Current*. 1st ed. Brill Handbooks on Contemporary Religion Ser. Leiden: Brill, 2013.

Hampton, Dave. "Ancient Modern: Lost Crafts of the Lemurians." *KPBS Public Media*, August 4, 2010. www.kpbs.org/news/arts-culture/2010/08/04/ancient-modern-lost-crafts-lemurians

Hanegraaff, Wouter J. *New Age Religion and Western Culture: Esotericism in the Mirror of Secular Thought*. Leiden: Brill, 1996.

Hartlaub, Gustav. "General Remarks on the Avifauna of Madagascar and the Mascarene Islands." *International Journal of Avian Science* 19, no. 3 (July 1877): 334–36.

Heie, Nolan. "Ernst Haeckel and the Redemption of Nature." Dissertation, Queen's University, 2008.

Hindes, Daniel. "Rudolf Steiner and Ernst Haeckel." *Defending Steiner*, 2004. www.defendingsteiner.com/articles/rs-haeckel.php

Hinsbergen, D.J.J. van, M. Mensink, C.G. Langereis, M. Maffione, L. Spalluto, M. Tropeano, and L. Sabato. "Did Adria Rotate Relative to Africa?" *Solid Earth* 5, no. 2 (2014): 611–29. doi.org/10.5194/se-5-611-2014

Holt, Stephen. "Ignatius Donnelly (1831–1901): Australian Echoes of an American Reformer." *National Library of Australia News* XI, no. 7 (April 2001). www.labourhistory.org.au/hummer/vol-3-no-6/echoes/

Hooker, Joseph Dalton. *Introductory Essay to the Flora of New Zealand*. London: Lovell Reeve, 1853. darwin-online.org.uk/converted/pdf/1853_Zealand_A944.pdf

Houle, Alain. "Floating Islands: A Mode of Long-Distance Dispersal for Small and Medium-Sized Terrestrial Vertebrates." *Diversity and Distributions* 4, no. 5/6 (November 1998): 201–16.

"Howard John Zitko," *The Ultimate Frontier*. May 27, 2003. the-ultimate-frontier.org/history/Zitco. htmIcke, David. *The Biggest Secret*. Derby: Ickonic Enterprises, 1999.

Ingle, S., D. Weis, and F.A. Frey. "Indian Continental Crust Recovered from Elan Bank, Kerguelen Plateau (ODP Leg 183, Site 1137)." *Journal of Petrology* 43, no. 7 (2002): 1241–57.

Isaksson, Stefan. "New Religious UFO Movements: Extraterrestrial Salvation in Contemporary America." *Anthrobase*, Spring 2000. www.anthrobase.com/Txt/I/Isaksson_S_01.htm

Jackson, Jr., John P., and Nadine M. Weidman. "The Origins of Scientific Racism." *The Journal of Blacks in Higher Education* 50 (Winter, 2005 /2006): 66–79.

Jenkins, Philip. *Mystics and Messiahs: Cults and New Religions in American History*. Oxford: Oxford University Press, 2000.

Jolly, Alison. *Lords and Lemurs: Mad Scientists· Kings with Spears and the Survival of Diversity in Madagascar*. Boston: Houghton Mifflin, 2004. archive.org/details/lordslemursmadsc00joll

Jones, Aurelia Louise. "Mount Shasta, Telos, And Lemuria." *Unariun Wisdom*, April 19, 2021. www.unariunwisdom.com/mount-shasta-telos-and-lemuria/

Joseph, Frank. *Atlantis and Other Lost Worlds*. London: Arcturus Publishing, 2014.

———. *The Lost Civilization of Lemuria: The Rise and Fall of the World's Oldest Culture*. Rochester, VT: Bear & Co., 2006. archive.org/details/lostcivilization0000jose

Joshi, Amitabh. "Vignettes of Haeckel's Contributions to Biology." *Resonance*, November 2018, 1177–1204.

Kaehr, Shelley. *Lemurian Seeds: Hope for Humanity*. Dallas: An Out of This World Production, 2006.

Kafton-Minkel, Walter. *Subterranean Worlds: 100,000 Years of Dragons, Dwarfs, the Dead, Lost Races and UFOs from inside the Earth*. Port Townsend, WA: Loompanics Unlimited, 1989.

Kalambakal, Vickey. "Solon." In *World History: A Comprehensive Reference Set*. Facts on File, 2016.

Kappeler, Peter. "Lemur Origins: Rafting by Groups of Hibernators?" *Folia Primatologica* 71 (2000): 422–25.

Kerins, Triumph. "Beyond the QAnon Shaman: The Disturbing Relationship Between New Age and Far Right Movements." *McGill International Review*, January 15, 2021. www.mironline.ca/beyond-the-qanon-shaman-the-disturbing-relationship-between-new-age-and-far-right-movements/

Kern, Emily Margaret. "Out of Asia: A Global History of the Scientific Search for the Origins of Humankind, 1800–1965." Dissertation, Princeton University, 2018. www.proquest.com/docview/2036927993/abstract/72CE08122A68431CPQ/1

King, Godfré Ray. *Unveiled Mysteries*. 3rd ed. Chicago: Saint Germain Press, 1939. archive.org/details/unveiledmysterie00kingrich

King, Godfré Ray, and Saint Germain (Spirit). *The "I Am" Discourses*. Chicago: Saint Germain Press, 1935. archive.org/details/iamdiscourses00king

Knight, J.Z. (Judy Zebra). *A State of Mind: My Story: Ramtha, the Adventure Begins*. New York: Warner Books, 1987. archive.org/details/stateofmindmysto00knigrich

——.*The White Book*. Yelm, WA: JZK Publishing, 2004. archive.org/details/whitebook0000ramt

Kossy, Donna. *Kooks*. Los Angeles: Feral House, 1994. archive.org/details/kooks0000koss

Kutschera, Ulrich. "Ernst's Haeckel's Biodynamics 1866 and the Occult Basis of Organic Farming." *Plant Signaling and Behavior* 11, no. 7 (2016).

Kutschera, Ulrich, Georgy S. Levit, and Uwe Hossfeld. "Ernst Haeckel (1834–1919): The German Darwin and His Impact on Modern Biology." *Theory in Biosciences* 138 (2019): 1–7.

Lachman, Gary. *Madame Blavatsky: The Mother of Modern Spirituality*. New York: Penguin Publishing Group, 2012.

Lagasse, Paul. "Cagliostro, Alessandro Conte Di." In *The Columbia Encyclopedia*. Columbia University Press, 2018.

——. "Pythagoras." In *The Columbia Encyclopedia*. Columbia University Press, 2018.

——. "Unitarianism." In *The Columbia Encyclopedia*. New York: Columbia University Press, 2018.

Lamson, Berenice McKeown. "Mount Shasta: A Regional History." Dissertation, University of the Pacific, 1984. scholarlycommons.pacific.edu/uop_etds/2111/

Landi, Val. "'Lost Continents Unveiled'-Antarctica's Prehistoric Buried Fossil Remnants 'Lead Back to the Breakup of the Supercontinent Gondwana.'" *Newstex*, November 8, 2018.

Lanser, Edward. "A People of Mystery." *Los Angeles Times*. May 22, 1932. www.newspapers.com/image/legacy/380412271

——. "Writers of the Desert." *The Desert Magazine*, May 1942: 23–24. archive.org/details/Desert-Magazine-1942-05

Larkin, Edgar Lucien. "The Atlantides." *San Francisco Examiner*. December 31, 1913. www.newspapers.com/image/legacy/457333304/

——. *The Matchless Altar of the Soul, Symbolized as a Shining Cube of Diamond, One Cubit in Dimensions, and Set within the Holy of Holies in All Grand Esoteric Temples of Antiquity*. Los Angeles: Edgar Lucien Larkin, 1916. archive.org/details/matchlessaltars00larkgoog

——.*Within the Mind Maze, or, Mentonomy, the Law of the Mind*. Los Angeles: Standard Printing Company, 1911. archive.org/details/withinmindmazeor00lark

Lawton, Ian. "The Seth Material." *Ian Lawton*, 2008. www.ianlawton.com/se1.html

Leadbeater, Charles W. *The Masters and The Path*. Adyar, Madras, India: Theosophical Publishing House, 1925. archive.org/details/in.ernet.dli.2015.201747

Le Plongeon, Augustus. *Queen Moo and The Egyptian Sphinx*. New York: Augustus Le Plongeon, 1896. archive.org/details/queenmooegyptian0000augu

——*Sacred Mysteries Among The Mayas and the Quiches*. 3rd ed. New York: Macoy Publishing and Masonic Supply Co., 1909. archive.org/details/sacredmysteriesa0000lepl

——. *Vestiges of the Mayas*. New York: John Polhemus, 1881. archive.org/details/PlongeonALeVestigesOfTheMayas1881

Lemuria The Incomparable: The Answer. Los Angeles: Lemurian Fellowship, 1943. catalog.hathitrust.org/Record/102292178

"Lemuria, the Lost Paradise." *Scientific American* 36, no. 10 (March 10, 1877): 144.

Lemurian Fellowship. "Into the Sun." Lemurian Fellowship, 2015. www.lemurianfellowship.org/purpose-of-life/into-the-sun-title-page/

Leslie, Desmond, and George Adamski. *Flying Saucers Have Landed*. New York: British Book Centre, 1953. archive.org/details/flyingsaucershav00lesl

Levit, Georgy S., and Uwe Hossfeld. "Ernst Haeckel in the History of Biology." *Current Biology Magazine* 29 (December 16, 2019): 1269–1300.

———. "Ernst Haeckel, Nikolai Miklucho-Maclay and the Racial Controversy over the Papuans." *Frontiers in Zoology* 17, no. 16 (2020).

Lewis, James R. "Excavating Tradition: Alternative Archaeologies as Legitimation Strategies." *Numen*, Alternative Archaeology, 59, no. 2/3 (2012): 202–21.

———. *The Gods Have Landed: New Religions from Other Worlds*. Albany: State University of New York Press, 1995. archive.org/details/godshavelandedne0000unse

Lewis, Ralph M. "Is Lemuria Legend or Fact?" *Rosicrucian Digest* 12 no. 7 (August 1934): 250–252. b45e1c3778bbf3ebb96c-637cca54df3fd347e9c3d5d35c2f839a.ssl.cf5.rackcdn.com/The_Rosicrucian_Digest_v12_n7_1934.pdf

Linden, Willem J.M. van der. "Walvis Ridge, a Piece of Africa?" *Geology* 8 (September 1980): 417–21.

"Lost Race Hunt Leader Sought." *San Francisco Examiner*. June 20, 1934. www.newspapers.com/image/legacy/458170689/

MacLaine, Shirley. *Dancing in the Light*. New York: Bantam Books, 1985. archive.org/details/dancinginlight0000macl

———. *Out On a Limb*. New York: Bantam Books, 1983. archive.org/details/isbn_0553263528

———. *The Camino: A Journey of the Spirit*. New York: Pocket Books, 2000. archive.org/details/caminojourneyofs00macl

———. *What If: A Lifetime of Questions, Speculations, Reasonable Guesses, and a Few Things I Know for Sure*. New York: Atria Books, 2013. archive.org/details/whatiflifetimeof0000macl_j6t2

Major, Trevor. "Ernst Haeckel: The Legacy of a Lie." *Firm Foundation* 108, no. 8 (August 1993): 9–11.

Masters, Judith C., Fabien Genin, Yurui Zhang, Romain Pellen, Thierry Huck, Paul P.A. Mazza, Marina Rabineau, and Moctar Doucoure. "Biogeographic Mechanisms Involved in the Colonization of Madagascar by African Vertebrates: Rifting, Rafting, and Runways." *Journal of Biogeography* 48 (2021): 492–510.

Mazza, Paul P.A., Antonella Bucciantl, and Andrea Savorelli. "Grasping at Straws: A Re-Evaluation of Sweepstakes Colonisation of Islands by Mammals." *Biological Reviews* 94 (n.d.): 1364–80.

McCall, Robert A. "Implications of Recent Geological Investigations of the Mozambique Channel for the Mammalian Colonization of Madagascar." *Proceedings of the Royal Society* 264 (1997): 663–65.

McClure, Tess. "Dark Crystals: The Brutal Reality behind a Booming Wellness Craze." *The Guardian*, September 17, 2019. www.theguardian.com/lifeandstyle/2019/sep/17/healing-crystals-wellness-mining-madagascar

McGovern, Una. "Mesmer, Franz Anton (1734–1815)." In *Chambers Dictionary of the Unexplained*. London: Chambers, 2007.

———. "Lévi, Eliphas (1810–75)." In *Chambers Dictionary of the Unexplained*. London: Chambers, 2007.

Mckee, Gabriel. "'Reality – Is It a Horror?': Richard Shaver's Subterranean World and the Displaced Self." *Journal of Gods and Monsters*, July 20, 2020. archive.nyu.edu/handle/2451/63884

Melton, J. Gordon. "Beyond Millennialism: The New Age Transformed." Celigny, Switzerland: Institut Oecumenique de Bossey, 2000.

———. "Edgar Cayce and Reincarnation: Past Life Readings as Religious Symbology." *Syzygy: Journal of Alternative Religion and Culture* 3, no. 1–2 (1994).

———. "New Age Movement." In *World Religions: Belief, Culture, and Controversy*. Santa Barbara: ABC-CLIO, 2022.

———. "New Thought and the New Age." In *Perspectives on the New Age*. Albany: State University of New York Press, 1992.

Meltzer, Marisa. "QAnon's Unexpected Roots in New Age Spirituality." *Washington Post*, March 29, 2021. www.washingtonpost.com/magazine/2021/03/29/qanon-new-age-spirituality/

Metcalfe, Tom. "Iceland May Be the Tip of a Sunken Continent." *Live Science*, July 28, 2021. www. livescience.com/iceland-tip-of-lost-sunken-continent.html

Miesse, William C. *Mount Shasta: An Annotated Bibliography*. Weed, CA: College of the Siskiyous, 1993. www.siskiyous.edu/library/shasta/

Mittermeier, Russell A., Ian Tattersall, William R. Konstant, David M. Meyers, and Roderic B. Mast. *Lemurs of Madagascar*. Washington, D.C.: Conservation International, 1994. archive.org/details/ lemursofmadagasc0000unse

Morgan, Kathryn A. "Designer History: Plato's Atlantis Story and Fourth-Century Ideology." *The Journal of Hellenic Studies* 118 (1998): 101–18.

Moyer, Christopher. "From 'Mother God' to Mummified Corpse: Inside the Fringe Spiritual Sect 'Love Has Won.'" *Rolling Stone*, November 26, 2021. www.rollingstone.com/culture/culture-features/love-has-won-amy-carlson-mother-god-1254916/

Muir-Wood, Robert. *The Dark Side of the Earth*. London: Allen & Unwin, 1985. archive.org/details/ darksideofearth0000muir

Murray, Andrew. *The Geographical Distribution of Mammals*. London: Day and Son, 1866. archive.org/ details/geographicaldist00murr

"Mystic Held for Selling Stock in Sunken Island." *Leader-Telegram*. October 4, 1941. www.newspapers. com/image/legacy/268792128

Nadis, Fred. *The Man From Mars: Ray Palmer's Amazing Pulp Journey*. New York: Jeremy P. Tarcher/ Penguin, 2013.

Niocaill, Conall Mac. "Calling Card of a Ghost Continent." *Nature Geoscience* 6 (March 2013): 165–66.

Noakes, Richard. "Spiritualism, Science, and the Supernatural in Mid-Victorian Britain." In *The Victorian Supernatural*, 23–43. Cambridge Studies in Nineteenth-Century Literature and Culture. Cambridge: Cambridge University Press, 2004.

Parmigiani, Giovanna. "Magic and Politics: Conspirituality and COVID-19." *Journal of the American Academy of Religion* 89, no. 2 (529 506): June 2021.

Partridge, Christopher. "Channeling Extraterrestrials: Theosophical Discourse in the Space Age." In *Handbook of Spiritualism and Channeling*, 390–479. Leiden: Brill, 2015.

"Paul Schliemann - Das Phantom Der Atlantisforschung." *Atlantis Forschung*. January 31, 2020. atlantisforschung.de/index.php?title=Paul_Schliemann_-_das_Phantom_der_Atlantisforschung

Pedersen, Rene. "Defining Theosophy in the Twenty-First Century." *Scripta Instituti Donneriani Aboensis* 20 (2008): 139–53.

Pelley, Virginia. "How a Former McDonald's Manager Convinced Millennial Women She Was God." *Marie Claire*, September 7, 2021. www.marieclaire.com/culture/a37417778/love-has-won-cult-amy-carlson-stroud-death/

"Pepe Deluxe Presents Queen of the Wave: An Esoteric Pop Opera in Three Parts: Pepe Deluxe Album Companion II," 2012. www.ignaciodarnaude.com/revelacion_extraterrestre/ Oliver(Phylos),Earth%20dweller%20return.pdf

Peters, Michael A. "New Age Spiritualism, Mysticism, and Far-Right Conspiracy." *Educational Philosophy and Theory*, (April 20, 2022): 1–9. doi.org/10.1080/00131857.2022.2061948

Phylos the Thibetan, and Frederick Spencer Oliver. *A Dweller on Two Planets, or, The Diving of the Way*. Los Angeles: Baumgardt Publishing Co., 1905. archive.org/details/dwellerontwoplan00oli/page/n9/mode/2up

——. *An Earth Dweller's Return*. Milwaukee: Lemurian Press, 1940. archive.org/details/phylos-the-thibetan-an-earth-dwellers-return

Plato. *Timaeus and Critias*. Baltimore: Penguin Books, 1971. archive.org/details/timaeuscritias00plat

Preece, Harold. "World Underground." *Rosicrucian Digest* 26, no. 10 (November 1948): 374-376. b45e1c3778bbf3ebb96c-637cca54df3fd347e9c3d5d35c2f839a.ssl.cf5.rackcdn.com/Rosicrucian_ Digest_v26_n10_1948.pdf

Preston Peet. *Disinformation Guide to Ancient Aliens, Lost Civilizations, Astonishing Archaeology & Hidden History*. San Francisco: Disinformation, 2013. archive.org/details/disinformationgu0000unse

"Pyramid and Crystal Myths, Powers and Pseudoscience." n.d.. web2.ph.utexas.edu/~coker2/index.files/pyracrystal.shtml

"QResear.Ch: The 8chan/8kun QResearch Board Search." Accessed August 16, 2022. qresear.ch/

Ramaswamy, Sumathi. *The Lost Land of Lemuria: Fabulous Geographies, Catastrophic Histories*. Berkeley: University of California Press, 2004.

Ramatherio, Sri. "Lemuria and Its People." *The Mystic Triangle* 4, no. 3 (April 1926): 60–63.

Rasmussen, Cecilia. "From L.A. Sprang Cult of I AM." *Los Angeles Times*, January 25, 1998. www.latimes.com/archives/la-xpm-1998-jan-25-me-11997-story.html

Reece, Gregory L. "The Shaver Mystery: The Most Sensational True Story Ever Told." *Los Angeles Review of Books*, August 26, 2013. lareviewofbooks.org/article/the-shaver-mystery-the-most-sensational-true-story-ever-told/

Reed, William. *The Phantom of the Poles*. New York: Walter S. Rockey Co., 1906. archive.org/details/phantompoles00reedgoog/page/n10/mode/2up?view=theater

Richards, Robert J. "Ernst Haeckel's Alleged Anti-Semitism and Contributions to Nazi Biology." *Biological Theory* 2, no. 1 (2007): 97–103.

——.*The Tragic Sense of Life: Ernst Haeckel and the Struggle over Evolutionary Thought*. Chicago: University of Chicago Press, 2008.

Ridge, Martin. *Ignatius Donnelly: The Portrait of a Politician*. Chicago: University of Chicago Press, 1962. archive.org/details/ignatiusdonnelly0000ridg

Roberts, Jane and Seth (Spirit). *Seth Speaks; the Eternal Validity of the Soul*. New York: Bantam Books, 1974. archive.org/details/sethspeakseterna00robe

Robertson, David G. "Conspiracy Theories and the Study of Alternative and Emergent Religions." *Nova Religio: The Journal of Alternative and Emergent Religions* 19, no. 2 (November 2015): 5–16.

Rudbog, Tim. "The I AM ACTIVITY." In *Handbook of the Theosophical Current*, 151–72. Leiden: Brill, 2013.

Rupke, N.A. "Continental Drift." In *Reader's Guide to the History of Science*. Routledge, 2000.

Ruse, Michael. "A Reappraisal of Ernst Haeckel." *The Lancet* 373 (February 28, 2009): 711–12.

Russell, Robert Jay. *The Lemurs' Legacy: The Evolution of Power, Sex, and Love*. New York: Putnam, 1993. archive.org/details/lemurslegacyevol0000russ

Rutter, Gordon. "Spiritualism." In *Chambers Dictionary of the Unexplained*. London: Chambers, 2007.

Santucci, James A. "The Notion of Race in Theosophy." *The Journal of Alternative and Emergent Religions* 11, no. 3 (2008): 37–63.

"Saturday Night Uforia: The Positively True Story of Kenneth Arnold - Part Four," *Saturday Night UFOria*. 2012. www.saturdaynightuforia.com/html/articles/articlehtml/positivelytruestoryofkennetharnold4.html

Sauther, Michelle L., Lisa Gould, Frank P. Cuozzo, and M. Teague O'Mara. "Ring-Tailed Lemurs: A Species Re-Imagined." *Folia Primatologica* 86 (2015): 5–13. doi.org/10.1159/000370321Schliemann, Paul. "How I Found the Lost Atlantis, The Sources of All Civilization." *Sacred Texts*. www.sacred-texts.com/atl/hif/index.htm

Sclater, Philip Lutley. "The Mammals of Madagascar." *Quarterly Journal of Science* 1, no. 1–4 (April 1864): 213–19.

Scott-Elliot, William. *The Lost Lemuria*. London: Theosophical Publishing Society, 1904. archive.org/details/in.ernet.dli.2015.222654

Scott, James M., Jingao Liu, D. Graham Pearson, Garrett A. Harris, Thomas A. Czertowicz, S.J. Woodland, Amy J.V. Riches, and R.W. Luth. "Continent Stabilisation by Lateral Accretion of Subduction Zone-Processed Depleted Mantle Residues; Insights from Zealandia." *Earth and Planetary Science Letters* 507 (Februrary 2019): 175–186. www.sciencedirect.com/science/article/abs/pii/S0012821X18306988

Selvius. "Descendants of Lemuria." *The Mystic Triangle* 3, no. 8 (August 1925): 113–4. b45e1c3778bbf3ebb96c-637cca54df3fd347e9c3d5d35c2f839a.ssl.cf5.rackcdn.com/The_Mystic_Triangle_v3_n8_1925.pdf

Sender, Pablo. "The Dawn of Civilization: An Esoteric Account of the First Three Root Races." *Theosophical Society in America*, Fall 2019. www.theosophical.org/publications/quest-magazine/4729-the-dawn-of-civilization-an-esoteric-account-of-the-first-three-root-races

Sengor, A.M.C. "The Founder of Modern Geology Died 100 Years Ago: The Scientific Work and Legacy of Eduard Suess." *Geoscience Canada* 42 (2015): 181–246.

Sgorbati, Sergio, Marco D'Antraccoli, Sandra Citterio, Rodolfo Gentili, and Lorenzo Peruzzi. "Was Charles Darwin Right in His Explanation of the 'Abominable Mystery'?" *Italian Botanist* 5 (2018): 25–30.

Shaver, Richard Sharpe. "An Ancient Language?" *Amazing Stories* 18, no. 1 (January 1944): 206–207. archive.org/details/Amazing_Stories_v18n011944-01.Ziff-Daviscape1736/page/n207/mode/2up

———."Cave City of Hel." *Amazing Stories* 19, no. 3 (September 1945): 6–29. archive.org/details/Amazing_Stories_v19n03_1945-09_cape1736

———.. "Earth Slaves to Space." *Amazing Stories* 20, no. 6 (September 1946): 9–53. archive.org/details/Amazing_Stories_v20n06_1946-09.Ziff-Daviscape1736

———.. *I Remember Lemuria*. Evanston, Illinois: Venture Books, 1948.

———. "Invasion of the Micro-Men." *Amazing Stories* 20, no. 1 (February 1946): 6–42. archive.org/details/Amazing_Stories_v20n01_1946-02_cape1736

———. "Luder Valley." *Amazing Stories* 20, no. 6 (June 1946): 98–117. archive.org/details/Amazing_Stories_v20n03_1946-06_cape1736

———."Quest of Brail." *Amazing Stories* 19, no. 4 (December 1945): 8–61. archive.org/details/Amazing_Stories_v19n04_1945-12_cape1736

———. "The Fall of Lemuria." *Other Worlds* 1, no. 1 (November 1949): 4–41. archive.org/details/Other_Worlds_01v01n01_1949-11_LennyS-EXciter

———."The Land of Kui." *Amazing Stories* 20, no. 9 (December 1946): 8–24. archive.org/details/Amazing_Stories_v20n09_1946-12_cape1736

———. "The Masked World." *Amazing Stories* 20, no. 2 (May 1946): 6–73. archive.org/details/Amazing_Stories_v20n02_1946-05_cape1736

———. "The Sea People." *Amazing Stories* 20, no. 5 (August 1946): 8–45. archive.org/details/Amazing_Stories_v20n05_1946-08_cape1736

———. "Thought Records of Lemuria." *Amazing Stories* 19, no. 2 (June 1945): 12–52. archive.org/details/Amazing_Stories_v19n02_1945-06.Ziff-Daviscape1736

Shaver, Richard Sharpe, and Bob McKenna. "Cult of the Witch Queen." *Amazing Stories* 20, no. 4 (July 1946): 8–38, 109–45. archive.org/details/Amazing_Stories_v19n03_1945-09_cape1736

Shipman, Pat. *The Man Who Found the Missing Link: Eugène Dubois and His Lifelong Quest to Prove Darwin Right*. Cambridge: Harvard University Press, 2002.

Snell, Merwin-Marie. "Modern Theosophy in Its Relation to Hinduism and Buddhism." *The Biblical World* 5, no. 3 (March 1895): 200–205.

Spence, Lewis. *The Problem of Lemuria: The Sunken Continent of The Pacific*. San Diego: The Book Tree, 2002.

Standish, David. *Hollow Earth: The Long and Curious History of Imagining Strange Lands, Fantastical Creatures, Advanced Civilizations, and Marvelous Machines below the Earth's Surface*. Cambridge: Da Capo Books, 2006. archive.org/details/hollowearthlongc0000stan

Stankiewicz, Jacek, Christien Thiart, Judith Masters, and Maarten de Wit. "Did Lemurs Have Sweepstake Tickets? An Exploration of Simpson's Model for the Colonization of Madagascar by Mammals." *Journal of Biogeography* 33 (2006): 221–35.

Staudenmaier, Peter. *Between Occultism and Nazism: Anthroposophy and the Politics of Race in the Fascist Era*. Leiden: Brill, 2014.

Steiger, Brad, and Sherry Steiger. *Conspiracies and Secret Societies: The Complete Dossier*. 2nd ed. Detroit: Visible Ink Press, 2013.

Steiner, Rudolf. *Cosmic Memory: Prehistory of Earth and Man*. West Nyack, New York: Rudolf Steiner Publications, Inc., 1961. archive.org/details/cosmicmemorypreh0000stei_x3t2Stephen. *Time's Arrow, Time's Cycle: Myth and Metaphor in the Discovery of Geological Time*. Cambridge: Harvard University Press, 1987. archive.org/details/timesarrowtimesc00step_0

Stockton, Steve, and Bill Melder. *National Park Mysteries and Disappearances*. Vol. 2. San Diego: Beyond the Fray Publishing, 2021.

Strickland, Tiffany Darlene. "Constructions of Mythology: Mount Shasta, Atlantis and the Ancient Lemurians." Thesis, California State University, Fullerton, 2006.

Sturdevant, Andy. "Nininger City, Ignatius Donnelly's Lost Atlantis on the Mississippi." *MinnPost*, March 26, 2014. www.minnpost.com/stroll/2014/03/nininger-city-ignatius-donnellys-lost-atlantis-mississippi/

Subramanya, Shivaya. *Lemurian Scrolls*. Kapaʻa, Hawaii: Himalayan Academy, 2006. archive.org/details/lemurianscrollsshivayasubramanya_128_OSutcliffe, Steven. *Children of the New Age: A History of Spiritual Practices*. London: Taylor & Francis Group, 2003.

Taffinder, Adelia H. "A Fragment of the Ancient Continent of Lemuria." *The Overland Monthly* 52 (December 1908): 163–167.

Tattersall, Ian. "Historical Biogeography of the Strepsirhine Primates of Madagascar." *Folia Primatologica* 77 (2006): 477–87. doi.org/10.1159/000095393

Tausk, Victor. "On the Origin of the 'Influencing Machine' in Schizophrenia." *Journal of Psychotherapy Practice and Research* 1, no. 2 (Spring 1992). www.ncbi.nlm.nih.gov/pmc/articles/PMC3330285/

Taylor Alfred E. *Plato The Man And His Work (1926)*. London: Methuen and Co., LTD, 1926. archive.org/details/in.ernet.dli.2015.476421

Thakur, Tanu, and Vikas Gupta. "Auditory Hallucinations." In *StatPearls*. Treasure Island, FL: StatPearls Publishing, 2022. www.ncbi.nlm.nih.gov/books/NBK557633/

"The First Ascended Master Organization The I AM Movement." *Light of Christ Truth*. n.d. lightofchristtruth.com/Asc_masters/IAM_Mvt.html

The Imperator. "A New Lemurian Mystery." *Rosicrucian Digest* 14, no. 8 (September 1936): 287–291. b45e1c3778bbf3ebb96c-637cca54df3fd347e9c3d5d35c2f839a.ssl.cf5.rackcdn.com/The_Rosicrucian_Digest_v14_n8_1936.pdf

"The Missing Continent That Took 375 Years to Find." *BBC*. February 7, 2021. www.bbc.com/future/article/20210205-the-last-secrets-of-the-worlds-lost-continent"The Mystery of Mt. Shasta," *Rosicrucian Digest*, May 1936. www.rosicrucian.org/rosicrucian-digest-archive

"The Shasta Indians." *Legends of America*, February 2020. www.legendsofamerica.com/shasta-indians/

The Supreme Secretary. "New Mystery at Mount Shasta." *Rosicrucian Digest* 13, no. 9 (October 1935): 337–41. b45e1c3778bbf3ebb96c-637cca54df3fd347e9c3d5d35c2f839a.ssl.cf5.rackcdn.com/The_Rosicrucian_Digest_v13_n9_1935.pdf

Thompson, Eve. "Mt. Shasta: Its Origin as Mecca for Spiritual Seekers." *Mount Shasta Herald*, March 14, 2012. www.mtshastanews.com/story/news/2012/03/14/mt-shasta-its-origin-as/49497962007/

Timothy Green Beckley (ed.). *Mysteries of Mt. Shasta: Home of the Underground Dwellers and Ancient Gods*. New Brunswick, NJ: Global Communications, 2008.

Toronto, Richard. "Lying Saucers or The Man Who Re-Invented Flying Saucers and Called Them Rokfogo." *Shaverton*, October 2016. www.shaverton.com/LyingSaucers.html

——*Shaverton: The Lettershop Years: Issues 12–17*. Vol. 2. San Francisco: Shaverton Press, 2014.

——. *Shaverton: The Mimeograph Years: Issues 1–11*. Vol. 1. San Francisco: Shaverton Press, 2013.

——. *War over Lemuria: Richard Shaver, Ray Palmer and the Strangest Chapter of 1940s Science Fiction*. Jefferson, NC: McFarland & Company, Inc., 2013.

Torsvik, Trond H., Hans Amundsen, Ebbe H. Hartz, Fernando Corfu, Nick Kuszmir, Carmen Gaina, Pavel V. Doubrovine, Bernhard Steinberger, Lewis D. Ashwal, and Bjorn Jamtveit. "A Precambrian Microcontinent in the Indian Ocean." *Nature Geoscience* 6 (March 2013): 223–27.

Trbovich, Pete. "The Shaver Mystery: An Account Of Congruent Insanity." *Geeky Domain*, October 22, 2021. geekydomain.com/the-shaver-mystery-an-account-of-congruent-insanity/

Trevithick, Alan. "The Theosophical Society and Its Subaltern Acolytes (1880–1986)." *Marburg Journal of Religion* 13, no. 1 (May 2008): 1–32.

Tumminia, Diana. "Brothers from the Sky: Myth and Reality in a Flying Saucer Group." Dissertation, University of California, Los Angeles. Accessed September 15, 2022.

——. "How Prophecy Never Fails: Interpretive Reason in a Flying-Saucer Group." *Sociology of Religion* 59, no. 2 (Summer 1998): 157–70.

———. "In the Dreamtime of the Saucer People: Sense-Making and Interpretive Boundaries in a Contactee Group." *Journal of Contemporary Ethnography* 31, no. 6 (December 1, 2002): 675–705. doi.org/10.1177/089124102237821

Tuttle, Russell Howard. "Human Evolution." In *Encyclopedia Britannica*, August 17, 2022. www.britannica.com/science/human-evolution

Tyree, J.M. "Ignatius Donnelly, Prince of Cranks." *The Believer*, August 1, 2005. culture.org/ignatius-donnelly-prince-of-cranks/

Tyson, Peter. *The Eighth Continent: Life, Death, and Discovery in the Lost World of Madagascar*. New York: William Morrow, 2000. archive.org/details/eighthcontinent00pete

Ullrich, Heiner. *Rudolf Steiner*. London: Bloomsbury Publishing, 2008.

"Understanding Reincarnation & Esoteric Teachings of Rosicrucians." *The Rosicrucian Order, AMORC*. n.d. www.rosicrucian.org/history

Unterman, Alan. "Kabbalah." In *Dictionary of Jewish Lore and Legend*. London: Thames & Hudson, 1997. search-credoreference-com.ezproxy2.apus.edu/content/entry/thjll/kabbalah/0

Urban, Hugh B. *New Age, Neopagan, and New Religious Movements: Alternative Spirituality in Contemporary America*. Berkeley: University of California Press, 2015. ebookcentral.proquest.com/lib/apus/detail.action?docID=2025592

Vidal-Naquet, Pierre. *The Atlantis Story: A Short History of Plato's Myth*. Exeter: University of Exeter Press, 2007.

Wallace, Alfred Russel. *Island Life or The Phenomena and Causes of Insular Faunas and Floras Including a Revision and Attempted Solution of the Problem of Geological Climates*. 2nd ed. London: MacMillan & Co., 1895.

———. "On the Zoological Geography of the Malay Archipelago." *Journal of the Proceedings of the Linnean Society: Zoology 4*. (1859): 172–184. darwin-online.org.uk/converted/Ancillary/1860_Wallace_A269.html

Walsh, J. "Tantrism." In *World History: A Comprehensive Reference Set*. New York: Facts on File, 2016.

Ward, Charlotte, and David Voas. "The Emergence of Conspirituality." *Journal of Contemporary Religion* 26, no. 1 (2011): 103–21.

Wegener, A. *The Origin of Continents and Oceans*. New York: Dover Publications, 1966.Williamson, George Hunt. *Secret Places of the Lion: Alien Influences on Earth's Destiny*. Rochester, Vermont: Destiny Books, 1996. archive.org/details/secretplacesofli0000will

Wilson, Colin. *The Occult: A History*. New York: Random House, 1971.

Wiseman, Eva. "The Dark Side of Wellness: The Overlap between Spiritual Thinking and Far-Right Conspiracies." *The Observer*, October 17, 2021. www.theguardian.com/lifeandstyle/2021/oct/17/eva-wiseman-conspirituality-the-dark-side-of-wellness-how-it-all-got-so-toxic

Wogawa, Stefan. "Urkontinent Lemuria." *Mysteria 3000*, September 24, 2021. web.archive.org/web/20210924125534/https://mysteria3000.de/magazin/urkontinent-lemuria/

Wong, Kate. "How Scientists Discovered the Staggering Complexity of Human Evolution." *Scientific American*, September 1, 2020. www.scientificamerican.com/article/how-scientists-discovered-the-staggering-complexity-of-human-evolution/

Woodward, Aylin. "A Lost 8th Continent Is Hidden Nearly 1,000 Miles under Europe, New Research Shows. Scientists Named It 'Greater Adria.'" *Business Insider*. September 17, 2019. www.businessinsider.in/a-lost-8th-continent-is-hidden-nearly-1000-miles-under-europe-new-research-shows-scientists-named-it-greater-adria-/articleshow/71175385.cms#:~:text=New%20research%20shows%20that%20an,across%20Europe%2C%20like%20the%20Alps

Wright, Bruce Lanier. "Fear Down Below." *Shaverton*, July 18, 2009. web.archive.org/web/20090718120923/http://www.softcom.net:80/users/falconkam/feardownbelow.htmlYoder, Anne D., Matt Cartmill, Maryellen Ruvolo, Kathleen Smith, and Rytas Vilgalys. "Ancient Single Origin for Malagasy Primates." *Proceedings of the National Academy of Sciences* 93 (May 1996): 5122–26.

INDEX